THE G
AND PHILOSOPHY

The Blackwell Philosophy and Pop Culture Series
Series editor: William Irwin

A spoonful of sugar helps the medicine go down, and a healthy helping of popular culture clears the cobwebs from Kant. Philosophy has had a public relations problem for a few centuries now. This series aims to change that, showing that philosophy is relevant to your life—and not just for answering the big questions like "To be or not to be?" but for answering the little questions: "To watch or not to watch *South Park*?" Thinking deeply about TV, movies, and music doesn't make you a "complete idiot." In fact it might make you a philosopher, someone who believes the unexamined life is not worth living and the unexamined cartoon is not worth watching.

THE GOOD PLACE AND PHILOSOPHY

Edited by

Kimberly S. Engels

WILEY Blackwell

Registered Office
John Wiley & Sons, Inc., 111 River Street, Hoboken, NJ 07030, USA

Editorial Office
111 River Street, Hoboken, NJ 07030, USA

For details of our global editorial offices, customer services, and more information about Wiley products visit us at www.wiley.com.

Wiley also publishes its books in a variety of electronic formats and by print-on-demand. Some content that appears in standard print versions of this book may not be available in other

Library of Congress Cataloging-in-Publication data applied for

9781119633280 (paperback)
9781119633020 (adobe pdf)
9781119633297 (epub)

Cover Design: Wiley
Cover Images: Sky: © spooh/Getty Images
Sofa: © Pitinan Piyavatin/EyeEm/Getty Images
Grass: © hadynyah/Getty Images

Set in 10.5/13pt Sabon by SPi Global, Pondicherry, India

10 9 8 7 6 5 4 3 2 1

Contents

Contributors

Leslie A. Aarons is a Professor of Philosophy at City University of New York. Her specializations are in environmental and public philosophy. She has published numerous chapters in the Philosophy and Popular Culture series, including *House of Cards and Philosophy: Underwood's Republic* (Wiley-Blackwell); *Philosophy and Breaking Bad* (Palgrave Macmillan); and *WikiLeaking: The Ethics of Secrecy and Exposure* (Open Court). As an amateur chef she is proud of her latest signature dish that captures the delectable "Full Cellphone Battery" flavor in a perfectly executed chicken piccata.

David Baggett is Professor of Philosophy at Houston Baptist University and works in ethics, philosophy of religion, and natural theology. He's the executive editor of MoralApologetics.com, and his most recent book is *The Moral Argument: A History*, co-written with Jerry Walls. Unapologetic about drinking almond milk, he remains just 520,000,008 points shy of The Good Place.

Marybeth Baggett, an English Professor (not a philosopher) at Houston Baptist University, studies contemporary American literature, science fiction, and the life and work of groundbreaking artist and popular icon Kamilah. The Eleanor to David's Chidi, Marybeth has authored two books and has been working for 18 years on her magnum opus, *Why Do Bad Things Happen to Mediocre People Who Lie about Their Identity?*

Steven A. Benko is a Professor of Religious and Ethical Studies at Meredith College. His research focuses on ethics, subjectivity, and culture. He is the co-editor of *The Good Place and Philosophy: Get an*

Afterlife, Ethics and Comedy (forthcoming) and has published articles on authenticity and *The Good Place*, religious humor in Monty Python's *Life of Brian*, critical thinking pedagogy, and posthumanism. He once asked Chidi for help with an ethics syllabus, but Chidi said that it gave him a stomachache.

Kiki Berk is an Associate Professor of Philosophy at Southern New Hampshire University and currently holds the Papoutsy Chair in Ethics and Social Responsibility. She received her PhD in Philosophy from the VU University Amsterdam in 2010. Her current research interests include value theory (especially happiness), analytic existentialism (especially the meaning of life), and the philosophy of death. If searching for meaning is philosophical suicide, then her days are numbered.

Andreas Bruns is a PhD candidate at the University of Leeds. His research focuses on deontological ethics and moral conflicts. He teaches moral and political philosophy, and medical ethics. The Accounting Department assigns a negative value of –143 points to doing a PhD in philosophy, and the job prospects are terrible. But, as his good friend Barack once told him during a skiing holiday with Michelle and the kids, "You are not here to fear the future. You're here to shape it. And where you are met with cynicism and doubts and those who tell you that you can't, tell them: Yes, I can."

Andrew Davison is a student at the Gatton Academy of Mathematics and Science, so you may be surprised to see him listed as a contributor to a philosophy volume. He researches applications of the Fourier Transform and other mathy stuff. This is his first philosophy chapter and his second publication. Clearly, Andrew is conflicted about what exactly he wants to do when he "grows up," but hopefully he can be as cool as his dad (see: Scott Davison). As Jason Mendoza once said, "I'm just trying to figure out what the fork is happening."

Scott A. Davison is Professor of Philosophy at Morehead State University. He is the author of two books, *On the Intrinsic Value of Everything* (Continuum, 2012) and *Petitionary Prayer: A Philosophical Investigation* (Oxford, 2017), and a number of articles in the areas of metaphysics, philosophy of religion, and value theory. He serves as the book review editor for the *International Journal for Philosophy of Religion* and the associate editor of the journal *Faith and Philosophy*.

In his spare time, he likes to build things and hang out with his children and his rabbits. Other than that, as Eleanor has told him repeatedly, "Ya basic."

Kimberly S. Engels is Assistant Professor of Philosophy at Molloy College. Her research focuses on existentialism as a contemporary living philosophy, applicable to all domains of modern life. She is co-editor of the book *Westworld and Philosophy: If You Go Looking for the Truth, Get the Whole Thing* (Wiley-Blackwell, 2018), and has published articles relating existentialism to issues in environmental ethics, medical ethics, and public policy. Jason Mendoza once told her, "You've got a dope soul and hella ethics."

T Storm Heter teaches Philosophy at East Stroudsburg University. He is author of *Sartre's Ethics of Engagement* (Continuum, 2006) and he writes about existentialism, music, and critical race theory.

Darren Hudson Hick is the author of *Introducing Aesthetics and the Philosophy of Art* (2017) and *Artistic License: The Philosophical Problems of Copyright & Appropriation* (2017), and co-editor of *The Aesthetics and Ethics of Copying* (2016). Unbeknownst to Sarah Worth, his bud-hole is mostly filled with velvet Elvis paintings.

Pamela Hieronymi is a Professor of Philosophy at UCLA. She has published on moral responsibility and on our control over our own states of mind. She is currently bringing these two strands together into a book, *Minds That Matter*, in order to unwind the traditional problem of free will. She and Chidi are still trying to decide which quotation to use for this bio.

Jake Jackson is a PhD Candidate in Philosophy at Temple University writing on depression, anxiety, and moral responsibility. His published work examines how to navigate depression and anxiety within a stigmatizing world. He's been compared to Chidi a few too many times and tries his best to ignore his point totals, but fears the Time Knife.

David Kyle Johnson is a Professor of Philosophy at King's College in Wilkes-Barre, Pennsylvania, who also produces lecture series for The Teaching Company's *The Great Courses*. His specializations include metaphysics, logic, and philosophy of religion, and his "Great

Courses" include *Sci-Phi: Science Fiction as Philosophy, The Big Questions of Philosophy*, and *Exploring Metaphysics*. Kyle is the editor-in-chief of *The Palgrave Handbook of Popular Culture as Philosophy* (forthcoming), and has also edited other volumes for Wiley-Blackwell, including *Black Mirror and Philosophy: Dark Reflections* and *Inception and Philosophy: Because It's Never Just a Dream*. Thanks to Lisa Kudrow, his six-year-old son Johney won't stop calling him a think-read-book-man.

Dean A. Kowalski is a Professor of Philosophy and Chair of the Arts & Humanities Department in the College of General Studies at the University of Wisconsin–Milwaukee. He regularly teaches philosophy of religion, Asian philosophy, and ethics. He is the author of *Joss Whedon as Philosopher* (2017), *Classic Questions and Contemporary Film*, 2nd edition (2016), and *Moral Theory at the Movies* (2012). He is the editor of The Big Bang Theory *and Philosophy* (2012), *The Philosophy of* The X-Files, revised edition (2009), and *Steven Spielberg and Philosophy* (2008); he is the coeditor of *The Philosophy of Joss Whedon* (2011). Like Chidi, he is vexed by what you might call directional insanity. Vexed. Just ask his wife (or any of his friends, really).

Being a fairly young soul, this is only **James Lawler**'s 322nd time for participating in *The Good Place and Philosophy*. Previously, some may recall, during his 321st time round his classic book *The God Tube: Uncovering the Hidden Spiritual Message in Pop Culture* (Open Court, 2010) won the Noble [*sic*] Prize, beating out Bob Dillon [*sic*] that year. Dillon (this time around he spells it Dylan) failed then to convince the jury with his song "The Times Are They Are Unchangin'." After 702 repetitions, he finally got the message, showing that humanity is indeed making progress. James is still at the State University of New York at Buffalo, but this time, for those who remember, in the Philosophy Department, not Astrophysics.

If **Greg Littmann** goes to The Good Place, he'll still get to be an Associate Professor of Philosophy at Southern Illinois University Edwardsville. But the exams will all magically grade themselves. He'll still publish in metaphysics, epistemology, philosophy of logic, and the philosophy of professional philosophy. He'll still write chapters relating philosophy to popular culture, like the ones he's written for books devoted to *Big Bang Theory, Black Mirror, Doctor Who, Game* *of Thrones, It's Always Sunny in Philadelphia, The Walking Dead,* and others. But there'll be no word limits or due dates, and his word processor will automatically underline bad ideas in red. If Greg goes to The Bad Place, the students will ask, "Will this be on the exam?" anytime he says anything in class. He'll still be allowed to write, but Plato and Aristotle will stand over his shoulder, sniggering.

Laura Matthews is an Instructor in the Department of Philosophy at Auburn University. Her research focuses on integrating phenomenology with 4E (embodied, embedded, enactive, and extended) approaches to cognition. She is particularly interested in the application of these approaches to philosophical problems surrounding the classification and treatment of mental illness. She is currently finishing her thesis on an enactive approach to mental illness at the University of Georgia. Chidi once sat in on one of Laura's lectures and complimented her that it was "so bleak."

Todd May is Class of 1941 Memorial Professor of the Humanities at Clemson University. He is the author of sixteen books of philosophy, most recently *A Decent Life: Morality for the Rest of Us* and *Kenneth Lonergan: Filmmaker and Philosopher.* When Jason tells Shawn, "You used to be cool. But you've changed, man," he was thinking of Todd. Except the cool part.

Michael McGowan is Professor of Philosophy and Religion at Florida Southwestern State College. He is co-editor of *David Foster Wallace and Religion: Essays on Faith and Fiction* (Bloomsbury Academic Press, 2019) and author of *The Bridge: Revelation and Its Implications* (Pickwick, 2015). He is currently interested in meaning-of-life questions and nihilism, or maybe he isn't. Whatever.

Matthew P. Meyer is Assistant Professor of Philosophy at the University of Wisconsin–Eau Claire. His main areas of study are existentialism, phenomenology, and psychoanalysis. He has written a book entitled *Archery and the Human Condition in Lacan, the Greeks, and Nietzsche: The Bow with the Greatest Tension* (Lexington, 2019) and has published articles and chapters on Nietzsche and film, and in several Blackwell Philosophy and Pop Culture series books, on Sartre (and *The Office*), Nietzsche (and *House of Cards*), and aesthetics (and *Westworld*). Chidi Anogonye once gave him the answer to life, but he is not willing to share it.

Traci Phillipson is Visiting Assistant Professor of Philosophy at Marquette University. Her research focuses on Medieval Latin and Arabic philosophy and its Aristotelian roots. She works primarily on issues of will and intellect in Aquinas and Averroes. She, like Michael, thinks that human beings can be "g-g-good, sometimes."

Alison Reiheld is Associate Professor of Philosophy at Southern Illinois University–Edwardsville. She is a regular contributor to the scholarly bioethics blog, IJFAB Blog, and hopes that her work there helps folks to think through tricky issues in medical ethics. In addition to her research on the ethics of memory, Dr. Reiheld deals with how power and social norms operate within social institutions to render some people and groups vulnerable in unethical ways. She tends to make folks question ethical conclusions that had at first seemed obvious. This is why everybody hates moral philosophers.

Catherine M. Robb is an Assistant Professor of Philosophy at Tilburg University in the Netherlands. At the moment she is interested in questions about the ethics and politics of self-development, and also writes on the aesthetics of music. In her spare time she "takes it sleazy" just like Eleanor, although she prefers red wine to margaritas.

Dane Sawyer is Senior Adjunct Professor of Philosophy and Religion at the University of La Verne. His research focuses on the interconnections among existentialism, philosophy of mind, Buddhism, and meditation. Tahani often brags that Dane offered her "exquisite" and "unsurpassable" meditation advice and philosophical reflections on the nature of mind during her time as a Tibetan Buddhist monk.

Michael Schur is the creator of *The Good Place*. He also co-created *Brooklyn 99* and *Parks and Recreation*.

C. Scott Sevier is Professor of Philosophy at The College of Southern Nevada in Las Vegas. His research focuses on medieval philosophy and aesthetics as well as the nature of beauty. He is interested in the history of ideas and in philosophy as a wisdom tradition. He contributed a chapter to *Psych and Philosophy: Some Dark Juju-Magumbo* (Open Court, 2013), and published articles relating to the aesthetics and morality of Aquinas, as well as the book *Aquinas on Beauty* (Lexington Press, 2015). If it seems like he talks too fast, it's because he still goes to Andy's Coffee, and he's got a full punch-card, Bro.

Eric J. Silverman is Associate Professor of Philosophy at Christopher Newport University, United States. He has twenty publications on topics in ethics, philosophy of religion, and medieval philosophy. His publications include two monographs, *The Prudence of Love: How Possessing the Virtue of Love Benefits the Lover* and *The Supremacy of Love: An Agape-Centered Vision of Aristotelian Virtue Ethics*, and a co-edited collection, *Paradise Understood: New Philosophical Essays about Heaven*. Although he shares much of Chidi's fashion sense, it has never taken him more than fifteen minutes to choose a fedora.

Zachary Swanson is in his final year as an undergraduate at Christopher Newport University. He is applying to graduate programs in psychology. He is still in the process of completing his 4000-page manuscript on the simple question: Why? Like Chidi, his brain makes noises as a fork in a garbage disposal.

Joshua Tepley is an Associate Professor of Philosophy at Saint Anselm College. He received his BA in philosophy from Bucknell University and his PhD in philosophy from the University of Notre Dame. His research focuses on the intersection between twentieth-century continental philosophy and analytic metaphysics. The thing he looks forward to the most when he gets to The Good Place is hanging out with Judge Gen.

Sarah E. Worth is a professor at Furman University. She writes at the intersection of aesthetics and epistemology. She published *In Defense of Reading* in 2017 and is now working on a book called *The Pleasures of Eating: A Philosophy of Taste*. Sarah teaches classes about food and eating as often as she can, and believes, ironically, that although hell is other people's tastes, frozen yogurt is pure heaven. She shares an office with Darren Hudson Hick that is decorated only with clown paintings.

Robin L. Zebrowski is Associate Professor of Cognitive Science at Beloit College. Her research focuses on artificial intelligence and human/computer interfaces, with a focus on the relationship between embodiment and conceptualization. Jason Mendoza thinks she's the Pam Anderson boob motorcycle of people, but she also once got lost on an escalator.

Editor's Introduction and Acknowledgments

Kimberly S. Engels

"We Are Not in This Alone"

> So, why do it then? Why choose to be good, every day, if there is no guaranteed reward we can count on, now or in the afterlife? I argue that we choose to be good because of our bonds with other people and our innate desire to treat them with dignity. Simply put, we are not in this alone.

When Chidi Anagonye reads this aloud in "Somewhere Else," he expresses the heart and soul of a show that succeeded in making philosophy both funny and mainstream. More than any work of contemporary pop culture, *The Good Place* explicitly explores the work of a variety of famous philosophers, yet it is anchored in one theme. As the show's creator, Michael Schur, said in a 2018 plenary session of the annual meeting of the North American Sartre Society, "The goal is to try to ask the question what it means to be a good person. That was the one line source of the show."

Despite Chidi's desire for the first three and a half seasons, perhaps there is no single philosophical answer to that question. There is, though, a narrative answer. Through the story it tells, *The Good Place* shows us that being a good person is social. It involves becoming better together through our relationships and bonds with other people—through our shared experiences, sacrifices, triumphs, and failures. Simply put, we are not in this alone. This is true not just for Chidi but for all of us.

Indeed, I have not been alone at any stage with this book, which has its origins in a meeting of the North American Sartre Society (NASS) in November 2018 at the University of Mary Washington. The NASS includes many supportive, collaborative, and remarkable individuals who are even better when together. Each year's meeting is filled with meaningful scholarship and companionship, but the 2018 gathering was extra special. The show's creator, Michael Schur, and one of the show's philosophical advisors, Todd May, joined us for a special plenary session about *The Good Place* and Sartre's work. It was one of the most rewarding experiences of my professional life.

My gratitude to all who organized and participated in the event—Michael Schur, Todd May, Jake Jackson, Kiki Berk, and Craig Vasey—cannot be overstated. NASS president T Storm Heter, conference organizer Craig Vasey, as well as other members of the NASS executive committee then entrusted me to carry this project to the next stages. Michael Schur graciously agreed to write the foreword for the book. He was kind, responsive, and generous with his time. Likewise, the philosophical advisors for *The Good Place*, Todd May and Pamela Hieronymi, graciously agreed to write an introduction for the volume.

William Irwin, the Blackwell Philosophy and Pop Culture Series editor, helped turn the project into a reality. He offered invaluable assistance in every stage of the process. The contributing authors worked diligently, met important deadlines, and helped create something wonderful. Did I mention that I was not in this alone?

Last but not least, my daughter, Moriah A. Khan, binge-watched the show with me on repeat. At this point she is a mega-fan as well as a budding philosopher.

Foreword

In the summer of 2015, I found myself sitting in heavy traffic on a freeway in Los Angeles. Sitting in heavy traffic is one of our favorite pastimes out here, along with sitting in moderate traffic, inching along in light traffic, and canceling plans because there's too much traffic. On this particular day, a man in a white sports car decided the rules of society didn't apply to him—he is special! He has a white sports car!—and he pulled into the breakdown lane and sped by all of us poor suckers who were foolish enough to abide by a social contract.

"That guy," I thought to myself, "just lost twenty points."

It was a game I played sometimes—a little soul-soother: I imagined that someone (or -thing) is omnisciently tallying up our moral triumphs and failures, filing them away for review *in toto* when our threads finally get snipped. I'm hardly the first person to imagine such a system, but in my version it was a real numbers game—a cold, computational, *Moneyball*-style analysis of our every action. This time, when I played my little accounting game, something else occurred to me: if this were the actual grand, eternal system, whose computational rules would we be using? Would all moral philosophers even agree that white sports car man had lost a few points in that moment? Would there be a consensus as to how many points his act had cost him? Would their reasons for believing so be the same? And then I had one more (slightly less lofty) thought: is there any way this is a television show?

In the months that followed I conceived of and wrote the pilot for *The Good Place*, a comedy on NBC that I've now run for the last four years. The basic premise, if you haven't seen it—though, if you haven't, why the hell are you reading this book?—is this: Eleanor Shellstrop wakes up in the afterlife, and is told that she is in The Good Place. Though it's explicitly nondenominational, The Good Place is a version of the Christian "heaven," full of everything she'd ever want, and reserved (she's told) for the very best people who ever lived. Humans' moral scores have been scrupulously kept, points added and subtracted for every action, great and small, and only the real cream of the moral crop get into this paradise. The problem is: she is decidedly *not* the cream of the crop. She is a very mediocre person, who certainly does not qualify for this VIP Club of ethical superstars. There's been a mistake.

Then a million other things happen, that would take too long to explain. Just watch the show, it'll be easier. (And also, again, if you don't know what happens in the show, why did you buy this book?)

In order to write the show the way it needed to be written—meaning, "not ignorantly"—I embarked on a self-designed course of study into moral philosophy, a subject about which I knew very little. From my few courses in college, I remembered that Kant was strict, Mill was results-oriented, and Socrates was forced to drink hemlock because he annoyed everyone in Athens until they couldn't take it anymore. That was about it.

I bought a few survey books covering the basics—virtue ethics, utilitarianism, deontology—designed to lay down a primer coat of knowledge: Ethics for Dummies Who Write TV Shows. The problem was, every book and article pointed me to five others, which led me to twenty others after that. I bought more and more volumes, spent more and more time reading, got deeper and deeper into the philosophical weeds. My eyes were never unstrained. My Amazon cart was never empty.

It was exhausting—but it was fun. Oh man, was it fun. It didn't feel like work, really—it felt like listening to a *conversation*, a 2500-year-long conversation these men and (far too late in the game) women were having with each other. The debates, and refutations, and criticisms.... Scanlon was talking to Rawls, who'd been talking to Kant, who'd been sniffing at Aristotle. Philippa Foot was talking to Mill, and then John Taurek snapped at the people who'd talked to her. The ideas were fascinating, but the *conversation* was the fun part. And as long as humans walk the planet, it occurred to me, it would never end. As T.M. Scanlon wrote, when concluding his magnum opus: working out the terms of moral justification is an unending task.

Which is why this volume delights me so much. When you start a TV show, you have very pedestrian goals: make something good, that entertains people. If you're lucky, you make something audiences care about, and invest in, emotionally and intellectually. But this show had another, clandestine goal: to add to the conversation. I hoped the show could toss out a few ideas, ask a couple questions, raise a hand from the back of the class. An entire book full of ideas based on its contents was something I never dreamed of.

I'm very grateful to the academics who contributed to the pages within—and to the writers, actors, editors, and crew members who made the show sturdy enough in its scholarship to warrant those pages. I'm doubly grateful for everyone who watched the show and felt it contributed, in some small way, to the conversation of philosophy.

Michael Schur
Creator of *The Good Place*
October 2019

Introduction

Pamela Hieronymi and Todd May,
philosophical advisors to The Good Place

The philosopher Ludwig Wittgenstein once remarked that "A serious and good philosophical work could be written consisting entirely of jokes."[1] But who, really, has tried this? Who would have the chutzpah, not to mention the fortitude, to write such a book? And if such a task were beyond most philosophers, what about this: a television show of philosophy composed largely of jokes?

If you're reading these pages you already know that it's been done. Tacking between the Scylla of cheapening philosophy and the Charybdis of unfunny humor (the dreaded philosophy jokes), *The Good Place* has sought to engage philosophy seriously while at the same time remaining an entertaining sitcom broadcast on network television. In particular, it has focused on the questions of how to be good and how to learn to be good in a world fraught with ethical complexities. Although the show engages in any number of philosophical arenas, for instance existentialism and the problem of personal identity, it always returns to the core issue of living an ethically decent life in a world that has the unfortunate tendency to push back.

In doing so, the show does not cleave to one or another of the ethical theories current in philosophical discussion. It presents Kant's view, through the behavior of the academic philosopher Chidi, as a blind set of imperatives whose key is hard to discover and even harder to act upon. Consequentialism, on the other hand, comes in for critique in the form of the point system for getting into The Good Place. Consequences are impossible to calculate in a world where good and bad are so deeply entwined that even the most diligent of consequentialists— and who is more diligent than Doug Forcett?—cannot pull off the trick of earning enough points to achieve proper Good Place standing. As Judge Gen discovers when she takes her short foray to the land of the living, acting rightly, if we base it on consequences, is far too complicated to master.

In the first and second season, T.M. Scanlon's *What We Owe to Each Other* looms large. Contractualism offers a contrast to both points and imperatives, with its update of the Golden Rule and its focus on respect and concern for other people. It is not so much the particularities of Scanlon's theory that inform the show in its early episodes—although Chidi does present Scanlon's idea that we should act on principles that others could not reasonably refuse—but rather the primary role that the theory gives to interpersonal relationships. In the first season, it is revealed that, in life, Eleanor never felt comfortable being part of any group; she was a distrustful loner ("Someone Like Me as a Member"). She turns a corner, though, when she convinces Jason and Janet that they all must return to The Good Place and sacrifice themselves, so that Chidi and Tahani are not sent to The Bad Place ("Mindy St. Claire"). Eleanor's first motive is friendship, but its connection to justice comes through.

If there is a philosophical view that comes closest to what *The Good Place* puts before us, it would be Aristotle's virtue ethics. And yet there is no wise person, no sage that stands as a model for those seekers of ethical living. Instead, all Eleanor, Chidi, Jason, Tahani, and Michael have are one another—flawed human beings (and a flawed immortal). What allows them to improve? What keeps them on the path even as, in the third season, they are convinced it will be impossible for any of them to enter The Good Place? In interview after interview about the show, Mike Schur returns to a single word: trying. Through their relationships with one another, they come to desire and then to try their hardest to become better people.

Trying, though, has its own hazards. Eleanor needs to try because she lacks the motivations of a good person. Aristotle would recommend that she do what the good person does, as a way to become a good person: in contemporary terms, "Fake it 'til you make it." But sheer effort alone will not transform poor motives—motives are not like muscles; mere repetition will not effect change. To become a better person, your motives must be transformed, and effort alone does not guarantee transformation. In the pilot, Eleanor volunteered to pick up trash as a way of becoming better. She tried, but she couldn't stick to it. Later, though, when she realized Chidi's disappointment in missing his real soul mate, she was moved to kindness, without effort (and the sinkhole closed). Eleanor's resolve again flags when she is back on earth, attempting to improve herself, but it revives when she hears Chidi's lecture on contractualism, with its emphasis on interpersonal relations. As the humans (re)unite on earth and form friendships, their transformations begin.

Aristotle's ethics is not, in the end, in tension with Scanlon's contractualism. Aristotle recognized that becoming good is not something that one does on one's own. Ethics, for him, is a part of politics: becoming good requires other people. *The Good Place* turns the Sartrean dictum that hell is other people on its head. Michael tries to create an interpersonal hell for Eleanor and the others, but it backfires. The four humans bond in bringing themselves to be better than they were. They recognize one another as people who are also seeking to live their lives as best they can, and they realize that they might do much worse than to try to help one another out.

As *The Good Place*'s characters learn this, we learn something important about them. It is a lesson that we would do well to heed in this period of profound polarization and mistrust. There is often more to people than our quick summary judgment of them leads us to believe. Eleanor, the "dirt bag from Arizona," becomes, through her moral education alongside others, the most morally courageous of the group. There is nothing in the early episodes of the series that would make us predict this. Yet her evolution that stems from her relationships with others, especially but not exclusively Chidi, is entirely believable. There is more to her, and more to most people, than our snap judgments would tempt us to think. We can each be better—or at least try to be better—than we currently are; and, relatedly, we should realize that others are often better—or at least might well be better—than we think they are.

The essays in this volume approach *The Good Place* from a variety of philosophical angles, although ethics is never far from the text. The contributing authors engage in conversation with the thinkers one might expect—Sartre, Camus, Nietzsche, Aristotle, and Scanlon among them—developing their ideas in order to bring forward aspects or implications of the show that are either implicit or cannot be treated at length philosophically in the episodes themselves. (Let's not forget that *The Good Place* is a sitcom, complete with fart jokes.) Although we cannot canvass those aspects and implications here— after all, that is the job of the essays themselves—perhaps a few quick gestures can indicate the rich resources of the show itself for philosophical reflection.

The final episode of the first season, "Michael's Gambit," calls to mind the quote from Sartre's *No Exit* that "Hell is other people." As several essays argue, and as is evident from the show itself, things are more complicated than those four words might, on their own, lead one to believe. To be sure, Michael designed The Good Place neighborhood with that very idea in mind. The frustration Chidi experiences in trying to teach Eleanor to be good (and the conflict he experiences, in keeping her secret), the exasperation Tahani feels in being unable to engage Jason in conversation, and so on lead to feelings of helplessness and self-torture among the four characters. Nevertheless, as the show develops we become witness to an alternative: just as they can make one another miserable, so they can encourage one another to be better. If hell is other people, might it not be that heaven is as well?

This theme leads to another one: that of moral development. Several of the essays note the journey of moral development and self-understanding that takes place. Eleanor, especially, comes to listen to the little voice in her head that warned her when she was about to do something wrong, a voice that she admits to Michael has always been there but that she had not been willing to pay attention to before. Likewise, Tahani comes to recognize that her feelings toward her sister have been one-sided, and that her sister has had struggles with her parents' expectations complementary to Tahani's own. Being with one another over the course of *The Good Place*'s episodes has fostered these recognitions, and so the characters provide one another opportunities to become better persons, instead of just torturing one another.

Another theme that appears in the essays, and looms large in the show itself, is that of reward and punishment. In the third season we learn that nobody has gotten into the real Good Place in 521 years. This is because, as Judge Gen discovers, there are so many unforeseeable consequences of our behavior; it seems impossible to try to be good without thereby causing bad. This raises a question—and it is a question not only for moral reflection, but also for such social institutions as the contemporary prison: how should we think about the ways in which we judge one another? Challenging a simple calculus of good and bad consequences, the show asks us to consider the complexity of our fellow human beings. In a period in which polarization has lent itself to the formation of simple binaries in our assessments of others, the sitcom asks for nuance and grace.

Finally, a fourth theme, one that plays an important but sometimes implicit role in the show, is that of our freedom of action, particularly in the contemporary world. If the characters of the show are to be capable of moral development, then they must have the freedom to be able to engage in that development. However, their freedom of action is hedged by the complexity of our world, one in which to buy a rose for a loved one might contribute to exploitation (of the workers who picked the rose), climate change (through the transportation of the rose), and deforestation (if the rose was an element of a farm that cleared forest land in order to create a rose farm that will itself be laid waste). Although the general theme of free will and determinism only appears once in the show during a conversation between Michael and Eleanor ("The Worst Possible Use of Free Will"), the pressing question of our freedom to be good in a world fraught with unforeseen consequences is an abiding concern throughout.

In all, *The Good Place* offers much food for thought without either spoon-feeding us or, as Wittgenstein worried about, unduly restricting our diet. By raising issues but refusing simple answers, by illustrating theories and dilemmas in ways that are at once provocative and entertaining, by allowing us to follow the moral development of four flawed individuals (and one flawed demon) through four seasons, the show displays how the reflective work of philosophy can be deep, engaging, and humorous all at once. And it has accomplished the trick that has eluded many of us in the field over these past several thousand years: it makes philosophy cool.

Note

1   Quoted in "A View from the Asylum" in Henry Dribble, *Philosophical Investigations from the Sanctity of the Press* (New York: iUniverse, 2004), 87.

Part I

"I JUST ETHICS'D YOU IN THE FACE"

How Do You Like Them Ethics?

David Baggett and Marybeth Baggett

As NBC's breakout sitcom opens, Eleanor Shellstrop finds herself in a dilemma. She has died, and a cosmic mismanagement lands her in The Good Place, a secular version of heaven, completely by mistake. Confessing the error will almost certainly mean her removal to The Bad Place and eternal torture. So what should she do? It is out of this predicament that all the series' hijinks ensue. In considering this tension, we find that two organically connected questions lie behind this delightful show: (1) whether morality requires that we do good for goodness' sake and (2) whether reality itself is committed to morality.

Starring Ted Danson as the demon Michael and Kristen Bell as Eleanor—sweet, teentsy, and no freakin' Gandhi—the show blazes a trail of brilliant fun from Nature's Lasik to "Ya Basic!" As proof that moral philosophy professors aren't as bad as the show's running gag suggests, consider ethicist Chidi Anagonye's *Hamilton*-style rap musical: "My name is Kierkegaard and my writing is impeccable! / Check out my teleological suspension of the ethical!" Or how one day in class Eleanor dismissively asks, "Who died and left Aristotle in charge of ethics?" to which an exasperated Chidi replies, "Plato!"

Although the show is a comedy, the picture that emerges is one of tragedy, tragicomedy at best. Nobody, it turns out at the close of Season 3, has made it into The Good Place for centuries. Not even Doug Forcett is likely to make the cut, even though he's the show's quasi-prophet who accidentally stumbled on the secret of the afterlife and has arguably led a faultless life ever since. The reason for this regrettable situation is life's complexity. Even good-intentioned behavior often results in a number of unintended bad consequences, yielding a net *loss* of "points" rather than a *gain*. The relative importance of intentions versus consequences is one of the vital philosophical questions the show raises. After discussing what the show has to say on the matter, we will offer our own view and why, if we're right, the context of *The Good Place*, it turns out, is much more tragic than comic. Then we will consider the evidence of morality itself to see if it might suggest a different outcome. But enough of this bullshirt. It's high time to take a swig from a putrid, disgusting bowl of ethical soup.

What Makes an Action Right?

Before reviewing how philosophers have answered the intentions/consequences question, let's first consider the question itself. Some might say that actions are neither right nor wrong. The whole enterprise of morality, they suggest, is misguided. Perhaps life is meaningless or the category of morality is confused. A committed nihilist might insist there's good reason to think there's ultimately nothing to this morality business at all. There are simply no moral truths to be found.

This isn't quite the position of Mindy St. Claire when she counsels Eleanor and company not to mess with ethics ("Mindy St. Claire"). Instead, she advises them to look out for number one. In principle that leaves open the possibility that she believes in objective morality and that we can know what such morality tells us to do, but that she is simply indifferent to it. Perhaps she sees morality and self-interest as so much at odds that she simply gave up on what morality had to say. As she sees it, the more reliable path to happiness concerns promoting what's best for oneself. Interestingly, the moral theory of ethical egoism says that doing what's in one's own ultimate best interest *is* our moral obligation. This is one way of maintaining a vital connection between what morality says and what's best for us. There's no particular evidence to suggest that Mindy held such an ethical account. What we know is simply that her life was about "making money and doing cocaine"—finding what happiness and fulfillment she could in her circumstances.

The better representation of a nihilistic approach is what Chidi flirted with after becoming aware of his impending eternal doom in the episode "Jeremy Bearimy." Making his vile Peep-M&M-chili concoction in the middle of class, quoting Nietzsche's immortal lines about the death of God, losing heart about morality and meaning—this is the stuff of nihilism commonly understood. Of course, defenders of Nietzsche would quickly suggest it's a bit of a caricature, and they have a point. But we'll leave that interesting discussion to the side for now.

Most people still think it's important to consider what makes actions right or wrong. This is the arena of "normative ethics," which has two main strains in the history of philosophy. Chidi discusses both of them in his lectures. One is the Kantian idea that what makes an action right is that it comes from the right motive. Immanuel Kant (1724–1804), the first philosopher mentioned in the show, serves as both ethical touchstone and punchline, a "lonely, obsessive hermit with zero friends" whose ideas nevertheless challenge the characters to wrestle with fundamental questions of right and wrong. The only truly good thing, he thought, is the "good will," which requires that our moral actions be motivated by respect for the moral law. Consequences, on Kant's understanding, don't capture the heart of an action. It's the motive that counts. We should do the right thing because it's the right thing to do, not for any other reason, at least if our action is to retain its moral worth.[1]

One reason Kant found the emphasis on consequences to be dubious is that we're notoriously bad at predicting them. We might try to do something that will result in a good outcome, but the effort can backfire and we end up doing far more bad than good. So it's not the consequences that matter morally.

Obviously ethical egoists would disagree. But a narrow focus on self-interest alone strikes many as myopic. A broader "consequentialism" called utilitarianism says an action is right if it produces the best overall consequences for *all* who are affected by an action. The philosophical nerd best known for being horny for utilitarianism is John Stuart Mill (1806–1873). Whereas Kant put the moral focus on intention, Mill generally put it squarely on *consequences*. Chidi's lecture on Mill has Eleanor initially enamored of utilitarianism's simplicity, Jason's convoluted but surprisingly apropos example of framing "one innocent gator dealer to save a 60-person dance crew" notwithstanding.

Mill did see the possibility that a good-intentioned action might end up doing more harm than good. He handled that sort of possibility by distinguishing between the worth of the moral action and the intention of the moral agent. A well-intentioned action that surprisingly backfires is, in retrospect, a wrong action, but the doer of the action is not necessarily culpable for it. So in this way Mill carved out some space for intention too.[2]

We might side with Kant, or with Mill, or argue for some sort of combination of the two views. As *The Good Place* goes on, it becomes clear that the world it depicts represents a sort of synthesis of Kant's and Mill's ideas. There's a strong emphasis on doing the right thing for its own sake—which sounds like Kant. There's also an important consideration of consequences, but without Mill's distinction between the status of an action and the quality of the agent who performs it. Unintended consequences, even those that can't be reasonably foreseen, can function over time—and almost inevitably will in this increasingly complicated world—to doom one to The Bad Place. For this reason, Doug buying his grandmother flowers actually costs him points, given that his purchase inadvertently supported labor malpractice, environmental abuse, and sexual harassment. This is why nobody has made it to The Good Place for centuries, leaving Chidi and the gang to work out a better system come the final season.

Should It Bother Us?

Should this seemingly unfair feature of the universe of *The Good Place* bother us—chap our nips, tug our nuggets, zip our tip? It would seem patently unjust to be held eternally responsible for the unforeseen and unforeseeable consequences of our best-intentioned actions. The surface problem is the complexity that renders moral decision making so complicated and uncertain. But the deeper problem is that the world of *The Good Place* is apparently governed by incompetent administration and a bad moral theory.

Some commentators have noted how secular *The Good Place* is. There is no positive mention of God, for example. There's the Judge, but she's enthralled by *NCIS* and blindsided by the world's complexity, so she doesn't qualify as God in any traditional sense. She's as much at the mercy of the system as anyone. There are also layers of various bureaucracies, like the superficially benign but actually feckless, benighted, and ineffectual "committee," which is more ready to create subcommittees than to correct injustices in the point system. Though they're impeccable rule-followers, questions of actual justice, fairness, and suffering don't drive them.

It's all portrayed hilariously, of course, but viewers find themselves rooting for Eleanor and Chidi, Jason and Tahani—and even Michael! It does *and should* bother us that the system is flawed, the presiding administration unjust, the reigning hierarchies uncaring.

It also understandably bothers the characters themselves, because they continue to make their case, expose the unfairness, and appeal to some standard of goodness and decency that could give humankind hope for a better fate.

But should the callous administration and flawed system of such a world detract from the characters' commitment to do the right thing, to grow morally, to become better people, to discharge their duties? The show suggests that it shouldn't. Its message is that, even if doing the right thing is inconsistent with happiness, it's still worth doing. Eleanor's an exemplar of this approach, especially in her public confession in Season 1 that she does not belong in The Good Place. She has all the reason to suspect this confession will land her in The Bad Place, but she comes clean nonetheless. Morality is worth doing for its own sake. Once the characters' eternal fate in The Bad Place seemed sealed, any effort on their part to do good—by helping those they love escape a similar destiny—must be coming from a pure motive since it would help only others, not themselves. In this seemingly Kantian spirit, the show implicitly extols the heroic virtues of commitment to the moral life irrespective of consequences for oneself.

This approach, though, doesn't really resonate with Kant. Although he downplayed the importance of consequences and counseled commitment to duty for duty's sake, Kant wasn't indifferent to the moral agent's well-being. He thought human beings reside in both the noumenal and phenomenal realms—the world as it is and the world of appearances, respectively. If we were purely noumenal creatures, he argued, then commitment to virtue for its own sake and nothing else would be enough, but because we're also phenomenal creatures, we're hardwired to care about issues like our own happiness. So, it's true that Kant thought that our moral motivations shouldn't include our desire to be happy. But it's also true that Kant thought our desire to be happy is morally legitimate.

The show gestures toward this with Eleanor's conclusions in "Pandemonium," the final episode of Season 3. Even though she thinks reality is basically meaningless, she finds she can't let go of the desire to find happiness. "I guess all I can do is embrace the pandemonium, find happiness in the unique insanity of being here, now." Kant might suggest that the heroic depiction of being moral for its own sake irrespective of consequences is both correct and incorrect. It's true that we should be motivated by morality alone, but it's false to think that we can set aside questions of ultimate happiness as if they're unimportant. They remain important—and even more, they remain important *to morality*. The very institution or enterprise of morality itself, to make full rational sense, to remain rationally stable, requires a greater correspondence between virtue and happiness than *The Good Place* seems to allow.

The Coincidence Thesis

Although Kant is the philosopher best known for talking about the need for such correspondence between virtue and happiness, several thinkers before him recognized the connection. Questions about morality and the afterlife have a long history in philosophy. In his *Pensées*, French mathematician and philosopher Blaise Pascal (1623–1662) asserted that the immortality of the soul is so important that one must have lost all feeling not to care about knowing the facts of the matter.[3]

Continuing on the same general theme, the great English philosopher John Locke (1632–1704) is well known for emphasizing the importance of rewards and punishments in moral motivation. The forthrightness with which he occasionally emphasized their centrality, in fact, has elicited from some quarters accusations that he fell prey to the misguided notion that the matter of moral motivation can be reduced to aiming for a beneficial outcome—something more practical or prudential than intrinsically moral.[4]

However bluntly or crassly drawn some of these connections may be, Locke was right to insist on an ultimate reckoning and balancing of the scales—something emphasized both by the Hellenistic Socrates in the *Apology* and by the Hebraic St. Paul in Acts 17. *The Good Place*, in its own way, underscores this insistence on justice. Although the characters find themselves in a skewed system, they cannot let go of the conviction that there's a standard above the broken system that ought to hold sway. Unless ultimate reality is itself committed to justice, many of our most cherished hopes for the rectification of wrongs and redemption of sufferings are in vain.

Locke thought that humans can appreciate the intrinsic goodness of virtue, and even its appeal, but this is not nearly enough to motivate virtuous behavior, especially when doing so is costly. To remedy this problem, on Locke's view, clear and explicit sanctions are needed to ensure that the virtuous course of action will always be the more attractive option.

What if being or doing good were to produce, rather than *good* consequences, *horrible* ones? What Locke seemed to recognize—as did many other major philosophers, from Augustine to Anselm, from Bishop Butler to George Berkeley (and that's just the A's and B's)—is that morality and ultimate happiness need to go hand in hand if morality is to be a fully rational enterprise. To retain its authority in our lives, morality requires the stability of cohering with ultimate happiness.

Some philosophers have called this the "Coincidence Thesis," which says that the moral life is, or is at least likely to be, good on the whole for the virtuous agent. The rationality of morality requires it, but certain experiences of evil can shake this conviction. How can we believe in such a thesis? How can Chidi and Eleanor, especially after they find out that nobody's made it to The Good Place for centuries? Scottish philosopher Thomas Reid (1710–1796), for one, saw no way to defend the coincidence of virtue and well-being apart from supposing that the world is under benevolent administration. Entering the final season, we had yet to see evidence that the world of *The Good Place* is.

Reid offered a few arguments in support of the Coincidence Thesis, according to which well-being and virtue go together. He made it clear that virtue and well-being are distinct, but a benevolent deity secures their coincidence. As Reid put it,

> While the world is under a wise and benevolent administration, it is impossible, that any man should, in the issue, be a loser by doing his duty. Every man, therefore, who believes in God, while he is careful to do his duty, may safely leave the care of his happiness to Him who made him.[5]

As it happens, Reid would agree with the writers of *The Good Place*, convinced that genuine virtue requires being committed to the moral life for its own sake, not for some reward. Importantly, though, he saw no way to make sense of that commitment apart from holding that there is just and benevolent administration of the world, ensuring that an agent's virtue and well-being coincide, if not in this life, then in the next. As Reid put it, "Virtue is his [i.e., God's] care. Its votaries are under his protection & guardianship."[6] Reid thought a commitment to the Coincidence Thesis, though virtuous, natural, and intuitive, goes beyond the evidence in some sense. Another step is needed. For Kant, these considerations provided the material for an argument for God's existence.

Kant held that a rational moral being must necessarily will "the highest good," which consists of a world in which people are both morally good and happy, and in which moral virtue is the condition for happiness. Kant was less concerned with questions of happiness per se than with questions of what makes us worthy of happiness. He held that a person can't rationally will a virtuous life without believing that moral actions can successfully achieve such an end, which requires that the world be ordered in a certain way. This conviction is equivalent to belief in God, a moral being who is ultimately responsible for the character of the natural world.

So Kant would reject both the suggestion that happiness is irrelevant to the moral life and the suggestion that the world features a huge disconnect between virtue and happiness. *The Good Place*, potentially anyway, seems to represent a thought experiment in which the Coincidence Thesis is simply false. But Kant would say that rather than such a scenario enabling the purest morality of all, it would render the moral enterprise less than rationally stable. What morality and what rationality would dictate us to do would be at odds. Morality wouldn't really make full rational sense. Thus the tragedy.

Incidentally, Kant was known for a second moral argument for God's existence (or rational belief in God), which we can call his "argument from grace."[7] In light of our corrupt motivations and inward bents, Kant thought we must believe in God to give us the needed resources to be virtuous—to cure us from privileging our desires and inclinations over our moral duties. More could be said about this, but it's only mentioned here to identify another critique he'd offer of *The Good Place* universe. It had become a world in which the moral life was irremediably impossible to achieve with no divine resource to rectify it. Rational commitment to the moral life requires believing it's possible. If it isn't possible, the moral enterprise, once more, is compromised.

Benevolent Administration

Many of us have a nagging conviction that the moral life is worth doing for its own sake. Morality has autonomy or independence; morality is its own thing and reward. If this is correct, what does it reveal about reality?

Earlier we mentioned Reid, who held that the Coincidence Thesis lies deep in the moral life. Reid thought it a virtuous coincidence that the moral life is, or is at least likely to be, good on the whole for the virtuous agent. At the same time, Reid recognized that certain experiences of evil can shake this conviction. Terence Cuneo explains that

"Reid sees no way to defend the coincidence of virtue and well-being apart from supposing that the world is under benevolent administration. There is an important sense, then, in which Reid's ethical views are ineliminably theistic."[8]

It might be thought that insisting that virtue and happiness ultimately coincide is self-centered. How is this different from Mindy St. Claire's me-first attitude? But if Kant was right, we as human beings can't help but to care about our eternal destinies and to desire enduring joy. It's not irrational to be concerned with such things, but rather quite natural and altogether human. The idea that happiness and virtue ultimately coincide is not, on this score, myopically selfish. Rather, morality, to be the fully rational thing we suppose it to be, must feature such resonance with happiness. Not all self-interest is selfish. So-called eudaimonists are so convinced of the inherent connection between virtue and happiness that they tread the verge of equating them. Kant was not inclined to conflate them, but still he saw them as connected. This is why moral action should be done for its own sake, and this is why the stability of morality requires benevolent administration. Kant happened to think that a personal and loving God not only could but absolutely would ensure the airtight correspondence between virtue and happiness.

Some might suggest that there is a good nontheistic way to ensure such ultimate correspondence. Consider the possibility of karma instead of a theistic universe. In "You've Changed, Man," something like reincarnation or transmigration of souls is hinted at as a potential solution to the broken system. Couldn't an atheist opt for something like that to make everything bonzer? Yes, but in light of the incalculable complexity of a system of karma featuring its plethora of precise calibrations, such a moral order postulated by nontheistic reincarnation paradoxically provides evidence for the existence of a personal God after all. Who else is crunching the numbers and directing the whole show? So Kant at least would be inclined to think theism—not a mechanistic universe, a rule-obsessed committee, or a free-for-all pandemonium—is the more plausible explanation of the benevolent administration that morality and rationality would be at odds without.

Tragedy, Comedy, or Cincinnati?

Until the final season, the question loomed whether the show's depiction of the afterlife constituted a comedy or a tragedy. Simon Critchley has written that the world is a tragicomedy defined by war, corruption, vanity, and greed, and entirely without the capacity for redemption. Perhaps this is why it is so hard for us to parse the difference between tragedy and comedy. Who knows, perhaps Socrates was right in the *Symposium* after all: the tragedian should be a comedian and vice versa.[9]

With the finale now in the books, *The Good Place*, in its own way, seems to contain elements of both tragedy and comedy.

The show's aforementioned steadfast adherence to secularity makes it stand in contrast to the robustly religious conception of the afterlife held by those earlier thinkers like Pascal or Locke, St. Paul or Kant. And the show's tragic elements are thrown in relief by these points of departure. At the beginning of this chapter, recall that two central questions reside at the heart of the show: (1) whether morality requires that we do good for goodness' sake and (2) whether reality itself is committed to morality.

Now we can qualify and clarify that claim. Doing morality for morality's sake echoes a recurring and resounding note in the show. But if benevolent administration is needed to make morality and rationality cohere, the universe of *The Good Place* is not really as committed to morality as it might first appear. The highest authorities are often benighted, callous, ineffectual, and little concerned with justice. In fact, absurdly, voices of good and evil are accorded the same weight in final determinations—as if fairness requires treating them equally and impartially. That Shawn might still mount a coup and set up a whole new and deeply unjust system remains a possibility. Whether the reformed system stays in place is a wholly contingent matter. But as we saw earlier, a world ungoverned by a just authority undermines the Kantian notion of the rationality of doing right for the sake of rightness alone.

The final season enables us to extend this analysis. A feature of secularism is what Charles Taylor calls its "immanent frame," which inclines the modern mind to find fulfillment without recourse to any transcendent source. Rather than the beatific vision as humanity's ultimate end and best destiny, the highest good becomes, at worst, garden-variety amoral trivial pursuits like the perfect video game performance or jamming with a Magic Guitar. But at least at moments the show seems to recognize an even deeper value: that bonding with other people may be a more satisfying endeavor. In this way, the show affirms Ernest Becker's conclusion that the modern relationship is all that many of us have left after the "death of God." We see this in Chidi and Eleanor's relationship. By the final episode, however, we also come to see that even this love ultimately falters.

Perhaps this is because even human loves fall short. They admit of boredom and fail to satisfy. Understandably so since, as Becker puts it, "No human relationship can bear the burden of godhood."[10] But what if that's all there is, as *The Good Place* intimates? What if all we have to look forward to is monotony-induced enervating ennui, relieved only by the dissolution of the self? What else is to be said but that this would be a tragic state of affairs? Such a picture is one in which the highest possible good isn't large or transcendent enough to satisfy forever. It would be profoundly sad if eternal joy were an oxymoron, a contradiction in terms. Only an infinite good could liberate us from such a fate. Who knows what joys of life redeemed may bring, when fecund light and love unending sing?

The Good Place, despite its recognition of the flaws in a broken system, either can't or won't imagine for its characters a source of unending bliss and eternal satisfaction. If the show is right, however much we might wish to follow Arthur Schopenhauer (1788–1860) in crediting morality as the source of meaning, life for Chidi and company is tragic indeed. Although *The Good Place* may be second to none as a brilliant sitcom, we have principled reason to hope for an even more divine comedy.

And that, in the words of our paragon of moral wisdom Eleanor Shellstrop (1982–2016), is how you get ethics'd in the face.

Notes

1　See Immanuel Kant, *Critique of Practical Reason and Other Writings in Moral Philosophy*, translated and edited with an introduction by Lewis White Beck (Chicago: University of Chicago Press, 1949), 258.

2　See John Stuart Mill, *Utilitarianism* (Indianapolis, IN: Hackett Publishing, 2002).

3　Blaise Pascal, *Pensées*, trans. Honor Levi (Oxford: Oxford University Press, 1995), 143.

4　John Locke, *The Reasonableness of Christianity*, ed. I.T. Ramsey (Stanford, CA: Stanford University Press, 1958), 70.

5　Thomas Reid, *Essays on the Active Powers of the Human Mind*, intro. B. Brody (Cambridge, MA: MIT Press, 1969), 256.

6　Thomas Reid, *Practical Ethics, Being Lectures and Papers on Natural Religion, Self-Government, Natural Jurisprudence, and the Law of Nations*, ed. K. Haakonssen (Princeton, NJ: Princeton University Press, 1990), 120.

7   Kant gave this argument in the Dialectic of the *Critique of Practical Reason*; at the beginning of *Religion within the Boundaries of Mere Reason*, trans. George Di Giovanni (Cambridge: Cambridge University Press, 1998); and at the end of the first and third *Critiques*.

8   Terence Cuneo, "Duty, Goodness, and God in Reid's Moral Philosophy," in *Reid on Ethics*, ed. Sabine Roeser (New York: Palgrave Macmillan, 2010), 256.

9   Simon Critchley, *Tragedy, the Greeks, and Us* (New York: Pantheon, 2019), 267.

10 Ernest Becker, *The Denial of Death* (New York: Free Press Paperbacks, 1997), 166. For further discussion on this, see Alan Noble's *Disruptive Witness* (Downer's Grove, IL: IVPBooks, 2018), chap. 3.

Don't Let the Good Life Pass You By: Doug Forcett and the Limits of Self-Sacrifice

Greg Littmann

How would you like to drink water that's recycled from your own composting toilet? How about living on radishes and lentils, undergoing painful cosmetics research, and going shoeless, just to amuse bullies? Welcome to the life of Doug Forcett. Should you live like Doug? Doug thinks so.

Doug's famous in the afterlife as the human who most closely guessed the afterlife's true nature. While tripping on mushrooms back in the '70s, Doug realized that the way to end up in The Good Place instead of The Bad Place is to score enough points by doing good things and avoiding doing bad things. So he's been trying to live morally ever since.

In "Don't Let the Good Life Pass You By," Michael and Janet visit Doug. They find him living a life of self-denial and sacrifice. He lives "completely off the grid," growing his own food and donating the surplus to the food bank. He recycles his toilet water, reasoning, "Why take fresh water away from the beavers and fish?" He's so careful not to do harm that he won't even kill snails. He rescues every stray dog that wanders onto his land, and he volunteers for painful cosmetics experiments so that animal test subjects don't need to be used.

Michael and Janet are strangers to him, yet he offers them food, water, a place to live, and one of his kidneys. He's given so much blood that the last time he went to the blood bank, they declared him anemic and gave blood to *him*. He even submits to the bullying of

The Good Place and Philosophy, First Edition. Edited by Kimberly S. Engels.
© 2021 John Wiley & Sons, Inc. Published 2021 by John Wiley & Sons, Inc.

Raymond, a kid he describes as "just a local sociopath who comes by my house to take advantage of me." Though he recognizes that Raymond is taking advantage of him, he still folds his laundry for him, and even gives him his shoe when Raymond demands it. Raymond, who already has two shoes, just throws Doug's shoe away and calls him an idiot.

"Michael, Face Facts. Doug Is Not the Blueprint of How to Live a Good Life. He's Become a Happiness Pump." —Janet

Michael and Janet had hoped that Doug's life would provide a template for how people should live. Instead, they decide he's living badly. Michael judges, "Doug is a complete disaster." He advises him, "Loosen up, bud. Have a little fun. Eat something besides lentils; just have ice cream or chicken parm. Live your life. You know, travel. Drink regular water that wasn't inside you. Okay? Just relax." Janet diagnoses the problem with Doug's life: "He's become a happiness pump. Remember from Chidi's lessons?... A happiness pump is someone who is obsessed with maximizing the overall good at his or her expense. Doug will do literally anything to make other people happy even if it makes him miserable."

Doug insists that the way he lives is only rational. He explains, "What if I relax and do something that loses me just enough points to keep me out of The Good Place and I'm tortured for eternity?" Doug's right that getting into The Good Place and staying out of The Bad Place, if they exist, is a lot more important than anything that happens to us in this short life. A few decades of drinking toilet water is nothing compared to an eternity of penis flatteners and bees with teeth (or teeth flatteners and bees with penises, whichever is worse). But is Doug right that he's living the morally right sort of life? The question of what sort of life we should live is one we all must face whether we think that living well will get us into The Good Place or not. In Season 3, Eleanor, Chidi, Tahani, and Jason no longer think that they have a chance of getting into The Good Place, but just like people who don't believe in The Good Place at all, they still have to decide how they will live. Eleanor finally decides, "Now that I know how it all ends, I just want to be virtuous for virtue's sake."

"We Are Here to Celebrate the Life of Martin Luther Gandhi Tyler Moore, the Snail." — Doug

One of the reasons that Michael and Janet's rejection of Doug's lifestyle is philosophically interesting is that there's a long tradition of regarding people who sacrifice for the sake of others as heroes. The tradition is old enough to be a common theme in religion. For instance, in Hinduism, the primordial man Purusha sacrificed himself to create the universe from his body. In Greek mythology, the titan Prometheus defied the gods by giving fire to humans, though he was punished by being bound to a rock, visited daily by an eagle that eats his liver. In Norse mythology, the god Tyr sacrificed his right hand to save us all from the monstrous wolf, Fenrir. The central story of Christianity is Jesus' crucifixion, by which he sacrificed his own life to save humanity. Likewise, many later Christians became famous after being martyred for their faith, like Saint Peter (crucified upside-down) and Joan of Arc (burned at the stake).

Perhaps the most famous examples of heroic self-sacrifice come from war. We still remember how 300 Spartans died holding off the Persians at the Battle of Thermopylae (480 BCE) two and a half thousand years after the event, and despite the intervening millennia, the basic story still resonates enough to have been the basis of the hit film *300* (2006). In the modern United States, the Purple Heart is a decoration reserved only for those wounded or killed while serving in the military.

But not all self-sacrificing heroes are military heroes. People also idolize the likes of Mary "Mother Teresa" Bojaxhiu (1919–1997), who worked to help the poor in Calcutta. Doug identifies his heroes when he names a dead snail Martin Luther Gandhi Tyler Moore, after Martin Luther King, Jr. (1929–1968), who suffered abuse, imprisonment, and assassination to promote the civil rights of black Americans; Mohandas "Mahatma" Gandhi (1869–1948), who went on hunger strikes to stop violence between Hindus and Muslims; and American actress and philanthropist Mary Tyler Moore (1936–2017), who gave time and money for medical research and animal welfare.

Popular fiction has long focused on self-sacrificing heroes, like Sir Gawain of the Round Table, who offers to let the Green Knight cut off his head to spare the honor of King Arthur in the fourteenth-century romance *Sir Gawain and the Green Knight*, or Rick and Lisa in the film *Casablanca* (1942), who sacrifice their love for the sake of the war effort. In modern times, the tradition of heroic self-sacrifice is as strong as ever. Examples include the wizard Gandalf holding off the demonic Balrog in the novel *The Lord of the Rings* (1954), the Jedi Obi Wan Kenobi letting Darth Vader strike him down in *Star Wars: A New Hope* (1977), Mr. Spock exposing himself to radiation to save the *Enterprise* in *Star Trek II: The Wrath of Khan* (1982) and Captain Kirk doing the same in *Star Trek Into Darkness* (2013), Harry Potter planning to let Voldemort kill him to save Hogwarts in the novel *Harry Potter and the Deathly Hallows* (2007), and the gladiator Katniss plotting to martyr herself for the rebellion in the *Hunger Games* novel *Catching Fire* (2009).

Even in *The Good Place*, self-sacrifice is often treated as heroic, such as when the Janets rebel against the Judge in "The Funeral to End All Funerals," facing marbleization rather than letting her reboot the universe. In the same episode, Eleanor decides that Chidi is the right person to tackle the "ultimate ethical question" of how the afterlife should be designed, on the grounds that he's "brilliant and empathic." She explains, "All he cares about is how best to treat other people, and he is willing to sacrifice his own happiness to do it." In the final episode, "Whenever You're Ready," Chidi sacrifices his happiness for Eleanor by staying in The Good Place when he's ready for non-existence, and then Eleanor sacrifices her happiness for Chidi by letting him go.

"I Should Donate More Blood. I'll Try, but the Last Time I Went Down There, They Said I Was So Anemic They Ended Up Giving *Me* Blood." — Doug

Given the tradition of thinking of self-sacrifice as heroic, it would be odd to see Doug's life as a "complete disaster" just because he's so self-sacrificing. Yes, he's suffering, but Mother Teresa wasn't exactly having a ball attending to the wounds of poor Indians. Then again, maybe she was a fool. English philosopher Thomas Hobbes (1588–1679) wrote in his book *Leviathan* (1651) that both reason and moral duty tell us to be selfish.[1] Eleanor sometimes takes a similar view. As she sits at a bar in "Jeremy Bearimy," she declares, "Here are my rules. Rule number one I get to do whatever I want, and you all just have to deal with it" and describes the United States as "the perfect system" because everyone takes this selfish attitude. Let's allow that Hobbes and Eleanor are wrong there and that there's nothing wrong with being self-sacrificing per se, to get at a more controversial issue, which is how far our duty to be self-sacrificing extends. Do we have a *duty* to live like Doug? Even if we regard individuals who live selflessly as heroic, can it be that we are morally *required* to be so giving? Must we turn ourselves into happiness pumps?

As Janet notes, the term "happiness pump" was coined as an objection to the moral theory of utilitarianism. Utilitarianism, as most commonly understood, is the view that the right thing to do is whatever will best promote happiness. In the words of the theory's most famous proponent, the English philosopher John Stuart Mill (1806–1873), in *Utilitarianism* (1861), it's the view that "actions are right in proportion as they tend to promote happiness, wrong as they tend to produce the reverse of happiness."[2]

Utilitarianism is a demanding view. You can almost always better promote happiness by helping others than by helping yourself. After all, a starving person would benefit a lot more from your next meal than you would, a homeless person needs your sweater more than you do, and if you have two functioning kidneys, someone with no functioning kidneys has a right to one of them. Hence the objection that utilitarianism requires us to turn into happiness pumps.

While the "happiness pump" objection has been directed at utilitarianism, utilitarianism isn't unique in the duty it places on us to be self-sacrificing. For instance, variations on the so-called Golden Rule are found in many cultures. The Hebrew book *Leviticus* (c. fourth century BCE) instructs us, "Love your neighbor as yourself," an injunction repeated by Jesus, who added, "Do to others what you want them to do to you" to boot. The Chinese philosopher Laozi (seventh century BCE) writes in the *Tao Te Ching* that "The sage has no interest of his own, but takes the interests of the people as his own," while the Chinese philosopher Mozi (470–391 BCE) beat the English utilitarians by about two and a half thousand years in declaring that we should show equal concern for the well-being of everyone. The Indian *Mahabharata* (fourth century CE) instructs us, "Treat others as you treat yourself." According to the Islamic *hadith*, the prophet Mohammed said, "As you would have people do to you, do to them." All of these formulations seem to require great sacrifice if we take them seriously. If I were starving, I'd want others to give me food, even if they were already almost broke from giving. So if I treat others as I want to be treated, I need to give food to the starving, even if I'm almost broke from giving.

To be fair to utilitarianism and other theories demanding great sacrifice, Doug's self-sacrifice goes further than merely treating everyone else's interests as being as valuable as his own. He often treats his own interests as not important at all. When Raymond demands Doug's shoe, Doug hands it over, though the bully already has two shoes of his own, and Doug is left shoeless. The utilitarian would tell him to keep his shoes, since they will benefit him more than Raymond. Likewise, the utilitarian would find it absurd that Doug gets so upset when he misremembers Michael's name, causing himself needless suffering over something that didn't bother Michael at all. Doug has a moral duty to care for Doug too! The sixteenth-century collection of Chinese folk tales, *Ocean of Stories from Past and Present*, includes the story of a foolish follower of Mozi who saves the life of a wolf by hiding it from a hunter, only for the wolf to decide to eat him afterward.[3] The story reminds us that the desire to help others shouldn't make us blind to the costs, including our own exploitation.

Even so, all these theories seem to leave us with a great burden. A lot of people find it implausible that we owe so much. Is there any argument that can be offered that we *should* care as much about the well-being of others as our own? As pointed out by the Scottish philosopher David Hume (1711–1776) in *A Treatise of Human Nature* (1738), the existence of a moral obligation can't be demonstrated in the way that ordinary facts about the world can, because moral facts can't be observed with the senses.[4] If you step on a snail, you can hear the snail's shell crack under your shoe, and you can see the squashed shape and glistening color of the departed snail's corpse, but you can't see any moral facts to use as proof for a moral theory. So, I don't think any *proof* can be offered that we are obliged to treat everyone the same.

Having said that, it seems to me that the fact that you are no more valuable than other people is good enough grounds to conclude that you should not be treated preferentially to anyone else—even by you. Western society has come far enough that most of us think that it's wrong to give someone preferential treatment because they are the same ethnicity, religion, or sex that we are. But it seems no more justified to give someone preferential treatment because they are the same *person* that we are, that is, because they are *us*. Doug's life, which seems so disastrous to Michael and Janet, might make more sense from the perspective of a hungry person fed by his donations to the food bank, or someone whose life is saved after Doug, a stranger, gives them one of his kidneys.

Snails and Radishes

The most striking thing about Doug's self-sacrifice is how wide his compassion is. Doug sacrifices for the animals and plants. A vegetarian, he rescues every stray dog that comes his way, minimizes his water use so that there is more fresh water for the beavers and fish, and strives never to kill so much as a snail. He volunteers his own face for cosmetics experiments, to spare the test animals. He explains, "It's fun ... for the animals who don't have to do it. For me, it's like wearing a mask of fire." He even leaves in place the radishes that were growing at his cabin when he moved in because "it seemed mean to dig them up."

Many utilitarians have believed that we have a duty to be concerned about animal suffering, perhaps most famously the Australian philosopher Peter Singer in his 1975 book *Animal Liberation*. In the eighteenth century, English utilitarian philosopher Jeremy Bentham (1748–1832) was an early advocate for animal welfare who argued that they should receive far greater legal protection. Unlike Doug, Bentham didn't think it was wrong to eat animals, or even to perform useful experiments on them, but he saw the way that animals were treated by humans as callous and tyrannical, comparing it to the exploitation of blacks by whites. He wrote in *Introduction to the Principles of Morals and Legislation* (1789),

> The French have already discovered that the blackness of skin is no reason why a human being should be abandoned without redress to the caprice of a tormentor. It may come one day to be recognized, that the number of legs, the villosity of the skin, or the termination of the os sacrum, are reasons equally insufficient for abandoning a sensitive being to the same fate.[5]

In "The Snowplow," Simone the neuroscientist explains to Eleanor what she takes the stages of moral development to be:

> As humans evolved, the first big problem we had to overcome was 'me versus us.' Learning to sacrifice a little individual freedom for the benefit of a group.... The next problem to overcome was 'us versus them,' trying to see other groups different from ours as equals. That one, we're still struggling with. That's why we have racism and nationalism and why fans of Stone Cold Steve Austin hate fans of The Rock.

Perhaps the next stage in human moral development is to see members of other species as our equals.

A common justification offered for treating animals so much worse than we treat humans is that animals are less intelligent than we are. But Bentham points out that infants and disabled people may be just as intellectually limited, and we don't think we are justified in treating infants and the disabled the way that we treat animals. Bentham writes, "the question is not, Can they reason? nor, Can they talk? but, Can they suffer?"

Doug gets a mixed report card by this standard. Dogs can suffer, so it's good to look after strays. Beavers can certainly suffer and fish can at least feel pain, so it's good for them to have the fresh water they need. What about snails?

It isn't clear whether snails can suffer or not. Other mollusks, like octopuses and squid, can feel pain and warrant more protection because of it. If you have a strong stomach, you can watch squid being dismembered alive by chefs on YouTube, and as you observe these intelligent animals being cut up, imagine someone doing that to a live cat. It may convince you that there's nothing foolish about Doug's donation to the Canadian Mollusk Fund.

Having said that, snails' brains are very simple. Doug is foolish to give his snails funerals, and to avoid naming them because "they might already have a name that they prefer," since a snail's stupidity prevents it from understanding or caring about funerals and names. But there's no reason to believe that suffering could only occur at a certain level of intelligence, or even that more intelligent creatures suffer more intensely than less intelligent creatures. We don't usually think that an unusually stupid human can't suffer as much as a more intelligent human, so why think that a very simple creature, even one like a snail, can't suffer as intensely as we can? Perhaps when Doug stepped on Martin Luther Gandhi Tyler Moore and shattered its shell, it hurt the snail as badly as it would hurt you to be run over by a car. If it's plausible that snails feel intense pain, the same goes for other creatures with simple nervous systems like mosquitoes and flies. Jain monks and nuns in India often sweep the ground when they walk to avoid harming any insects. Perhaps we should all be doing the same!

Do I really think that we need to be going out of our way for the snails and insects? No—my best guess is that they don't have what it takes to feel good or bad. But that's open to revision in light of fresh evidence. Too often in the past, people have dismissed the possibility of animal pain in cases where it turned out to be all too real, as with squid and fish. The point is not that we must pamper the snails, but that the extent to which we need to self-sacrifice can depend in radical ways on what we learn about the world.

As for the radishes … now Doug is just being silly. When Doug moved in to his home, he left the radishes in place because it seemed mean to uproot them. But radishes don't have the intelligence to miss their plot of soil, any more than snails have the intelligence to have names they prefer. With no brain or nervous system, radishes are presumably incapable of physical discomfort from being uprooted either. It's unlikely that humans can make the plants happier or sadder, and so there are few grounds for worrying that we are treating them less kindly than we should. Go ahead and walk on the grass—stomp on it if you like.

"I Just Want to Be Virtuous for Virtue's Sake." —Eleanor

So is Doug "the blueprint of how to live a good life"? I don't think so. He's too hung up on things that don't matter, like snail funerals, and he's too uncaring about himself. On top of this, he shows no sign of political involvement to make the world a better place. Having said that, I disagree with Michael that Doug's life is a "disaster." Yes, Doug is miserable, but he donates the excess food he grows to the hungry, and he runs a refuge for stray dogs, all while hurting nobody. He does good in the world, very likely more than enough to outweigh his own unhappiness. If his determination not to harm the environment is excessive, what with living on lentils and recycling his waste just to save water, he's doing better than everyone who cares about the environment too little. The world could support a lot of Dougs without coming to harm, but ordinary folk are wrecking it.

It's not up to me to tell you how to live. That's the Judge's job. But whatever the blueprint of how to live a good life is, I think it's probably a miserable existence. The world is full of suffering, and relieving the suffering of others is almost always going to be the best use of our time. We don't have to ignore our own well-being, as Doug does. We just need to treat everyone else's well-being as just as important—and that's trouble enough. The mere fact that you're reading this book suggests that you are one of the lucky 15% or so living in a developed, first-world country, a rich person by world standards, with much less need for most of your possessions and spare time than billions of needy people. And however bad your life is, there's almost certainly plenty of people with worse lives to whom you should be directing your attention. So don't let the good life pass you by—go out there and make yourself unhappy doing what's right. Not a very cheerful conclusion, is it? But as Eleanor finally realizes when she believes she is doomed to go to The Bad Place, making yourself happy is not the point of being good.

Notes

1 Thomas Hobbes, *Leviathan* (Baltimore: Penguin Books, 1968).
2 John Stuart Mill, *Utilitarianism* (Indianapolis, IN: Hackett Publishing, 2002), 7.
3 Lee Dian Rainey, *Confucius and Confucianism: The Essentials* (Chichester, UK: Wiley-Blackwell, 2010), 218.
4 David Hume, *A Treatise of Human Nature* (Oxford: Oxford University Press, 2000).
5 Jeremy Bentham, *Introduction to the Principles of Morals and Legislation* (Mineola, NY: Dover Publications, 2007), 211.

3

Luck and Fairness in *The Good Place*

Scott A. Davison and Andrew R. Davison

We are often told that "Life is not fair." But is that right? In some ways, this is the central question of *The Good Place*. The story begins with a common picture of what happens to us after we die—either we go to The Bad Place, which involves eternal suffering, or we go to The Good Place, which involves eternal happiness. The Bad Place is a fitting punishment for moral failure during life on Earth, whereas The Good Place is a fitting reward for moral success.

But then things take a strange turn. We discover that Eleanor, Chidi, Jason, and Tehani are not in The Real Good Place, as we previously thought, but rather in The Bad Place. They are being tormented in creative ways by Michael, a demon who pretended to be an architect of happiness in The Real Good Place. We also discover that there is The Medium Place, and it is possible to escape (at least temporarily) from The Bad Place into The Medium Place. We watch Michael develop sympathy for the four main human characters and become friends with them, which leads to various attempts to get them into The Real Good Place (the last of which is finally successful).

One of the key philosophical issues in the story involves how to assess correctly the moral goodness or badness of a person's life on Earth, since this is the basis of the judgment concerning their eternal destiny. The four main human characters from *The Good Place* represent people from all over the world, who differ from one another in many respects, so they are designed to give us some kind of sample of humanity as a whole. Even if earthly life is not fair, as people often say, we would like to think that if there is an afterlife, the system of the universe treats everyone fairly in the end. But is the system of judgment in *The Good Place* fair?

The Good Place and Philosophy, First Edition. Edited by Kimberly S. Engels.
© 2021 John Wiley & Sons, Inc. Published 2021 by John Wiley & Sons, Inc.

Fairness and Judgment

In order for a system of judgment to be fair, equal cases must be treated equally, and people must get what they really deserve. Determining what people really deserve turns out to be a complicated matter, though, and seems to require a great deal of knowledge about their intimate lives.

In *The Good Place*, we discover things about our main characters that we would typically never know about other people, even our closest friends and family. We see crucial events from their past lives, for example, and come to know their inner motives and intentions. We see them put to various tests, with varying degrees of success. The idea of God in *The Good Place* is not clear, but as the show develops, we come to know some of the intimate details that an all-knowing God would know about our main characters.

As we come to know their true moral selves, we recognize our own selves in them. Once we have identified with our four main characters, we become deeply concerned for their welfare, and we want to see them treated properly—we want them to be judged fairly, and to get what they deserve. Since we have come to know them so well, we feel confident in our judgments about them—and we don't think they deserve to go to The Bad Place.

Morality and Control

When we discover that someone has literally no control over something, we tend not to praise or blame that person for it. For example, if Jason had killed Janet by pushing the big red button just to see what it was for (in Season 1, Episode 7, "The Eternal Shriek"), we would have blamed him for being careless. As it happened, though, Chidi actually pushed the button and killed Janet by accident, in the process of trying to prevent Jason from doing so. In this case, we do not blame Chidi for killing Janet, because it was an accident. Let's call this the control/blame connection.

People often assume that our moral goodness or badness is within our control, so that we deserve to be held responsible for our own moral character. The famous and influential Prussian philosopher Immanuel Kant (1724–1804) seems to have thought that this was true, and so did the ancient Stoic philosophers.[1] According to this approach, the only things that matter morally are things within our direct control, such as our freely chosen intentions. Sometimes the system of judgment in *The Good Place* seems to reflect this idea: for example, we are told that Eleanor cannot earn good points in the afterlife for her good actions if she does them only to earn good points, because that is selfish (Season 1, Episode 11, "What's My Motivation").

But is this common assumption correct? Is it really true that the only things that matter morally are those things that are within our control? We mentioned earlier that Kant, the famous philosopher, accepted this view, but many later philosophers disagreed with him about this. Friedrich Nietzsche (1844–1900), for example, famously criticized the idea that the value of an action is determined by the intention behind it:

> [T]he origin of an action was interpreted in the most definite sense possible, as origin out of an INTENTION; people were agreed in the belief that the value of an action lay in the value of its intention.... [N]owadays when, at least among us immoralists, the suspicion arises that the decisive value of an action lies precisely in that which is NOT INTENTIONAL, and that all its intentionalness, all that is seen, sensible, or "sensed" in it, belongs to its surface or skin—which, like every skin, betrays something, but CONCEALS still more.[2]

Here Nietzsche seems to say that the value of an action comes from what is not intentional about it, and that the intentional aspect of an action merely points to other aspects of the person that the action reveals. He also suggests that sometimes what appears to be intentional about an action actually conceals other things about the person, things that are morally relevant. The system of judgment in *The Good Place* takes account of the consequences of our actions, not just our intentions, so it departs from Kant's idea significantly. As Michael discovers, for people living today, the choice about which flower to purchase or which tomato to eat has ethical implications because of the interconnectedness of the modern world (Season 3, Episode 10, "Janet(s)"). Whether these consequences of our actions are good or bad, though, is typically not entirely up to us—there is quite a bit of luck involved, and we can rarely foresee the long-term consequences of our actions.

According to some recent prominent philosophers, this is not the only way in which morality is subject to luck. Thomas Nagel, the most prominent philosopher to develop this idea, claims that there are four kinds of "moral luck": luck in the circumstances in which we find ourselves, luck with respect to our constitution or character, luck with respect to the results of our actions, and luck with respect to having free choices at all.[3] We can see clear examples of each of these kinds of moral luck in *The Good Place*.

Moral Luck in *The Good Place*

For example, we know that Eleanor's selfishness, dishonesty, and insecurity stem in part from growing up with her mother Donna, a completely unreliable caretaker who resorted to fraud and deceit whenever she got into a bind (Season 3, Episode 7, "A Fractured Inheritance"). This is a case of bad moral luck for Eleanor. Of course, she is not completely morally bankrupt—she has virtues also, such as creativity, resourcefulness, and determination. These qualities appear to have developed in response to her difficult personal history, so Eleanor's earthly life also involves some good moral luck.

Chidi was always indecisive, even as a child—he wasted an entire recess period because he was unable to choose teammates ("Chidi's Choice"). So this seems to be clearly beyond his control, and this character trait led to all kinds of terrible consequences for those around him. But like Eleanor, he has his strong points—he sees both sides of every question, and he is worried about harming others, even if he can't seem to prevent it completely. So Chidi's earthly life includes moral luck, both good and bad.

Tahani's parents forced her to compete with her sister Kamilah from a young age ("A Fractured Inheritance"), leading to a distorted sense of self and permanent insecurities that would dominate her earthly life and often leave her blind to the suffering she caused others. This is a case of bad moral luck. However, she also knows what it means to be overlooked and neglected, and this means she can identify with the suffering of others in a morally positive way. Her moral luck also cuts both ways.

Jason grew up in an unstable environment, learning from his unreliable father Donkey Doug and his adopted family of shady friends ("The Ballad of Donkey Doug"). Predictably, he makes many bad choices in life as a result. In the end, he dies after locking himself in a safe accidentally with a snorkel, falsely believing it will permit him to breathe. Knowing Jason's history, we find it difficult to blame him for his ignorance and the harm he caused to others, because it seems to flow from his life circumstances in ways we would not expect anyone to overcome completely. He suffers from bad moral luck. But he is also honest and compassionate and generous, thanks to his difficult life history—in fact, by retelling the story of his hard-luck friend (Big Noodle), Jason even persuades the Judge that "you can't judge humans, because you don't know what we go through" ("Chidi Sees the Time-Knife"). So he also seems to benefit from good moral luck.

Unfairness in the System

Earlier we observed that in order for a system to be fair, equal cases must be treated equally, and people must get what they really deserve. With respect to the first part of fairness, the system of judgment in *The Good Place* seems to be unfair—equal cases are not treated equally. We are told, for instance, that there is arbitrariness in the administration of the bureaucracy of the afterlife—some people in The Bad Place are tormented horribly by expert demons, whereas others are afflicted by bungling amateurs who are still learning the trade. Sometimes Judge Hydrogen is clearly distracted by highly irrelevant information when she makes important rulings ("The Burrito"). Nobody has made it to The Good Place in 521 years because the consequences of ordinary actions today, in a deeply interconnected world filled with systematic injustice, are much worse than they were many years ago ("Janet(s)"). Even Doug Forcett, the one human being in history who figured out the system of judgment and how the afterlife works, has only half of the required points to enter The Real Good Place ("Don't Let the Good Life Pass You By").

Now consider the second part of fairness: what our main characters deserve. Luck is opposed to control in the following way: if something happens to you in a lucky way, then it was not something over which you had control. But as we noted in the "Morality and Control" section (under the control/blame connection), if what you deserve is connected to what you control, then it is not fair to hold you responsible for things that happen to you because of luck. In *The Good Place*, it seems that our main characters are judged on the basis of things that involve a significant degree of luck, including the remote consequences of their actions, so the system of judgment seems to be unfair in this sense also. The whole thing seems to be one big clusterfork.

Judgment and Ideals

Even if we believe already that life on Earth is not fair, it is deeply troubling to think that judgments about the afterlife might be unfair, because they seem to be irreversible and involve the most significant consequences imaginable. Since we care about the four main human characters, and identify with them, we hope that they can find some way to defeat the system and somehow enter The Good Place, because the formula of judgment seems unfair to us. But perhaps we are misled here; perhaps we are thinking about them in the following way:

> Our main characters do not deserve to go to The Bad Place.
> Either people deserve to go to The Good Place or they deserve to go to The Bad Place.
> So our main characters deserve to go to The Good Place.

This way of thinking seems to be logically flawed. Just because our main characters do not deserve to go to The Bad Place, it does not follow that they do deserve to go to The Good Place. It could be that the second statement in this list is false because the entire system is simply unfair—sometimes people get worse than they deserve, but people never get more than they deserve.

If God existed, and served as the judge for the afterlife, as many people assume, then this would seem to be a really serious philosophical problem. The unfairness of the afterlife would seem to be a kind of evil. God is supposed to be all-knowing, all-powerful, and perfectly good. If God existed, why would there be any evil in the world? Some popular answers to this question include the idea that evil is due to human free will, that evil is permitted in order to test us, and that God will eventually eliminate all evil from the world after it has served a purpose. But if we are talking about how people are judged in the afterlife, these explanations do not seem to help very much. The elements of moral luck that we mentioned in this chapter are not cases in which our main characters have exercised free will badly—if they were, then they would not be cases of luck, they would be cases of control. If evil is permitted to test us, then the system of judgment should focus only on how our main characters responded to the test— the point system should not be measuring things beyond their control, like the unforeseeable consequences of their actions in the distant future. And if God will eventually eliminate all evil from the world, how could there be a Bad Place at all?

Some philosophers of religion who write about the existence of God have recently wondered whether moral luck might affect judgment in the afterlife; the philosophical debate about this is usually described as a debate about "religious luck" or "salvific luck."[4] One of the key questions in this debate has to do with having correct religious belief. If one single religion is true, and God requires belief in that true religion for acceptance into The Real Good Place (that is, heaven), then what about those who were never exposed to the one true religion, and so could not be expected to believe in it? Would God judge someone on the basis of something unlucky like this?

Some of the philosophers who work on this problem have suggested that God's system of judgment concerning the afterlife might include knowledge not just of what we actually did in our lives on Earth, but also knowledge of what we would have done differently in different circumstances.[5] In *The Good Place*, something like this idea is explored through Michael's 802 "reboots" of the main characters involving slightly different initial conditions, where proportions of similar outcomes are supposed to reveal something about a person's true self ("Dance Dance Resolution"). But the information gained from Michael's "reboots" does not seem to figure in the decision about where our main characters belong, since that decision appears to have been made right after they died. The same idea seems to motivate Judge Hydrogen's decision to permit our four main human characters to return to Earth to see if they would make different decisions under similar conditions ("Somewhere Else"). But Michael and Janet cannot resist the temptation to nudge the humans in the direction of goodness when they seem to revert to their former selves, and this introduces an element of good moral luck that spoils the experiment.

The New System

Of course, in the end, the Judge is convinced to try a new system invented by Chidi that is designed to address the apparent unfairness of the point system. Humans are tested in creative ways by the demons, who design tests based on individual personalities and experiences, and these tests can be repeated indefinitely. If someone passes the test, that person gets to go to The Good Place. But there is no guarantee that everyone will pass the test, as Michael is told before he becomes human ("Whenever You're Ready"), and the test will be different for everyone.

Earlier we mentioned two criteria for fairness—equal cases must be treated equally, and people must get what they deserve. Chidi's system has no time limit, which seems to create something like equal (infinite) opportunity for everyone—this is directed at the first criterion. And the demonic tests are tailored to fit each individual person, rather than imposing a "one-size-fits-all" point system—this is directed at the second criterion. But because the demonic tests in Chidi's new system depend upon the details of one's earthly life, there is still quite a bit of luck involved. Also, different demons approach the task differently— some are inexperienced, others are suspicious of the whole testing approach, and still others can't seem to let go of chainsaw bears. So the amount of time one might spend repeating a test varies significantly, depending upon one's demonic facilitator—Vicky seems to be the most reliable one of all ("Mondays, Am I Right?"), but not everyone is lucky enough to fall under her supervision. Finally, there is no guarantee that a given person will pass the test—we see Brent struggling mightily with his test, for example ("Whenever You're Ready"). So elements of unfairness persist, even in the revised system.

It is hard to know how to respond to the problem of apparent unfairness in *The Good Place*. As we mentioned, the problem is not just theoretical—it is personal. As viewers, we are given lots of information about our four main human characters, information from behind the scenes, so to speak. We learn about their childhoods, their good and bad choices, and the accidental elements in their lives that led to their current selves. We also watch them learn and develop in good ways as a result of their cooperation with one another. We put ourselves in their places, identify with their flaws and strengths, and wonder what we would do in similar circumstances.

Perhaps one moral of the story of *The Good Place* is that life is really complicated, morally speaking—people are not simply good or evil, and cannot be judged easily (don't forget the story of Big Noodle). It is not clear what we deserve, really, and so we should not judge one another quickly. We should also ask ourselves what really matters to us in this life, because that might define us forever.

Notes

1   See Immanuel Kant, *Groundwork of the Metaphysics of Morals* (1784), ed. and trans. M. Gregor (Cambridge: Cambridge University Press, 1998); and James N. Jordan, *Western Philosophy from Antiquity to the Middle Ages* (New York: Macmillan Publishing, 1987).

2 Friedrich Nietzsche, *Beyond Good and Evil* (1886), trans. Helen Zimmern, http://www.gutenberg.org/files/4363/4363-h/4363-h.htm, sec. 32.

3 Thomas Nagel and Bernard A.O. Williams, "Moral Luck," *Aristotelian Society Supplementary Volume* 50.226 (1976), 115–151, reprinted in Thomas Nagel, *Mortal Questions* (Cambridge: Cambridge University Press 1979), 24–38.

4 For example see William Lane Craig, "'No Other Name': A Middle Knowledge Perspective on the Exclusivity of Salvation through Christ," *Faith and Philosophy* 6.2 (1989), 172–188; and Linda Zagzebski, "Religious Luck," *Faith and Philosophy* 11.3 (1994), 397–413.

5 For example, see Craig, "'No Other Name'"; Scott A. Davison, "Salvific Luck," *International Journal for Philosophy of Religion* 45.2 (1999), 129–137; Mark B. Anderson, "Molinism, Open Theism, and Soteriological Luck," *Religious Studies* 47.3 (2011), 371–381; and Robert J. Hartman, "How to Apply Molinism to the Theological Problem of Moral Luck," *Faith and Philosophy* 31.1 (2014), 68–90.

Part II

"VIRTUOUS FOR VIRTUE'S SAKE"

4

Can Eleanor Really Become a Better Person?

Eric J. Silverman and Zachary Swanson

We first meet Eleanor Shellstrop when she arrives in The Good Place—a paradise where the most moral people spend eternity. They get to live with their ideal soulmate in homes that perfectly reflect their preferences and personality in an ideal community populated exclusively by moral saints. Yet, Eleanor is no saint! Her presence in The Good Place appears to be a cosmic mistake.

Eleanor lacks care for others, the environment, and even basic manners. Her career was selling fake health supplements made of chalk to senior citizens. She took advantage of her earthly "drinking buddies" by repeatedly failing to take her turn as the designated driver. After agreeing to watch her friend's dog, she neglected it and let it become morbidly obese. She intentionally littered and was repeatedly rude to an environmentalist. She borrowed her roommate Madison's dress without permission and ruined it. When Madison sued the drycleaners for damaging the dress, Eleanor profited by selling shirts mocking her roommate as "The Dress Bitch." In short, Eleanor simply was not a good person.

Eleanor's bad character continues into the afterlife where she gets drunk on the first night and takes almost all of the shrimp at a welcome party, even going so far as to stuff her bra with extra shrimp. Eleanor initiates a petty rivalry with her neighbor Tahani Al-Jamil, criticizing her height, accent, and extravagance. Beyond that, she causes a trash storm by hiding garbage when she was supposed to be cleaning it up. An equal opportunity offender, Eleanor even treats her supposed soulmate Chidi Anagonye poorly, pressuring him to lie to help her stay in The Good Place, even though she could hardly be bothered to learn to pronounce his name correctly.

The Good Place and Philosophy, First Edition. Edited by Kimberly S. Engels.
© 2021 John Wiley & Sons, Inc. Published 2021 by John Wiley & Sons, Inc.

Eventually, Eleanor realizes that her vicious character could have eternal consequences. So she decides to become a better person in the hope of remaining in The Good Place. Her plight raises important philosophical questions: can we really become better people? Is moral growth something we can control and cultivate? Or is our character simply the result of forces outside of our control such as God, destiny, our parents, genetics, or our culture? Can Eleanor—or any of us—really become better people?

Aristotle's Guide to Moral Growth

Eleanor has a pretty tall order for Chidi: "Teach me.... How to be good. That was your job, right? A professor of ethics.... Let me earn my place here. Let me be your ethical guinea pig" ("Everything Is Fine"). Aristotle (384–322 BCE), one of the philosophers Chidi teaches her about, believed in the possibility of changing one's moral character. Aristotle's theory of moral character focuses on developing virtues, the deep internal dispositional traits from which external actions naturally flow. These character traits include the values, perceptions, emotions, desires, and tendencies toward action that constitute our reactions to various situations.

Aristotle describes moral virtue as a human excellence that can be developed through practice, much like other excellences such as technical skills, playing musical instruments, or becoming an expert DJ—as Jason Mendoza believes himself to be. Aristotle proposes that we can develops virtues by forming habits, by repeatedly practicing behaviors, which eventually become the natural patterns of life that constitute our moral character. Aristotle says, "For the things we have to learn before we can do them, we learn by doing them, e.g. men become builders by building and lyre-players by playing the lyre; so too we become just by doing just acts, temperate by doing temperate acts, brave by doing brave acts."[1] We learn moral habits the same way we learn other practical skills: by practice.

However, Aristotle warns that both positive and negative habits are developed by practice. So, the bad habits of being selfish or cowardly can be developed by practice, just like the good virtuous habits of becoming altruistic or brave. He explains:

> [B]y doing the acts that we do in our transactions with other men we become just or unjust, and by doing the acts that we do in the presence

of danger, and being habituated to feel fear or confidence, we become brave or cowardly.... Thus, in one word, states of character arise out of like activities.... It makes no small difference, then, whether we form habits of one kind or of another from our very youth; it makes a very great difference, or rather all the difference.[2]

For Aristotle, virtuous character is tremendously important and helps constitute our earthly happiness. So, developing the right habits early on is both a practical and a moral concern. Accordingly, flashbacks to Eleanor's high school years reveal that she developed selfish habits from an early age.

Aristotle's Four Levels of Moral Character

There are three foundational aspects of Aristotelian virtue, and mastering each of the three aspects constitutes moral growth. The fully virtuous person knows the right thing to do, does the right thing, and experiences the proper internal emotions and desires while doing the right thing. We can illustrate a fully virtuous person with a trait that Aristotle called temperance: to know and recognize the right types and amounts of foods appropriate for one's health, to eat the right foods, and to desire these right foods. Fully temperate people have all three of these traits: the right knowledge, the right desires, and the right actions. They eat the proper foods in the proper portions and are actually satisfied! Not only do they eat the proper amount of shrimp, but it wouldn't even occur to them to stuff extras in their bras.

A less than fully virtuous person—but still quite good—is the strong-willed person who knows the right things to do and does the right things, even though their desires are not really in line with virtue and their motives are sometimes mixed. The strong-willed person might manage to eat the proper foods in the right quantities—despite really wanting to hog all the shrimp herself! Both the strong and weak-willed person know the proper thing to do. The difference between the strong-willed person and the virtuous person is that while they both act similarly externally, internally the strong-willed person successfully resists the temptation of her desires in order to control herself. Her desires are not fully in line with virtue. Doing the right thing is a struggle and is not automatic, easy, and unreflective. Michael seems aware of the difference between the strong-willed person and the fully virtuous person when he discusses Brent's moral improvement in the new neighborhood in Season 4. Michael says that "his behavior is changing. Remember, that's the roadmap. First we change their behavior, then we work on motivation" ("A Chip Driver Mystery").

Morally worse than the strong-willed person is the weak-willed person: who knows the right thing to do, but neither desires to do it nor actually does it. For example, Eleanor agrees to pick up trash during her second day in The Good Place instead of getting to fly ("Flying"). She knows this is the right thing to do and even tries to do the right thing. Yet, as often happens with the weak-willed person, Eleanor failed to follow through on her commitment and hides a bunch of trash rather than cleaning it up properly.

The morally worst person is the vicious person: who does the wrong thing, desires the wrong thing, and doesn't even know the right thing to do—perhaps even mistaking the wrong thing to do for the right thing. This was the sort of person Eleanor was when she entered The Good Place. In her earthly life, Eleanor treated people badly and took advantage of them, whether they were strangers she sold fake medicine to ("Everything Is Fine") or her roommate whose dress she damaged ("Most Improved Player"). She didn't care about people—her friendships were just shallow relationships of convenience. She didn't treat people well, and she didn't even realize that treating people well was something she should be trying to do. Eleanor seemed to think that her selfishness was the proper way to live and that most people live this way.

Yet, early in the afterlife she starts to realize that not everyone lives this way. Being surrounded by people who seem to be moral saints made her realize that there are other ways to live. The possibility of eternal punishment in The Bad Place made moral growth desirable as a practical necessity. So, she used the Aristotelian strategy of seeking an experienced mentor, Chidi, to help her become a better person. Through her classroom sessions with Chidi, she at least learned about living morally. But, even in The Good Place, her actions were inconsistent, making her a good illustration of Aristotle's weak-willed person. Eleanor knew the right thing to do and even desired to do the right thing—at least theoretically—even though she rarely did the right thing.

By the end of the first season, though, we see a real change in Eleanor. She really wants to do the right thing and is even willing to sacrifice herself and her happiness for the larger group. Despite her strong desires and instincts toward self-protection and self-preference, she confesses, "Michael, the problem in the neighborhood is me. I was brought to The Good Place by mistake, I'm not supposed to be here" ("The Eternal Shriek"). In this case, Eleanor is a strong-willed person. She did the right thing by publicly admitting she didn't belong in The Good Place and risking her own eternal happiness, even though she only did it after looking for other possible ways to avoid telling the truth. If this sort of behavior continues, then she might even become fully virtuous and start doing the right thing out of habit.

Kohlberg's Model of Moral Development

Aristotle was not the only thinker to offer a theory of moral development. The psychologist Lawrence Kohlberg (1927–1987) gave a differing account of what he took to be normal, healthy moral development, dividing it into pre-conventional, conventional, and post-conventional stages.[3]

Kohlberg's pre-conventional stages of moral development are typically displayed by young children. At this stage, behavior is driven by simple self-interest or a desire to avoid punishment. In this sense, childhood morality is pre-conventional, not driven by moral motives. Such a pre-conventional person might follow the rules, such as "Don't steal a cookie," but only out of fear of getting caught and punished. One problem with pre-conventional morality is that if one's only motives for behavior are self-interest and fear of punishment, one might seek to live as selfishly as possible so long as one can avoid getting caught. When Eleanor arrives in The Good Place she seems stuck in the pre-conventional stage, motivated by strictly selfish motives. Even her initial desire to become a better person is only based in fear of punishment in The Bad Place. As Chidi tells her, "Look the only thing you're concerned with is your own happiness, that's your problem" ("Everything Is Fine"). So, even Eleanor's desire to become moral isn't based in anything resembling morality. It's just an extension of her own selfish self-interest and desire to avoid punishment.

The conventional stages of moral development are often found in adolescents as well as many adults. At this stage of development, the person simply wants to live up to and uphold their familial or cultural moral standards. Law and social order are valued with minimal reflection.

A child's relationship with her parents is important for moving into conventional morality. So, we can understand why Eleanor's development was so poor: she has a terrible relationship with her parents and was never motivated to please them by following the rules. Her parents are divorced and are apathetic toward her. Her mother accidentally kills her childhood dog, gets caught lying about it, and then demands that Eleanor not respond to it emotionally. She wastes Eleanor's college fund, forgets her birthday, and fakes her own death to avoid her gambling debts. Eleanor even has to lie to her own mother and claim that she has free WrestleMania tickets to get her to meet. In her teen years, Eleanor demands early emancipation from her horrible parents, but her lack of bonding with her parents foreshadows an ongoing lack of bonding in relationships and a lack of concern for what others think of her. Apathy undermined Eleanor's moral development; she never really cared if others noticed that she lived immorally.

In The Good Place, for the first time, Eleanor develops relational bonds with Chidi, Tahani, Jason, and even Michael. While her quest for moral growth begins with sheer self-interest, she eventually comes to care about her relationships and they enable her to grow. As Kohlberg himself says, "A person at this stage is aware of shared feelings, agreements, and expectations, which take primacy over individual interests. The person relates points of view through the 'concrete Golden Rule,' putting oneself in the other person's shoes."[4]

Post-conventional moral development is found only in adults, but not all adults. Abstract reasoning that grounds moral values is the ultimate basis for a person's moral behavior at this stage. Moral behavior is based in either respecting human rights, bringing about the greatest good for the most people, or some other higher-level abstract justification for morality. Knowledge of these abstract ethical theories is what professional ethicists specialize in, yet there is a tremendous gap between knowing ethical theory and living morally. One might have an excellent understanding of the theories of morality, yet choose to live selfishly. Or, like Chidi, someone might be an expert in understanding theories of moral behavior but have a serious character flaw like indecisiveness that prevents him from actually living out his morality. Chidi is indecisive about the ethics book he is writing, about his feelings toward Eleanor, and about practical matters like how to be a good best man in a friend's wedding. It even takes Chidi over an hour to choose between two fedoras in the afterlife. This deep indecisiveness shows that one can have knowledge about ethics, and even possess good intentions, while failing to actually live ethically.

Does Character Actually Matter?

One objection to the possibility of moral development is called situationism: the claim that people don't really live according to moral character but are overwhelmingly shaped by the situations around them. The evidence for this claim is that in various experiments, psychologists were able to manipulate human behavior despite the individual's supposed "moral character". For example, in the famous Milgram experiment participants were told by a scientist—displaying the symbols of authority, including the scientist's white lab coat—that it is important for the participant to train an unseen learner to repeat certain sequences of words and deliver increasingly dangerous electric shocks to them when the learner fails. However, the learner was actually an actor (rather than a participant in the experiment) who intentionally failed his tasks.

Stanley Milgram (1933–1984) expected that the participants' basic morality and common sense would cause them to stop delivering the shocks. To Milgram's surprise, all of the participants were willing to inflict significant electrical shocks (of at least 300 volts) to the learner. Worse, nearly two-thirds of the participants continued to deliver shocks up to the maximum amount on the device (450 volts) even after the learner begged them to stop, even when the learner appeared to be incapacitated by the shocks, and even though the maximum electrical shock was marked as fatal.

As Milgram explains,

> What is surprising is how far ordinary individuals will go in complying with the experimenter's instructions.... Despite the fact that many subjects experience stress, despite the fact that many protest to the experimenter, a substantial proportion continue to the last shock on the generator. Many subjects will obey the experimenter no matter how vehement the pleading of the person being shocked, no matter how painful the shocks seem to be, and no matter how much the victim pleads to be let out.[5]

According to Milgram, the individual's moral character had minimal impact on their reaction to the situation. Virtually everyone obeyed the authority figure and ultimately ignored any directive from their conscience to do otherwise. Therefore, the claim of situationism is that the situation shaped the individual's actions.

If situationism is correct, then personal moral progress isn't possible because it is our circumstances rather than our moral character that actually shapes our actions. According to this view, anyone might become a slaveholder or a Nazi if they lived in the relevant situation. So perhaps, Eleanor's, Chidi's, Jason's, and Tahani's moral characters are merely reflections of their situations. Perhaps, anyone who was born into Tahani's indulgent and lavish lifestyle would be corrupted by it and become a self-absorbed narcissist.

Does situationism succeed in debunking the idea of moral character and progress? Probably not. There are three reasons we should resist this inference from the experiments. First, the Milgram experiment itself seems flawed. The participants were lied to and manipulated in various ways. For example, if any were concerned about the shocks' effects on the "learner," they were manipulated and assured that the shocks were painful but would not result in any permanent tissue damage to the learner. Furthermore, the participants were coerced and told that they had no other choice but to continue the experiment once it began. It should be no great surprise that the participants followed instructions. The entire experiment included manipulative components and relied on intentionally misleading statements from the trusted authority figure in order to get the participants to act out of character.

Second, even though the Milgram experiment demonstrated that a situation can be orchestrated to manipulate an individual, not all the participants reacted identically. About a third refused to finish the experiment despite being repeatedly told to continue and that they had "no other choice" but to continue. Furthermore, some of those who continued actually complained and raised concerns about the experiment, only finishing the experiment under a significant degree of manipulative duress. Reluctant participants in the Milgram experiment might be thought of as Aristotelian weak-willed characters who did the wrong thing, but who at least recognized its problematic nature.

Third, even if we agree that the situation within the Milgram experiment shaped the actions of the participants, it is difficult to argue that the entirety of one's life is similar to a carefully orchestrated experiment employing manipulative "confederates" designed to coerce a single person's behavior. Perhaps, our actions would be largely out of our own control in a situation where we were being deliberately manipulated by several conspiring actors, but most of our lives are not lived under such circumstances. A mistake of situationism is to claim that because people can be manipulated in a short-term, carefully designed situation, they also lack agency in the bigger-picture situation constituting their entire life. The truth is that character develops over time and is tenacious, even if it can be manipulated in some situations. Thus, it is unlikely that our broad life "situation" controls our actions in the way that the specific "situation" of a carefully orchestrated experiment might.

According to situationism, Eleanor is a selfish person simply because she had terrible parents and a hard childhood. But, is this simplistic view correct? Undoubtedly, her parents were bad examples and gave her moral journey a bad start. But, is it correct that Eleanor never really had a choice? No. Surely, she had other opportunities to belong and find alternative role models and bond with other people.

Many children of bad parents grow up to reject their parents' vices, sometimes even defining their own characters in opposition to the bad examples set by their parents. As Aristotle saw, people become virtuous or vicious through habits developed over time that begin in their youth. Eleanor—like all of us—had many choices along the way. In high school, she might have joined a nerdy clique where she aspired to academic success rather than being a loner. Even a "Mean Girls" clique might have provided some social context for limited moral growth. At the very least, Eleanor must share some responsibility for her own character.

The Moral of the Story

So why do it then? Why choose to be good, every day, if there is no guaranteed reward we can count on now or in the afterlife? I argue that we choose to be good because of our bonds with other people and our innate desire to treat them with dignity. Simply put, we are not in this alone.

—Chidi ("Everything Is Bonzer")

The moral of the story seems to be something like this: Eleanor can become a more moral person. Moral growth starts by bonding with other people and caring about them. When we bond with others, we care what they think of us, and we care that we have a positive influence upon them. As Eleanor learns in *The Good Place*, the road to being a better person starts with caring about those close to us.

The Good Place is ultimately optimistic about human potential—as Aristotle was. As the Judge suggests, there is reason for hope: "Humans are not fixed at one level of morality, they can always get better" ("The Funeral to End All Funerals").

Notes

1 Aristotle, *Nicomachean Ethics*, in *The Basic Works of Aristotle*, trans. W. D. Ross (New York: Random House, 1941), 1103a–b.
2 Ibid., 1103b.
3 For a feminist alternative to Aristotle and Kohlberg, see Chapter 12 in this volume, "Not Knowing Your Place: A Tale of Two Women," by Leslie A. Aarons.
4 Lawrence Kohlberg, *The Philosophy of Moral Development: Moral Stages and The Idea of Justice*, vol. 1 (New York: Harper & Row, 1981), 410.
5 Stanley Milgram, *Obedience to Authority* (New York: HarperCollins, 1974), 5.

5

The Good Place and The Good Life

C. Scott Sevier

The most obvious guiding structural feature of *The Good Place* is Jean-Paul Sartre's (1905–1980) play *No Exit*, specifically his proclamation that "Hell is other people."[1] Eleanor suggests this view in the pilot episode when she speculates that her parents might be used to torture one another ("It would work," she mused), and it is confirmed by the revelations at the end of Season 1.[2] However, the central questions posed by the series are "Who is a good person?" and "How does one become a good person?" Or, in the show's idiom, "Who gets into The Good Place?" Maybe hell is other people, as Sartre claims, but the show suggests that heaven (The Real Good Place) may also be other people. Since in "Michael's Gambit," it is revealed that our protagonists are actually in The Bad Place, this claim will require some justification.

Being Happy and Being Good

We all want happiness and we need to know how to get it. For most pre-modern philosophers, questions about the good life and the happy life were inseparable. If this sounds strange, it is because of the difference between classical and contemporary conceptions of "happiness." Today when someone says she is happy, we assume that means she *feels* a certain way. To *feel* happy is to *be* happy. Happiness is primarily a subjective notion. The only sure way to know whether someone is happy is to ask her. In the classical view, the happy person is the one who lives an admirable life. Happiness was conceived of as an objective state, and the best way to determine whether someone is happy is

The Good Place and Philosophy, First Edition. Edited by Kimberly S. Engels.
© 2021 John Wiley & Sons, Inc. Published 2021 by John Wiley & Sons, Inc.

not to ask her, but to examine her life. Is it admirable, one worth imitating, the kind of life one might wish for one's children? If I want to be happy, on this view, I need to become good. Being happy and being good are more or less the same thing. The distinction between these different conceptions of happiness is important because, according to many ancient thinkers, the desire for happiness is innate and unavoidable. We might disagree about what we think will make us happy; but whatever it is, we must have it. And everything we do is in the service of obtaining this one thing.

Who Died and Left Aristotle in Charge of Ethics?

Aristotle (384–322 BCE) believed we are drawn to those things we believe are good, including the kind of life we think is best. Since Aristotle believed some goods (and some kinds of lives) are objectively better than others, I can be right or wrong about which life is best for me. Given the finite nature of my life, and that the clock is already ticking, sorting out which life is best to pursue is incredibly important, urgent, and more than a little scary!

The Good Place suggests (and Aristotle claims outright) that relationships are key to the good life. Depending on the company I keep, I can be made to suffer or to succeed. The main story arc of Season 1, revealed in "Team Cockroach," is that while Michael is convinced that this particular group of people will cause each one to suffer "for thousands of years," instead they help each other become better people. How can this happen? How can they help one another to become the "best versions" of themselves?

The Good Place is a laboratory for testing moral theories, providing the show's writers opportunities to see which (if any) theories help the protagonists become better persons. In the end, while each theory provides *some* guidance, the most successful theory (in terms of significant moral improvement) is virtue ethics.

The defining feature of virtue ethics is its focus on character rather than action. Chidi summarizes Aristotle's *Nicomachean Ethics*, telling us, "Aristotle believed that there were certain virtues of mind and character, like courage and generosity, and you should try to develop yourself in accordance with those virtues" ("Jeremy Bearimy").[3] By way of contrast, other ethical systems focus on outcomes (utilitarianism), intentions (Kantianism), or adherence to a fixed set of moral laws (Divine Command Theory).

For the virtue ethicist, moral education aims at training people to become morally good *actors*—people who want to do good, who have reliable intuitions about the good and how to achieve the good, and who then actually perform good actions. An ethics of virtue is difficult and messy because it does not reduce morality to a simple formula. Instead, it involves an inner transformation of character that leads to virtuous actions. Repeatedly practicing good actions forms habits of acting well, which further improves the character. In "Tahani Al-Jamil," Chidi advises Eleanor, "In order to be a good person, you have to do good things." However, merely acting well isn't the ultimate goal. Instead, we aim to develop a character that produces good actions naturally.

The process of character development is difficult, however. For one thing, Aristotle believes that learning to think well about ethics is largely a waste of time unless you are already a good person. Without good moral intuitions already in place, formal education would simply produce an ethically sophisticated bad person. Eleanor illustrates this throughout much of Season 1. We see her regularly appeal to one moral theory or another to justify her bad behavior or induce Chidi's support. For example, in "The Eternal Shriek," after rationalizing her decision to let Michael assume responsibility for the bad effects she was having on the neighborhood (on the grounds that Michael is ultimately responsible for bringing her to the neighborhood and so ultimately responsible for whatever she does), Eleanor revels in her successful ethical reasoning: "Ha! How do you like them ethics? I just ethics'd you in the face, Chidi!" As her response illustrates, moral education does not necessarily make one morally good. Ethical reasoning may be employed to rationalize one's behavior after the fact or merely to win an argument. Chidi is acutely aware of this danger and constantly worries that helping Eleanor might be morally wrong. From this exchange, his concern seems justified. This is the primary way that Eleanor is used to torment Chidi, and it is quite effective. Since he operates mostly on the basis of moral *duties*, Chidi remains in a perpetual state of agony, torn between his conflicting moral obligations to Eleanor (his "soulmate") and to his community.

Aristotle's aim is not to make bad people good, but rather to make good people better: first, by refining their good character through the development of more sophisticated moral reasoning, which makes them wiser; and second, by repeated practice of good actions, which creates good habits. But how does one know which good actions to practice?

The first step in moral improvement is to find a mentor or exemplar who represents the good life and begin to imitate her behavior. Rather than following universal *rules* to guide behavior, the virtue approach involves following a good *example* as that person navigates the actual world. "Because that's what Chidi would do" is sufficient justification to motivate Eleanor to help Michael in "Team Cockroach" when it otherwise seems counterintuitive. Eleanor looks to Chidi as her moral standard, and whenever she is in doubt about what to do, she acts as she believes he would act. For Aristotle, the ultimate goal is to internalize the behaviors of the moral exemplar so that you change and eventually become like the moral exemplar. Speaking of Chidi in "…Someone Like Me as a Member," Eleanor says, "I'm a different person now because of the person who helped me, and I want to be like him." By repeatedly acting as she believes her exemplar would act, she is becoming the sort of person who will eventually do such actions without having to imagine the exemplar or even think about it. To become happy, on this view, means that good actions become "second nature."

Why Kant We Be Good?

One of Chidi's favorite moral guides is Immanuel Kant (1724–1804). In contrast to Aristotle, for whom becoming a better person is somewhat natural, Kant believes (according to Chidi, in "Team Cockroach") "it is our duty to improve ourselves."[4] For Kant, morality is grounded in *duty* to live autonomously and rationally. I am autonomous when my actions are governed by free choice, in contrast to actions that are determined. As a physical thing, my body obeys physical laws just like every other physical thing. Reason, which can operate contrary to one's physical inclinations, is the only thing that escapes physical determinism.[5]

According to Kant, when I act solely on my biological drives, I am no different from other animals. When I am hungry, I eat whatever will satisfy that hunger. But whereas other hungry animals might eat a small child, I will not. Reason dictates that human beings refrain from doing so since humans have intrinsic value and are not to be used as food. As a rational being, I have a moral duty to obey the dictates of reason when they conflict with my appetitive urges.

Kant expects our moral obligations to conflict with our natural inclinations, and the only way to become a good person is to consistently choose to do what is right (rational) out of a sense of duty (to reason) and in defiance of our physical compulsions. When I choose to act on the basis of reason rather than biological instinct, I am thwarting the determinism inherent in the physical world, and placing myself outside of it to a degree.

Chidi repeatedly teaches Eleanor, with some success, that the moral value of actions is determined by motivation.[6] Since any hint of self-interest voids an action's moral value, it is extremely difficult to accrue moral points in the universe of *The Good Place*. Our protagonists complain about the arbitrariness of the system, but part of the problem is that they exist in a largely Kantian moral universe. Many of the problems with the accounting system in the universe of *The Good Place* are problems inherent in a Kantian moral system.

In "Janet(s)," Michael determines that someone from The Bad Place must be "tampering the point system." However, the results are just what we ought to expect in a Kantian universe. Even when someone acts out of duty, it is rare that this is her *sole* motivation. It is rational to be concerned about the consequences of our actions to ourselves and to others, as well as other considerations. But these other concerns count *against* Kantian moral goodness.

We can see why a Kantian universe would not maximize the number of people getting into The Good Place. But why should we *care* about that? Concern with numbers is a worry of consequentialist moral systems, which are antithetical to Kantianism. In utilitarianism, for example, the best action is that which produces the greatest amount of overall happiness in the world. On that view, the best world would be one in which the greatest number of people end up in The Good Place and the fewest in The Bad Place. Obviously, that is not the world we find in *The Good Place*. For the Kantian, this is perfectly acceptable since consequences are not morally significant.

Utilitarianism: It's So Simple!

Of course, the world of *The Good Place* is not really a purely Kantian world since one's eternal destination depends on the cumulative point value of all of one's actions in life. From the first episode, we are told that each individual action has a precise point value, based on the amount of good or bad the act produces in the world. That sounds rather consequentialist in nature.

Herein lies another explanation why so few people are in The Good Place. Michael discovers in Season 3 that as the world becomes more complex and interconnected, it becomes more difficult to anticipate the consequences of one's actions. In "The Book of Dougs," we are told that the same act (giving roses to his grandmother) performed by a medieval "Doug" and a contemporary "Doug" have different point values because of indirect consequences. An act that once had a small positive point value now has a negative point value. The negative consequences attending each action are so pervasive today that it has become impossible for anyone to earn enough points to make it into The Good Place.

The problem of accurately predicting the consequences of one's actions was acknowledged long ago in the book *Utilitarianism* by John Stuart Mill (1806–1873). Mill believed this objection could be met by appealing to collective human experience. We can generally tell which actions will produce mostly good or bad results. For the world of *The Good Place*, though, general impressions are not good enough. The accounting system, we are told in the pilot episode ("Everything Is Fine"), is "perfectly accurate." The precise point value of every action is calculated to a degree impossible for humans. Thus, in a strictly utilitarian moral universe, the deck would be stacked against us by the complexity of modern life.

Another issue is that in a purely utilitarian universe, one's character or intentions would have no significant moral value (outside of their consequences). Utilitarianism and Kantianism are in tension with one another. A Kantian moral universe values intention but not consequences. A utilitarian universe reverses these values.

The universe of *The Good Place* seems to embody an internal incoherence. Near the end of Season 1, Eleanor's moral point value suddenly and dramatically increases when her *motivation* changes. Yet, in Season 3, we discover that the *consequences* of one's actions ultimately determine who is good enough to get into The Good Place. Part of the frustration our protagonists experience navigating the moral universe of *The Good Place* stems from the inherent tension in a world in which both Kantianism and utilitarianism compete for preeminence. In such a universe, moral failure seems inevitable. This is the conclusion reached by the Judge in Season 4's "The Funeral to End All Funerals."

In real life, one need not choose between Kantianism and utilitarianism alone. Consequences and motivation *both* seem relevant to moral decision making. The key is finding balance. If that is what *The Good Place* is attempting, it illustrates the difficulty of the task.

We Are Not in This Alone

In Aristotle's ethical system, true moral progress toward the good life is within reach. Though Aristotle was pessimistic about training adults to be moral, the show suggests that even someone as selfish (and occasionally mean) as Eleanor Shellstrop can become a good person. She needs motivation (desire to stay in the neighborhood), instruction, and friends who provide both the opportunity to act virtuously and the encouragement to do so. Having good friends, it turns out, is an essential ingredient.

Aristotle devotes roughly 20 percent of the *Nicomachean Ethics* to the integral role of friendship in becoming good and happy.[7] According to the philosopher, there are three types of friendship. Some are based solely on usefulness (a friend with a pool, for example). Some friendships are based on pleasure, revolving around shared activities or enjoyment (basketball teammates, for example). Of course, these categories need not be mutually exclusive. For Aristotle, however, the best type of friendship is one based on neither utility nor pleasure, but virtue.

A friendship based on virtue is one in which I am attracted to another person because of her good character, or virtue, irrespective of any utility or pleasure she might bring. I like and respect who she is. I want to be around her and I want to be like her. Additionally, according to Aristotle, friendships of this sort are also useful and pleasant. Having multiple grounds of goodness, they are the most fulfilling and the most stable of friendships.

Friendships based on virtue are not only the best sort of friendships, they are also necessary for moral development, according to Aristotle. You cannot exercise virtue in a vacuum. In order to be courageous, you must face risk. In order to be prudent, you must be presented with choices to make. In order to be kind or generous or patient, you must spend time with people who test these traits. It is relatively easy for me to express these virtues toward strangers because of the brevity of those interactions. It is harder to be truly patient with someone with whom I spend a large amount of time.

To really practice the virtues, I need to spend time with people. To become good, I need an ideal to shoot for and an accurate measure of how I'm doing. The virtuous friend with whom I spend time provides both of these and becomes a goad to improvement. I want to be like her, and my actions toward her reveal how far I've gotten and how far I've still got to go.

Eleanor has no obvious interest in actual goodness at the beginning of the series. In fact, part of Eleanor's torture is that she is uncomfortable being around people she believes are better than her. She is suspicious of their goodness, as in "Tahani Al-Jamil," when Tahani gives her a "housewarming" plant. However, Eleanor seeks Chidi's help out of necessity: she needs to fit in so that she doesn't get caught and get sent to The Real Bad Place. Eleanor does not appear to enjoy spending time with Chidi. She repeatedly calls him derogatory names ("nerd," "dork," "super-dork Jones," and "talking sweater vest") and she complains about how boring he is. Eleanor doesn't value virtuous character and certainly isn't attracted to Chidi because of it. Her relationship with Chidi is, therefore, initially based solely on utility: she needs his help to stay in what she falsely believes is The Good Place.

In Aristotelian terms, we could say that Chidi's relationship to Eleanor is also one of utility. Eleanor lacks virtue, and Chidi finds spending time with her unpleasant, since it often requires him to act questionably and stresses him out. The relationship is useful to Chidi because it provides him the opportunity to exercise his moral duty to help others. In fact, Eleanor seems to provide the only opportunity for him to exercise this duty since presumably no one else there needs his help. In "Flying," Chidi tells her, "It's The Good Place; you can get anything you want at any time." If the neighborhood is filled with good people who can have whatever they ask for, it is difficult to imagine many opportunities to truly help others in need. Their relationship is at first, then, a friendship based merely on utility.

Over time, the nature of their relationship changes, especially as Eleanor begins to become a better person. In "…Someone Like Me as a Member," Eleanor can say, with complete honesty, that she wants to *be* (and not merely *thought* to be) a good person. She can say this honestly because she has already begun to change. She is already becoming a better person. We see the change especially in some of the decisions she makes, as when she confesses that she is the source of the problems in the neighborhood in "The Eternal Shriek" or when, in "The Burrito," she is the only one of the four humans to pass the Judge's test (yet conceals this from the others and accepts their fate).

It is revealed in "Dance Dance Resolution" that at some point in their time in the afterlife, Chidi and Eleanor fall in love. This presumably means that they have moved beyond a relationship based on utility and into something else—perhaps one based on utility and pleasure or perhaps one based (at least partly) on virtue. Chidi is attracted to virtue, to goodness, and to truth. He has spent his life in pursuit of these ideals.[8] It seems unlikely that he could fall in love with Eleanor if she lacked these qualities altogether. In "Best Self," Eleanor claims that this incarnation was "the best version" of herself.

This suggests (and it is later confirmed) that in the world of *The Good Place* moral development is possible (even when it's not supposed to be), and it is possible because of the help one receives from one's friends. This is reiterated in a number of ways throughout Season 4—by the title of Episode 7, "Help Is Other People"; by Chidi's discovery that the "answer" (to the ultimate questions) "is Eleanor"; and in the series' penultimate episode, "Patty," when the ancient philosopher (and resident of The Good Place) Hypatia asserts that what ultimately "saved" our four protagonists (as well as everyone else in The Good Place) was their friendships. As mentioned earlier, the show gives the writers a kind of laboratory in which to test-drive various ethical theories. In spite of the verbal commitments made to Kant's ethics, the show ultimately proves to be a vindication of virtue ethics. A universe governed by Aristotelian morality is one in which moral development is possible. I can become a better version of myself if I want to and if I have help. It is, therefore, a universe in which people have good reason to help one another. And if Aristotle is right about the nature of friendships, this universe in which we help one another become better versions of ourselves is also a pleasant universe. As Eleanor advises Mindy, near the end of the final episode, "There is greater happiness waiting for you if you form bonds with other people." In helping each other to become good, we make our world a good place.

Notes

1   Jean-Paul Sartre, *No Exit*, in *No Exit and Other Plays* (New York: Vintage, 1989).
2   That the humans are intended to torture each other is first revealed in "Michael's Gambit."
3   Aristotle, *Nicomachean Ethics*, in *The Complete Works of Aristotle*, 2 vols., ed. Jonathan Barnes (Princeton, NJ: Princeton University Press, 1984).
4   Kant's ethical theories are expressed over several works, but perhaps the most basic foundation for a duty to self-improvement can be found in his first formulation of what he calls the "Categorical Imperative," also referred to as the "Formula of Universal Law," which states: "act only in

accordance with that maxim through which you can at the same time will that it become a universal law." Immanuel Kant, *Groundwork of the Metaphysics of Morals*, in *The Cambridge Edition of the Works of Immanuel Kant: Practical Philosophy*, ed. Mary J. Gregor (Cambridge: Cambridge University Press, 1996), sec. II, p. 73 (4:421).

5 This point is not unique to Kant. In fact, Plato (427–347 BCE) includes an extended discussion of the ways that reason can conflict with the appetitive drives. Plato, *Republic*, in *Plato: Complete Works*, ed. John M. Cooper (Indianapolis, IN: Hackett, 1997), Book IV.

6 See, for example, "Flying" and "What's My Motivation." Even Tahani is seen to have internalized this lesson in "Michael's Gambit."

7 *Nicomachean Ethics*, Books VIII and IX, are devoted to the subject of friendship and its relationship to the good life.

8 See, for example, "Everything Is Fine" and "Everything Is Great!"

6

The Ethics of Indecision: Why Chidi Anagonye Belongs in The Bad Place

Traci Phillipson

Let's face it, it's easy to see why Eleanor, Tahani, and Jason are in The Bad Place. But what about Chidi? Not only is he a practicing moral philosopher, aware of the various theoretical frameworks we can use to judge morality, but he is obsessed with the practical application of these theories. Sure, he can talk the talk of moral philosophy, but he also wants to walk the walk! Yet, he is continually plagued with moral doubt and often finds himself questioning what he should do, paralyzed by indecision and his desire to do the right thing. This indecision and the resulting inaction often produce bad results, as the time for action expires while he is still weighing his options. Still, one might ask: should a person really be punished for their sincere moral efforts? Chidi is *trying* to be good. Isn't this more than can be said for the other residents of The Bad Place? Isn't this more than can be said for many people in our everyday lives?

Aristotle's (384–322 BCE) Virtue Theory is a character-based system in which morality is a matter of having the appropriate character traits rather than following a set of strict moral rules. As Chidi himself points out when explaining the theory to Eleanor, Aristotle thinks that morality and immorality—virtue and vice—are voluntary. People can morally improve with effort and practice, and they can achieve the ultimate goal of developing a virtuous character. The virtuous person will habitually do the right thing, at the right time, in the right way, for the right reason without having to laboriously examine the situation first. Key among the virtues, according to Aristotle, is practical wisdom (*phronesis*), which allows a person to reason through a practical situation, make the moral decision, and act upon that decision.

The Good Place and Philosophy, First Edition. Edited by Kimberly S. Engels.

So, as Aristotle would see it, Chidi's inability to make moral decisions constitutes his immorality. Thus, despite his conscious attempts to be a good person, Chidi still belongs, for most of the show, in The Bad Place.

Aristotle's Virtue Theory: Learning to Be Good

According to Virtue Theory, morality is about the person performing the actions. It's not about just doing the right thing—it's about being the right kind of person. If we understand the appropriate character traits and cultivate those traits in ourselves, moral actions will simply follow as a result of being a person with a moral character. A moral person becomes habituated to morality, and it becomes second nature to them to act in the way that is morally best in any given situation. Similarly, vice can also become part of our nature; instead of cultivating virtuous character traits, a person can cultivate vicious ones.[1] In this case the person becomes habituated to viciousness and immorality, and it becomes second nature to them to act immorally. Insofar as we are responsible for our own moral training and habituation by acting in the course of our everyday lives, both virtuousness and viciousness are voluntary. As Aristotle puts it, "we are ourselves somehow part-causes of our states of character."[2]

With this basic understanding of Virtue Theory we can already see how Chidi is, at the very least, an imperfect example of virtue and morality. He is characterized not by habitual moral action but by pained decision making and insecurity. In the very first episode, Chidi tells Eleanor that he has "spent [his] entire life in pursuit of fundamental truths about the universe" and that as a moral philosophy professor he has dedicated his life to understanding morality ("Everything Is Fine"). Yet, he gets a stress-and-anxiety-induced stomachache when he has to decide whether or not he should help Eleanor. Now, one might say that this is a weighty decision—he would, presumably, be acting contrary to the system put in place by whatever higher powers exist and would be risking his own position in The Good Place. However, we repeatedly see Chidi at an impasse even when making the simplest of decisions with little moral consequence—no actions seem to be habitual for him. Michael notes that he never decided on a name for his dog and that his life's work, a book on moral philosophy titled, in part, *Who We Are and Who We Are Not: Practical Ethics and Their Application in the Modern World; A*

Treatise, remained unfinished after 18 years of work. These are just a couple of the many instances of everyday decisions Chidi is not able to make confidently. He clearly has failed to cultivate a character resulting in habitual action.

Decision Making 101: The Practical Syllogism

One might say that Chidi can be forgiven for not having yet perfected his character because he is, after all, still acting voluntarily and making moral decisions most of the time. Indeed, we could say that this fits quite well within Virtue Theory, which values our decision making and control our actions. To further this point we should note that Aristotle does discuss the process by which we make decisions at some length. He says it is a process that is difficult at first, but should become easy and habitual with practice. This decision-making process is called the practical syllogism and it includes several steps. First, a person must wish for an end; he must decide upon a goal he would like to achieve. Second, the person must deliberate about the means by which to achieve that end. He must enumerate all of the ways that a person could achieve the goal he has in mind; sometimes there is only one possible way to achieve a goal, and sometimes there are many. Third, he must decide upon the best course of action from the list generated by his deliberations. Finally, he must act upon this decision and, if everything goes well, achieve his goal.[3]

For the person in the early phase of moral development these steps are carefully and deliberately made, but for those who have already habituated themselves and developed a moral character these steps happen so quickly that they seem not to happen at all. For example, a person who has been living a life in which they have paid no attention to their health may wish to become healthier. At first they must analyze what this means, deliberating about the types of actions that will lead to health and deciding upon a course of action. Each time an unforeseen health-related dilemma presents itself this person must consult their plans, reworking the practical syllogism. On the other hand, the person who has made healthfulness a part of their life for years no longer needs to think about whether or not skipping the gym could fit with their goal. They have cultivated a character that habitually, seemingly naturally, decides not to forgo the gym.

On the pro-Chidi side of things, we certainly see him engaging the practical syllogism frequently throughout the series, both in the present and in flashbacks to his life. He is constantly making (or attempting to make) decisions. In fact, the care he gives to even simple decisions is a hallmark of his personality. Surely this careful consideration is a good thing. After all, Aristotle would not have been so careful in detailing the process if we were not meant to follow it closely. Alas, Chidi is not able to get beyond the careful application stage of moral decision making to reach the part where it becomes easy, habitual, and indicative of a moral (or immoral) character. He has great trouble making even the simplest decisions. In "Chidi's Choice," Chidi is trying to figure out how to help Eleanor stay in The Good Place. First, he wishes to help her stay. Next he must deliberate about how to do that. This is where he runs into trouble. He gets sidetracked by his inability to choose a writing implement with which to make his list of ways to help her. He eventually makes a decision in the spur of the moment by "trusting his gut" rather than deciding deliberately. While he is stuck trying to work out his decision, we see several flashbacks to other points in Chidi's life when he was unable to make a choice. As a child he takes so long picking his team for a recess soccer match that recess ends, much to his friend Uzo's disappointment; he dies when an air conditioner falls on him as he is 30 minutes into trying to find a bar to go to with Uzo, who he has disappointed yet again. Seconds before Chidi's death an exasperated Uzo exclaims, "it is literally impossible to be your friend. You're incapable of making a single decision!"—and he's right! Chidi is unable to follow through on the practical syllogism, let alone make decision making a habitual activity.

Practical Wisdom (*Phronesis*): "I Have to Consider All the Factors"

So, we must ask, what is Chidi missing? Why can't he seem to make decisions without debilitating anxiety? Of course, part of the problem is his obsession with trying to take every detail and possible outcome into account, an astronomical and impossible task. As we saw in the soccer flashback, he couldn't choose who to draft onto his team without taking into account "athletic strategies, the fragile egos of [his] classmates, and gender politics!" But Aristotle would explain his problem differently. Chidi simply lacks what Aristotle called practical wisdom (*phronesis*). Practical wisdom is an intellectual virtue that Aristotle defines as "a true and reasoned state of capacity to act with regard to the things that are good or bad for man."[4] It is an excellence of human reasoning; the ability to reason well about practical matters and determine the virtuous course of action.

Practical wisdom is the lynchpin in Aristotle's moral system. As we know already, Virtue Theory is character based, and a person is moral if she has a virtuous character—if she is the kind of person who habitually does virtuous actions and makes virtuous decisions. But, we have yet to define virtue. According to Aristotle, virtue or moral excellence is

> a state concerned with choice, lying in a mean relative to us, this being determined by reason and in the way in which the man of practical wisdom would determine it. Now it is a mean between two vices, that which depends on excess and that which depends on defect.[5]

Virtue, and thus morality, is a middle ground between vices. Furthermore, it is relative to the individual. What is appropriate for one person may be excessive or deficient for another. This is not, however, a pernicious type of relativism. It's not that whatever a person wants is moral. Rather, what the *rational* person would want, after taking into account the particulars of the situation, is moral. The rational person is the person with practical wisdom.

Thus, it is practical wisdom that allows one to deliberate well about what virtue requires, to decide upon a course of action when there are several possibilities, and to take the initiative to act upon those decisions appropriately. Chidi, though, is routinely unable to deliberate clearly, well, or in a timely fashion about what is best in a given situation. His desire to take the smallest minutiae of every situation into account leaves him morally stagnant and ultimately acting out of intuition or expediency when time is up. This is comically demonstrated in "The Trolley Problem." Michael decides to bring Philippa Foot's (1920–2010) classic trolley problem to life by placing Chidi in a seemingly real trolley simulation and repeatedly having him decide what to do, all the while running over fake people who experience real pain, including strangers and people from Chidi's past. In these scenarios Chidi repeatedly runs out of time when trying to make a choice, and he suffers through the bloody and gruesome deaths of hundreds of people as a result. Chidi's indecision becomes other people's demise!

Chidi often wavers and changes his mind about what he should do. Even when he seems to have a good moral intuition about what is right, he second-guesses himself and overcomplicates things. The situation of his friend Henry's red boots, recounted via flashback in "The Eternal Shriek," offers a good example of this. We see Chidi encounter his friend Henry, who is wearing outlandish red boots and asks Chidi if he likes them. Chidi says yes but almost immediately regrets it, asking himself, "My God, what have I done?" as soon as Henry leaves. He continues to worry and loses sleep over the situation, unsure whether or not it was moral to lie to Henry. Although he resolves to tell Henry the truth, Chidi puts it off, even when Henry presents him with his very own pair of the expensive boots, and *again* when Henry is about to go into surgery for an aneurysm and may die. Only after Henry survives the surgery and is in recovery does Chidi blurt out "I hate your boots!" This flashback occurs while Chidi is trying to wrestle with the fact that he and Eleanor have been lying to Michael about her presence in The Good Place and now Michael will be going into retirement, the Eternal Shriek. Chidi tells Eleanor that "lying is always wrong," memories of the dreaded red boots flooding his mind.

What most people might see as a small "white lie" (albeit one that got out of hand and was resolved awkwardly) is a source of continued anxiety for Chidi, not only while the situation is unfolding, but even after his death when he can't do anything about it and despite the fact that, as far as he knows at the time, he has made it to The Good Place regardless. The anxiety and wavering stance may be explained by a guilty conscience—he values the truth and so feels guilty for lying—but it is also easily explained by the fact that he was not able to successfully employ practical reason and complete the practical syllogism, thus remaining unsure and insecure about his moral choices. Even after the situation is long resolved, Chidi is still anxious about it because the resolution was not the result of clear application of practical wisdom, but rather the anxiety and guilt that led him to blurt out the truth at a less than ideal time.

Can't We Just Give Chidi a Break?!

At this point, it seems reasonable to ask if this isn't all a bit too much. The standard we are employing is very high, perhaps too high. Aristotle asks a lot of us fallible human beings. Everyone faces moral dilemmas, and everyone questions their choices and actions at some point in their lives. Isn't there hope for Chidi? Isn't there hope for us? These are especially apt questions in the context of the show, where Eleanor makes the good point that there should be a Medium Place, for people who were not morally perfect but were also not totally morally corrupt. Her stance is strengthened when we learn in "Janet(s)" that no one has made it into The Good Place in 521 years. Surely something fishy is going on in the afterlife!

Aristotle is often criticized for his elitist views, including his high standards for virtue and morality. A person is not truly moral, Aristotle thinks, unless she has achieved a virtuous character with respect to each of the particular virtues. He lists five intellectual virtues, the most morally relevant of which is practical wisdom, and at least eight moral virtues, each of which is accompanied by corresponding vices of excess and deficiency. There are also what he calls pure vices, which do not have a corresponding virtue, such as murder. There are thus more than twice as many ways to get things wrong as there are to be successful, and one must be successful in every instance in order to be considered truly moral.

There is, however, some hope, even in Aristotle's system. This comes in the form of the scale of moral development. In *Nicomachean Ethics*, Book 7, Aristotle offers a discussion of several characters that one might have. The most important for our purposes are incontinence and continence, ways in which a person can be partially moral. The incontinent (or weak-willed) person has some understanding of virtue coupled with a desire to be virtuous. Thus, they are not truly vicious people. But, they lack the ability to fully control themselves when confronted with conflicting desires and often end up doing the wrong thing—that thing which the person with practical wisdom would recognize as immoral—despite their best intentions. The incontinent person regrets their actions when they make these mistakes and strives to do better next time.[6] The continent (or strong-willed) person is further along in their moral development since they not only understand what virtue demands but also are able to follow through on this understanding, even in the face of non-virtuous desires. The problem with the continent person, according to Aristotle, is that the continent person has any non-moral desires at all. A fully virtuous person, by contrast, only desires virtuous things and so never experiences a conflict of moral understanding and desire.[7]

Chidi falls, for the most part, in the category of incontinence. He has a deep desire to be moral. He has a generally good sense of what a moral person would do in a given situation and a generally reliable moral intuition. Yet, his anxiety and indecisiveness often cause him to act contrary to that understanding, or to come to a full understanding only after the fact. He regrets his immoral actions and he continually strives for moral improvement. Our analysis of Chidi also fits with Aristotle's claim that an incontinent person cannot have practical wisdom since practical wisdom entails the marriage of understanding and action—and this is the exact disconnect the incontinent person experiences.[8]

A Medium Place for Medium People

Where does this leave Chidi? If we consider Aristotle's scale of moral development we can say that Chidi is not a vicious or fully immoral person, even by the stringent standards of Virtue Theory. However, he is clearly also not a fully virtuous or moral person. Maybe he belongs in Eleanor's desired "medium place for medium people." But, Mindy St. Claire's Medium Place seems to be a one-off, the result of a very rare cosmic tie, and not a genuine option for most medium folks. Thus, in the absence of a Medium Place, the only options are The Good Place and The Bad Place. Because The Good Place requires near moral perfection, we can confidently say Chidi Anagonye deserves his spot in The Bad Place.

In the final season we finally see Chidi make moral progress. Chidi sacrifices his memories to allow Michael and his friends to conduct the final Bad Place experiment; he has learned to make decisions with authority, rather than being paralyzed by indecision. Indeed, he is instrumental in devising the new testing system, which is quite Aristotelian, in which the Good Place and Bad Place architects work together to help their human charges develop their moral characters before being granted entry to The Good Place. Finally, he is confident in his final decision to leave The Good Place in the series finale, not even stopping to sit at the bench by the door but striding through unflinchingly. While Chidi's life on Earth was plagued by indecision and immorality, his ability to develop his character in the afterlife leads him, ultimately, to morality and peace.

Notes

1　These general ideas are the basis of much of Aristotle's argument in his major ethical work, the *Nicomachean Ethics*. See Aristotle, *Nicomachean Ethics*, vol. 2 of *The Complete Works of Aristotle*, ed. and trans. Jonathan Barnes (Princeton, NJ: Princeton University Press, 1984).
2　Ibid., Book 3, chap. 5, 1760.
3　Ibid., Book 3, chaps. 2–4, for Aristotle's extended discussion of the process and his detailed analysis of each of the steps and their precise relation to one another.
4　Ibid., 1800.
5　Ibid., 1748.
6　Ibid., Book 7, chaps. 6–7.
7　Ibid., Book 7, chap. 9.
8　Ibid., Book 7, chap. 10.

Part III

"ALL THOSE ETHICS LESSONS PAID OFF"

Moral Absurdity and Care Ethics in *The Good Place*

Laura Matthews

French playwright, novelist, journalist, and philosopher Albert Camus (1913–1960) famously argued that human life is absurd because we seek objective meaning in a meaningless world.[1] As an atheist, Camus believed that there is no God and no objective source of meaning or morality. On *The Good Place*, there may or may not be a God, but there is definitely an objective meaning to life, namely to live in accord with morality. The objective moral standards placed on Eleanor and friends are too high, however. No one can live up to them, not even the illustrious Doug Forcett. As we'll see, the ethics of care can provide a better basis for the moral point system.

Moral Absurdity

During Eleanor's first lifetime on Earth, before she learns about The Good Place, before she meets Chidi and decides to become all ethical and boring, she believes life is meant to be lived, enjoyed, savored to the very last drop. For example, in a flashback Eleanor discusses with her then-boyfriend the coffee shop whose owner is accused of sexual harassment. Her boyfriend wants to boycott the coffee shop, but Eleanor thinks this is, to say the least, dumb. In the exchange, Eleanor sarcastically suggests that they "stay in, watch a Roman Polanski movie, listen to R. Kelly, and eat Chick-fil-a.... There's bad stuff everywhere, man, it's impossible to avoid." Exasperated, then-boyfriend responds, "But shouldn't we just try?" To which Eleanor retorts, "Why? It's so much harder to live that way, and it's not like

The Good Place and Philosophy, First Edition. Edited by Kimberly S. Engels.
© 2021 John Wiley & Sons, Inc. Published 2021 by John Wiley & Sons, Inc.

someone's keeping score" ("Tahani Al-Jamil"). Ironically, of course, someone *is* keeping score.

So life is not absurd for our characters on *The Good Place*, at least not in Camus's sense. The existence of The Good Place—and The Bad Place—restores the meaning to life that Camus argued was lacking. The traditional view of human existence comes back into play, albeit in a slightly distorted and sometimes warped way. We live this life for the sake of some otherworldly reward or punishment. This life is a test. Someone is watching over us. Why, then, be good? Not for some personal gain, like the respect and friendship of others. Not for fear of being arrested, tried, and convicted. Not because if we help others they will ultimately be in a better position to help us in return. Instead, we must be good because someone is keeping score. And upon our death we will be given one of two extreme deserts: eternal bliss or eternal torture.

As it turns out, the price for morality as the meaning of existence is the entrance of another kind of absurdity, a *moral* absurdity. Clearly, there is something absurd about life on *The Good Place*. It's not the type of existence we've been yearning for—one that satisfies our desire for deeper significance and purpose. That's because even though purpose is grounded in being a good person, there's a lot to be desired about the moral point system employed.

First, there are the extremes of the rewards and the punishments. Moral worth, both on *The Good Place* and in our real-life existence, comes in degrees. Actions are given a score—they can be barely good or barely bad, or extremely good or extremely bad. People are very rarely entirely good or entirely evil. So, the extremes of The Good Place and The Bad Place don't correlate well to the moral reality of the situation. Why is there no Medium Place? Eleanor's dismay at this question is entirely warranted. In her own words, she "was a medium person. [She] should get to spend eternity in a medium place!" ("Everything Is Fine").

Second, there is the extreme difficulty of getting into The Good Place. The scales seem to be drastically tilted in favor of The Bad Place. It's not enough for our actions to have good consequences, as in the case of Tahani's lifelong philanthropy. Our intentions must be good as well, hence Tahani's failure to earn her spot in The Good Place. It's also not enough for our intentions to be good, as in the case of Chidi's incessant moral deliberation—the consequences must be good as well. Not only does this set an exceedingly difficult standard to achieve, but the cutoff appears to be entirely arbitrary. The standard is a random and virtually unattainable number according to an opaque scoring system. The result is that no one has made it into The Good Place for 521 years. This means that for the duration of this Good Place drought, the universe has existed as a kind of torture farm, where people are born, live, and die for the sole purpose of being tortured in The Bad Place.

Third, there is the unsatisfactory nature of our characters' epistemic position, in other words, their inability to *know* how to be good. One can devote one's life, as Chidi does, to seeking out the good, to determining the best way to live and adhering to those standards. But even Chidi doesn't know how to be a good person until the rules of the game are revealed, and this only happens when it's already too late.

Good Enough for The Good Place

Thanks to the point system, everyone who has been born and died in the last 521 years is suffering in The Bad Place for all eternity. As a combination of deontological and consequentialist systems of ethics, the point system virtually guarantees this outcome. Deontological views, most famously associated with Immanuel Kant (1724–1804), hold that the morality of an action is determined based on whether or not it adheres to a moral rule. For example, a deontologist might hold that lying is morally impermissible, even if, all things considered, lying may in some circumstances bring about more pleasure or happiness than not lying. Consequentialist theories, by contrast, judge the morality of an action based on the consequences of that action. For example, John Stuart Mill (1806–1873) argued that we ought to choose those actions that bring the greatest amount of pleasure for the greatest number of people.[2] Unlike the deontologist, a consequentialist might hold that lying is sometimes permitted in circumstances when lying would bring about better consequences.

When Michael goes to the accountant with Janet in order to argue that The Bad Place has been tampering with the point system, the accountant explains that it's impossible for The Bad Place to tamper, because every action is quantified and double-checked by the whole system of accountants ("Janet(s): Extended Cut"). The actions are judged on a variety of factors: their use of resources, the intentions behind them, and their effects on others. Considering the effects on others is a consequentialist way of scoring an action. Any action could in principle be scored good or bad in different circumstances, just like the case of lying. Considering the intention behind an action is a deontological way of scoring—whether you intended to do good or not. In the point system on *The Good Place*, both consequences and intentions are tallied.

In the pilot episode, Michael explains to the inhabitants of the fake Good Place neighborhood that every action is scored, then tallied over the course of each individual's lifetime to produce their point total. When you blow your nose by "pressing one nostril down and exhaling," for example, you receive –6.46 points. When you use the term "bro-code," you receive –8.20 points. If you're a commissioner of a professional football league, well, that's an automatic –824.55 points. If you "fix a broken tricycle for a child indifferent to tricycles," that's +0.04 points. If you "fix a broken tricycle for a child who loves tricycles," you'll get +3.46 points. The tricycle is the clearest example we get of the combination of the deontological and consequentialist elements of the point system. When you fix the tricycle for a child who doesn't care, you're not making a positive impact on that child, but it's still considered good. Perhaps the moral principle is something like: it's good to lend a helping hand whenever you're able. But when the impact is more positive, the action is judged more positively, suggesting that the point system is also consequentialist in nature.

The problem with the consequentialism of the point system is that it doesn't account for the immorality that emerges naturally from the increased complexity of human society. Michael and the gang point this out to the Judge in the hopes of winning their appeal—the same types of actions generate different point scores than they would have 50, 100, or 200 years ago. As Michael puts it, "Life now is so complicated, it's impossible for anyone to be good enough for The Good Place" ("Chidi Sees the Time-Knife"). Because of the growth, development, and interconnectedness of human society, each choice we make has many unintended consequences. Michael continues: "These days, even buying a tomato at the grocery store means you are unwittingly supporting toxic pesticides, exploiting labor."

The result is that no one is good enough to get into The Good Place. Even Michael thinks this means that there must be something messed up about the point system. But in bringing this to the Judge's attention, Michael and the gang don't get the reaction they want. The Judge tells them to suck it up—just because the world has become more complex and being a good person has become that much more difficult, this doesn't excuse us from our moral obligations. In the Judge's view, we should just try harder.

But maybe there's another solution. Maybe the point system could be calculated in a different way, and people could be judged by a different, fairer measure.

A Different Moral Calculus

What if the point system were determined by a different ethical system? The contemporary American philosopher Virginia Held defends an alternative moral view, which she calls the ethics of care.[3] All human beings are dependent on the care of others, in childhood, in old age, and throughout adulthood. Since we are dependent on one another, care ethicists argue, we shouldn't consider ourselves substantially separate from one another. We should view our relationships as essential to our identity, and we should foster them for their own sake. On this view, morality becomes less about which actions are permitted or forbidden and more about caring for other human beings, other living creatures, and the planet as a whole.[4] If the point system were based on an ethics of care, it would promote a different type of world and perhaps allow more people into The Good Place.

Consider Doug Forcett, for example. Doug is what philosophers call a "happiness pump." If we're morally obligated to promote the greatest amount of good for the greatest number of people, then this implies that we're morally obligated to sacrifice our own happiness if it could lead to the greater happiness of someone else. This is what Doug does when he lets Raymond, the local sociopath, come over and take advantage of him. Doug is so worried about his point total that he does anything to promote others' happiness at the great expense of his own ("Don't Let the Good Life Pass You By"). But is Doug making the world a better place? In some instances yes, but in some instances no. From a care perspective, Doug shouldn't allow Raymond to walk all over him; rather, Doug should *care* about Raymond. As parents know, care comes in all different forms, and it often involves decreasing a child's overall happiness. Denying the child its desires is sometimes the best way to care for the child. Likewise, fostering Raymond's sociopathic tendencies is probably not the right thing to do.

Care doesn't involve acquiescing to others' every request, nor does it involve adhering strictly to predetermined rules. Care requires being flexible in different situations so as to best foster caring relationships with others. Thus, care ethicists advocate for contextuality in moral reasoning—there's no one-size-fits-all when it comes to living our best lives. A care perspective might have helped Chidi avoid the moral pickle he gets into with Henry's red cowboy boots. Chidi hates the boots because they are (objectively) hideous. At first Chidi tells a white lie and says he loves the boots. The lie spirals out of control, as these things are wont to do. And Chidi, under the sway of a strict deontological rule forbidding lying, is wracked with guilt. He's so tied up in knots about the whole ordeal that he wakes his girlfriend up in the middle of the night to weigh his options. Chidi assumes she'll take his side, because she's also influenced by Kant, and Kant believed it was always impermissible to lie. Instead she retorts, "Kant was a lonely, obsessive hermit with zero friends" ("The Eternal Shriek"). Instead of taking this to heart and choosing a different course of action, Chidi decides to wait at Henry's hospital bed as he recovers from surgery to confess the truth about the horrendous red cowboy boots. Perhaps Chidi could also be described as a "lonely, obsessive hermit." The obsessive part, at the very least.

Let's consider how a care ethicist might have tackled this problem differently. She would be more inclined to restrict the domain of universal rules to a more appropriate realm, such as the legal system. A care perspective would suggest that impartiality is not to be favored at all costs, and in the sphere of our private lives—with our friends, family, and coworkers—context is key. Was Chidi fostering a caring relationship with Henry by confessing the lie? Certainly not in the hospital room at the moment Henry regains consciousness. Perhaps the lie could be confessed in a more appropriate context, but the motivation and execution would be different. From the perspective of care, Chidi's actions should be guided *not* by abstract universal reasoning, but by the emotions of sympathy, empathy, sensitivity, and responsiveness. Chidi is obviously lacking sensitivity in this case, and he could certainly take a more empathic approach.

Other details of *The Good Place* give us further evidence that a more relationship-oriented approach might be preferable. For example, Eleanor blames her lack of virtue on her crappy parents. A care ethics approach would give some support to Eleanor's claims, insofar as a caring home life is essential to the development of the child in a variety of ways. Indeed, Eleanor is only able to overcome her childhood environment and become a better person when she has other caring relationships through which she can grow as a person.

Then there's Michael, who prides himself on being all-knowing. He can perceive in nine dimensions, so he can sense when there's tension cluttering up the room. But Michael has a transformative experience when he becomes friends with Eleanor and the others. His character takes a drastic turn, from a demon who loves to torture to a reliable and loyal friend. At the beginning of this turn, Michael makes a point to demonstrate how stupid he finds Chidi's ethics lessons. But the real reason he does this is because he's embarrassed at not knowing how to make moral choices. Michael is supposed to know everything, but it's not until he makes meaningful relationships with others that he comes to develop a moral compass. In particular, it's not until he can feel empathy for others, sympathize with them, and be responsive to their needs that he can use moral decision making. In other words, it's not until he learns to care for others.

The power of caring relationships is perhaps nowhere more salient than in the show's final few episodes. For example, after integrating the memories from over 1,000 different versions of himself, Chidi comes to realize that "There is no 'answer.' But Eleanor is the answer" ("The Answer"). Then, after achieving salvation for all living souls, the gang finally enter The Real Good Place, only to find out that it is not the promised land they had imagined. Everyone in The Real Good Place has turned into hedonistic zombies, having had all their wildest desires immediately satisfied for the entire duration of their afterlives. Not only does this give us further indication that the maximization of pleasure or happiness ought not be the ultimate aim of morality, but it also gives the group one last opportunity to band together and save humanity. Once they come up with their solution—to allow people the choice to leave The Good Place—Chidi says to Patty, "We're lucky we ran into you. It saved us," to which she replies, "That's not what saved you. It was your friendships" ("Patty"). Finally, once settled into their eternal home in The Good Place, Chidi and Eleanor bask in the newfound time they finally have. Chidi tells us, "That's what The Good Place is. It's not even really a place ... it's just having enough time with the people you love" ("Patty"). These moments show us that caring, loving relationships are powerful forces of good.

How would care ethics change the point system? Would we be scored on how many relationships we have? Or how outgoing we are? No, that would be its own kind of moral absurdity. To make sense and be fair, the system would have to score us only for things we can reasonably control. So, we could be scored on the extent to which we care about other human beings. Care has both emotive and behavioral aspects. This means that to be a caring person, you have to feel for other people, empathize with them, and be sensitive to their experiences, desires, goals, and needs. But it's not enough to feel these feelings; we have to act on them. We must engage in caring behavior, looking out for other people, helping them when they need it, and generally being a caring and supportive presence in this increasingly complex world.

The Remedy to Absurdity

As we've seen, the absurd existence that results from Camus's meaningless landscape need not be replaced by an equally absurd moral system of an impossible moral standard coupled with eternal punishment. Perhaps the remedy to absurdity lies in something more basic—our innate desire to take care of each other. And perhaps this has been part of the message in *The Good Place* all along. In one of the most touching moments of the show, in "Pandemonium," Chidi prepares to get rebooted so that he can help the people in the new neighborhood improve, knowing that this means his memories of his relationship with Eleanor will be erased. But he assures Eleanor that he isn't scared, because, he says, "I know that you'll be here, taking care of me."

Notes

1 Albert Camus, *The Myth of Sisyphus and Other Essays* (New York: Random House, 1955), 9–12.
2 J.S. Mill, *Utilitarianism* (Indianapolis, IN: Hackett Publishing), 6–8.
3 Virginia Held, *The Ethics of Care: Personal, Political, and Global* (New York: Oxford University Press, 2006), 9–13.
4 Ibid., 154–158.

8

The Medium Place: Third Space, Morality, and Being In Between

Catherine M. Robb

I mean, I wasn't freaking Gandhi, but I was okay. I was a medium person. I should get to spend eternity in a medium place! Like Cincinnati. Everyone who wasn't perfect but wasn't terrible should get to spend eternity in Cincinnati.

— Eleanor ("Everything Is Fine")

When Eleanor first arrives in The Medium Place with Janet and Jason, after escaping on the Trans-Eternal Railway, she looks around with her bags still on her shoulders and concludes that this neutral zone is "truly nothing." The desert landscape is sparse and dry, and the neighborhood doesn't even have a name—it's simply called "n/a" ("Mindy St. Claire"). Even though The Medium Place is overshadowed by the dramatic events that unfold in the fake Good Place neighborhood, it is more significant to *The Good Place* than we might have originally thought. In fact, The Medium Place turns out to be pivotal to the overarching narrative, with its very own ethical and metaphysical importance. This means that Eleanor's first impressions turn out to be wrong—The Medium Place is not "truly nothing" after all.

What makes The Medium Place so "medium"? It is described as an individually tailored "eternal mediocrity," a place of neutrality and compromise. But it is also a place of self-exploration, where meaningful realizations are made. After all, it is here that Eleanor first finds out she has told Chidi she loves him, where Janet and Jason figure out how to have sex for the first time, and where Michael and the humans build and test out their new experimental Good Place neighborhood

The Good Place and Philosophy, First Edition. Edited by Kimberly S. Engels.
© 2021 John Wiley & Sons, Inc. Published 2021 by John Wiley & Sons, Inc.

in Season 4. This is all possible because The Medium Place is uniquely privileged as being *in between* The Good Place and The Bad Place, allowing the characters to creatively experiment with who they are, what they believe in, and how they interact with each other.

Having understood the metaphysics of The Medium Place—and by this, I just mean an understanding of what The Medium Place is and why that's important—we will be in a good position to uncover its strange ethical implications, as neither good nor bad, but something in between the two. Mindy, as the original resident of The Medium Place, is consistently self-centered and unapologetically seeks the pleasures of sex, drugs, and alcohol. What does this say about the ethics of The Medium Place? Is there really such a thing as a "medium" morality, in between good and bad? I'm going to try to convince you that because The Medium Place makes room for more personal concerns and self-realizations, in the end it turns out to be the most human and realistic neighborhood in *The Good Place* universe.

Escape, Neutrality, and Stomachache

Throughout most of *The Good Place*, we aren't told very much about The Medium Place. In the beginning the characters only visit it a few times, and elsewhere it's mentioned only in passing. But we do know more about it than the *real* Good Place, and by the end of Season 2, it is the only "authentic" neighborhood that the four humans have visited. We also know that The Medium Place is used by the characters as an escape and retreat. At the end of the first season, Janet and Jason go to Mindy's house in order to avoid Michael rebooting Janet. Eleanor follows them not to avoid capture from another character, but to sidestep the moral trap she's fallen into ("What's My Motivation"). Eleanor realizes that her intentions to become a better person were in fact self-centered, and so the only hope she has to gain more Good Place points is to leave and then start acting on selfless motivation. But by choosing to go to The Medium Place rather than The Bad Place, Eleanor is choosing to be morally neutral. She flees to a place that is neither good nor bad, but what Janet calls a "neutral zone." Exploring this idea of "neutrality" between two oppositions will help us determine what kind of place The Medium Place really is.

Being neutral is often assumed to be negative. If you describe someone as neutral, you're probably not giving them a glowing review. Ethically speaking, being neutral means that you refuse to take sides, and if you do make a choice, it will be to rest firmly in the middle of two contrasting alternatives. Neutrality allows us to shirk responsibility or to lack conviction, to stand on the sidelines and fail to stand up for what is right. Chidi is a prime example of why this kind of neutrality gets bad press—he regularly fails to decide between one thing or another, and often ends up with a stomachache or something he doesn't really want. This was the case during Pick-a-Pet day, when Chidi failed to choose between two cute puppies and ended up with an owl ("The Worst Possible Use of Free Will"). Chidi's indecision also has more significant consequences—not being able to choose whether to go for drinks with his friend is ultimately the cause of his death ("Chidi's Choice").

If The Medium Place was neutral in this negative way, it would neither be good nor evil, but some kind of stalemate between the two, where both good and evil are sidelined and decisions about them are not made. But this doesn't seem to be the case, as there is so much going on for the characters in The Medium Place concerning their own personal and moral development. Decisions *are* made. At the end of Season 1, Eleanor decides to go back to save Chidi and Tahani even though Jason objects ("Mindy St. Claire"). At the beginning of Season 2 Eleanor and Chidi ask, "What should we do?" when trying to formulate a plan to defeat Michael ("Dance Dance Resolution"). At the end of Season 3, the eternal beings decide how to build the new experimental neighborhood ("Chidi Sees the Time-Knife"), and in Season 4, the humans are in Mindy's house when they decide whether or not to trust Michael against Glenn's accusations that he is really Vicky in a Michael suit ("Tinker, Tailor, Demon, Spy"). Yes, the characters do use The Medium Place as an escape, but this is not because they are shunning their moral responsibilities. Instead, Mindy's house and her backyard end up being a space of self-discovery, where the characters explore who they are and what they stand for. So, if The Medium Place is neutral, this neutrality must be active and meaningful, rather than passive and morally indifferent.

Eleanor's "Third Possibility"

Just three years before he died and probably went to The Bad Place, Roland Barthes (1915–1980), a philosopher of literature and language, gave a series of lectures on the topic of *The Neutral*. He claimed that neutrality had been wrongly defined as something negative, passive, and cowardly, and instead should be thought of as something active and morally worthy. According to Barthes, being neutral means that we are not forced into choosing between two opposite extremes, but this doesn't mean that we don't choose anything at all. What we do choose is a "moment of exception" between those two extremes, an *in-between* space that seems to disrupt the status quo.[1] In this in-between space, we find a "third possibility" that, Barthes says, allows us to explore our subjectivity, our own personal experience of the world and the search for our "own style of being present to the struggles of [our] time."[2]

This rings true of how The Medium Place is used. In the first season, Eleanor escapes to The Medium Place to avoid choosing between either staying in The Good Place or sacrificing herself to The Bad Place ("What's My Motivation")—this is just a case of Eleanor refusing to choose between two extremes. And in the second season ("Team Cockroach"), when faced with the choice to either stay and help Michael trick Vicky, or be taken by Shawn to The Bad Place for eternal torture, Eleanor initially chooses to sneak away to The Medium Place—this is another example of Eleanor choosing the middle (or neutral) option between the two original extremes. If Barthes is right, then Eleanor's choices here are not cowardly or passive. Instead, she actively refuses to be bound by choices that are made for her, so that she can autonomously determine her own way to respond to the ethical struggles she's facing.

Dialectics, Contradictions, and Mindy's Weird Beige House

So far, it seems like The Medium Place is neither good nor evil but, as Barthes would say, a "third possibility" between the two. This means that The Medium Place is not just a moral void. Going there is not an ethical cop-out—the characters use it as somewhere *in between* good and evil, as a way to overcome being forced to choose between two moral extremes. The idea of overcoming two oppositional extremes is a central part of *dialectics*. In ancient philosophy, dialectics was a method of engaging in discussion, where two people who had opposing views about a topic would reason with each other, bringing up arguments and counterarguments in the hope that they would finally reach a conclusion about the truth. The most famous example of this method is Plato's (c. 428–348 BCE) use of Socratic Dialogue, where the character Socrates would pose a question about a topic, and consistently raise contradictions to the answers he would get from his audience, until finally they reached the truth together.[3] This dialectical method of philosophical reasoning has had lasting impact, and is arguably the most prominent way of doing contemporary philosophy.

Even though Eleanor and the other characters make lots of important decisions in The Medium Place, it doesn't seem like they're engaging in this kind of dialectics, using Socratic Dialogue to discover the truth. For example, Eleanor is so independent that she usually makes her decisions impulsively and by herself, and Mindy doesn't seem to care about the truth of morality when she explicitly tells Eleanor that "there's no time for that morality nonsense" ("Mindy St. Claire"). Similarly, Janet and Jason don't engage in any philosophical discussion but spend most of their "honeymoon" trying to figure out how to have sex with each other (which in the end, after drawing quite a few instructional diagrams, proves really quite impossible).

This means that The Medium Place is not a space where the characters resolve the contradictions between good and evil by talking or hugging it out, philosophically speaking. It seems more apt to think about The Medium Place as a space where these ethical contradictions are not resolved, but where the characters *explore* what it's like to be stuck in the middle between them. Mindy is a good example of this. Throughout her life, in her own words, she "mostly sucked." But just before dying she came up with, and followed through on, an idea for a highly effective relief-aid charity. Mindy's life was, as a result, a moral contradiction—on the one hand she lived an immoral life, but on the other hand, her charity resulted in extreme moral goodness. In order to decide whether she deserved to be in The Good Place or The Bad Place, the two sides reached a compromise. Mindy ended up in her own neighborhood, provided with all the things she requested by The Good Place, but modified by The Bad Place to make sure that she would live in "eternal mediocrity." Mindy is now subjected to a "weird beige house" with an outdated '80s interior, warm beer, and a jukebox with only live versions of songs by the Eagles and William Shatner's spoken word poetry ("Mindy St. Claire").

It might seem like The Good Place and The Bad Place managed to resolve their conflict about Mindy with a compromise. But importantly, the contradiction that Mindy embodies did not disappear and was not overcome. There was no new truth discovered about whether Mindy was moral or immoral, or whether she belonged in The Good Place or The Bad Place. Mindy ended up stuck in the middle between those two options. This means that The Medium Place is a kind of holding space, where the contradictions between good and evil, moral and immoral, get to play themselves out, eternally.

In his theory of dialectics, the German philosopher Georg Hegel (1770–1831) claims that contradictions are a necessary part of reality, and that in order to discover the truth about the way the world really is, we should follow a three-step process: thesis-antithesis-synthesis. First, we present a statement or claim (thesis), then we negate that claim with a contradictory counterargument (antithesis), and finally we resolve the differences between the two claims by arriving at a common ground, or synthesis. For example, a Kantian might claim that being moral just involves having good intentions, but a consequentialist would argue against this claim, stating that our intentions are not all that should count, and that the consequences of our actions are morally important. In order to find the truth about morality, according to Hegel's three-step process, we would find a way to resolve these two positions and arrive at a compromise or "synthesis" between them.

Hegel did not actually use the terms "thesis," "antithesis," and "synthesis" to describe his own theory (in fact, he only used those terms to argue against Kant's theory).[4] One of the reasons for this is that the idea of a synthesis makes it sound like the two opposing sides can really be resolved, so that the contradiction disappears and creates some new truthful realization about the world. Hegel didn't think that contradictions could disappear so easily. For Hegel, contradictions are just part of reality, and our task as philosophers is to explore these contradictions head on, to confront them and find out what it's like to be stuck in the middle between them, just like Mindy is stuck in The Medium Place in her weird beige house.[5]

Self-Exploration and Becoming

Being in this contradictory *in-between* space is not just a compromise, but a dynamic and active refusal to choose between two conflicting extremes. This is not cowardly or neutral. It is not an avoidance of responsibility, but a choice to spend time confronting the contradictions that are always a part of our world. Yes, good and evil might seem incompatible and contradictory, but what the humans in *The Good Place* show us is that in most of our lives, good and evil come together as part of the whole package. The contradiction between the two doesn't disappear, and it is something that we battle with and try to constantly balance. The Medium Place seems to be the spatial embodiment of this battle or struggle, as a place in the middle of good and evil that doesn't try to resolve this all-pervasive conflict.

What's interesting about this in-between place is that it allows for and produces meaningful realizations and moments of self-exploration. Although Eleanor uses the Medium Place as an escape, while she is there she also figures out what she stands for and who she loves. She eventually does go back to save Chidi and Tahani in the first season ("Mindy St. Claire"), and in Season 2 she discovers that she and Chidi have declared their love for each other ("Dance Dance Resolution"). In Season 3, we also see that Derek (Janet's self-made "son-rebound-booty-call") comes into his own as Mindy's lover and butler, eventually finding his own identity ("Chidi Sees the Time-Knife"). And in Season 4, Eleanor comes to realize her leadership skills when others seem to doubt her ("A Girl from Arizona Part 2"). In The Medium Place, the contradictions between good and evil, prudence and morality, life and death, are all explored and confronted in a space that seems to be all about *becoming*—becoming empowered to stand for what you really believe in, becoming sure of who you are, and becoming proud of who you love.

Third Space and Medium Morality

One of the most prominent contemporary cultural theorists, Homi K. Bhabha, calls this space of becoming, where contradictions and differences are explored rather than resolved, a "Third Space." (You'll notice that Bhabha's idea here is very similar to Roland Barthes's idea of the "third possibility" that was discussed at the beginning of this chapter.) Bhabha explains that the Third Space between two extremes provides "the terrain for elaborating strategies of selfhood—singular or communal—that initiate new signs of identity, and innovative sites of collaboration."[6] We have already seen how, on an individual level, the characters of *The Good Place* come to discover new aspects of themselves when they visit Mindy's house. But on a communal level, this is most obviously the case for our characters at the end of Season 3 and during Season 4, when the infinite beings and humans come together collaboratively, despite their differences, to design the new experimental neighborhood and then an entirely new afterlife system in the backyard of The Medium Place.

Bhabha claims that despite its importance, being "in-between" is usually "unrepresentable," and Barthes too refers to his idea of the "third possibility" as having "no place" of its own.[7] But the writers of *The Good Place* have proved them wrong—they have found a way to represent this middle "in-between" space it as a geographical neighborhood. This means that we have a perfect vantage point to witness the moral implications of trying to remain firmly in the middle of a contradiction between good and evil. What would this kind of medium morality, between good and evil, actually be like?

I have three suggestions. First of all, it might be that a morality in between good and evil is a *compromise* between the two. For example, if we are trying to determine whether we should act on a moral requirement to give 10 percent of our income to charity, we could find a compromise that would involve neither giving the full 10 percent nor giving zero, but giving only 5 percent. However, if we followed this approach, we would never really be doing what's completely right or morally good, but only something that is "half-moral" or "mediocre." This isn't what Mindy did—she was fully immoral for most of her life, and fully moral when she withdrew her life savings to start her charity. There was no moral compromise or mediocrity in the way she lived. Likewise, this isn't what Eleanor did—she chose in the end to do the morally right thing and rescue her friends from being tortured in The Bad Place. A compromise isn't what we're looking for if we are interested in confronting contradictions and exploring what it's like to be stuck in the middle of them.

The second suggestion is to characterize "medium morality" using Aristotle's theory of virtue. Aristotle (384–322 BCE) claimed that acting virtuously means choosing the appropriate action for the particular situation that you're in.[8] In order to do this, we have to use our moral wisdom to pick out the middle ground (the mean) between two extreme vices—the vice of *excess* and the vice of *deficiency*. Being moral, according to Aristotle, is being able to determine the virtuous action that is *between* doing too much and doing too little. For example, the virtue of courage is just the appropriate middle ground between the vices of cowardice and rashness; the virtue of honesty is just the middle ground between understatement and boastfulness;

and modesty is just the appropriate virtuous middle ground between the vices of shyness and shamelessness.[9]

Despite its importance, Aristotle's virtue ethics is not going to give us the right characterization of a medium morality as we find it in The Medium Place. This is because Aristotle's "middle ground" is a way to achieve moral goodness and resolve the conflict between good and evil. His theory of virtue ethics provides us with a way to determine what is good, rather than telling us how to explore the contradiction between good and evil, morality and immorality. It's clear that The Medium Place really isn't a place of undeniable moral virtue—there's just too much self-concern and scheming to allow for that (remember in "Dance Dance Resolution" when Mindy filmed Eleanor and Chidi having sex so she could watch it repeatedly as porn?).

Don't Let the Good Life Pass You By

The medium morality of The Medium Place is not a compromise between good and evil, and it can't be understood in terms of Aristotle's middle-ground virtue ethics. So, my third and final suggestion is to characterize the medium morality of The Medium Place as *suspending* good and evil, to make room for more personal concerns and self-discovery. The contemporary philosopher Susan Wolf, in her article "Moral Saints," provides a good explanation of why this is desirable.

Moral saints, she claims, are morally perfect—they are as morally worthy as it is possible to be, and their actions are always morally good. This kind of moral perfection can occur in two ways. First, as a result of being truly loving, you can devote yourself to others out of the goodness of your heart. Second, you can be morally perfect by sacrificing your own happiness for the interests of others, but feeling the loss that comes with that sacrifice and not being too happy about it. However, according to Wolf, a moral saint is not really the kind of person that we should want to be, because it would involve ignoring and neglecting personal characteristics that contribute to a good life.[10] Someone who is morally perfect would, for example, neglect personal excellences such as developing a talent for sports or music, or cultivating good humor: "A moral saint will have to be very, very, nice. It is important that [they] will not be offensive. The worry is that as a result, [they] will have to be dull-witted or humorless or bland."[11]

The character Doug Forcett, who appears in Season 3, is a perfect example of a moral saint. He spends his life sacrificing his own well-being for the sake of others' interests, partly out of the goodness of his heart, but mostly out of fear of not making it into The Good Place ("Don't Let the Good Life Pass You By"). Despite his moral perfection, Doug is boring—he doesn't allow himself to enjoy good food or home comforts, and doesn't have a sense of humor—and so he's not the kind of person that we should try to emulate. Wolf concludes that there's more to living a good life than merely aiming to be the most moral that we can be—and the example of Doug Forcett shows us why this is probably good advice.[12] This doesn't mean that we ought to ignore morality altogether, or find a compromise between moral and immoral behavior. Rather, Wolf's claims about moral perfection show us that sometimes we can suspend morality and admit that it should not always tell us how to act.

We're All Medium People!

At the end of Season 3, Michael and the humans try to convince the Judge that human life is so complicated that it's almost impossible to be morally good enough to make it into The Real Good Place ("Chidi Sees the Time-Knife"). Michael tells Judge Gen that "life is chaotic and messy and unpredictable," and Jason pleads that "you can't judge humans, because you don't know what we go through." The Judge confirms and agrees with this "big revelation" about human morality after a short visit to Earth, exclaiming with disbelief that "Earth is a mess, y'all!" So there's no doubt that it's impossible to be excellently moral given the messiness and chaos of human life. We should have realized this from the very beginning of *The Good Place*. In the first episode ("Everything Is Fine"), Eleanor tells Chidi that she's not a bad person but a "medium person," and that she doesn't belong in The Bad Place but some kind of "medium place." By the end of the fourth season, The Medium Place becomes the space in which the messiness between good and evil is constantly experimented with and tested. It is here that the "new" humans learn about themselves, discover how to improve, and explore their identities.

What we learn from The Medium Place, and the way that it embodies a third space between good and evil, is that the exploration of this chaos, confusion, and mess is precisely what allows for new and meaningful personal discoveries—realizations about who we are, and what we do in the face of moral challenges. It is when we are stuck in the middle of good and evil, suspending the choice between the two, that we allow for the development of an interesting and well-rounded life. We see this explicitly in the final season when the new afterlife is being designed. Eleanor's idea of creating a third option of a personal "Cincinnati" for people who don't meet the criteria for either The Good Place or The Bad Place is rejected ("You've Changed, Man"). But what Chidi designs is basically like a glorified Medium Place—a space where Good and Bad Place architects work together on neutral ground, and a place where humans have the chance to improve, experiment, and discuss their moral characters before a final decision is made. This is not a place of escape, but a place where humans and eternal beings alike are made to confront and reflect upon their own identities, in amidst the chaos and messiness of existence.

The morality of The Medium Place is the most human and realistic of all *The Good Place* neighborhoods. As a third possibility in between The Good Place and The Bad Place, The Medium Place turns out to be the only neighborhood where we can comfortably rest assured that, as Eleanor famously says, "Pobody's Nerfect!"

Notes

Author's note: Thanks to Emma Reid and Katie Reid for their extremely helpful comments on an earlier draft of this chapter. I wouldn't mind being stuck with them in The Medium Place for eternity!

1 Roland Barthes, *The Neutral,* trans. Rosalind E. Krauss and Denis Hollier (New York: Columbia University Press, 2005), 33, 38.

2 Ibid., 37, 6.

3 Julie E. Maybee, "Hegel's Dialectics," in *The Stanford Encyclopedia of Philosophy*, ed. Edward N. Zalta (Winter 2016 ed.), https://plato.stanford.edu/archives/win2016/entries/hegel-dialectics/.

4 Georg Wilhelm Friedrich Hegel, *The Phenomenology of Spirit*, trans. and ed. Terry Pinkard (Cambridge: Cambridge University Press, 2018), see particularly paragraphs 50 and 51 of the "Preface," 31–32.

5 See Theodor Adorno, *An Introduction to Dialectics*, ed. Christoph Ziermann, trans. Nicholas Walker (Cambridge: Polity Press, 2017), specifically Lecture 2, 12.

6 Homi K. Bhabha, *The Location of Culture* (London: Routledge, 1994), 1–4.

7 Barthes, *The Neutral*, 39, 91, 153. This is also discussed in Ana Parvalescu, "The Professor's Desire: On Roland Barthes's The Neutral," *Women, Gender and Sexuality Studies Research* paper no. 24 (2017), 34, http://openscholarship.wustl.edu/wgss/24.

8 Aristotle, *The Nicomachean Ethics*, trans. David Ross (Oxford: Oxford University Press, 1986), particularly Book I.13 and Book II.24–47.

9 Ibid., Book III.6–9, 63–72 and Book III.10–12, 72–78.

10 Susan Wolf, "Moral Saints," *The Journal of Philosophy* 79 (1982), 419–439.

11 Ibid., 422.

12 Ibid., 434.

9

What We May Learn from Michael's Solution to the Trolley Problem

Andreas Bruns

What do a two-year-old child and an immortal torturer-demon have in common? That's right—they might propose quite similar solutions to the "trolley problem," one of philosophy's most famous moral dilemmas.

Introduced by the British philosopher Philippa Foot (1920–2010), the trolley problem asks us to imagine a trolley heading toward five unfortunate workmen.[1] They can only be saved from being crushed and killed if the trolley is diverted to a side track, occupied by a sixth unfortunate workman who would meet the same fate. What should we do? Should we let the trolley go its default way and kill the five? Or should we save them even if this means putting another, previously unthreatened workman into harm's way?

In a video uploaded to YouTube in 2016, a two-year-old tackles the trolley problem with a toy train and several toy figures.[2] The child considers his options, then comes to a decision to move the lonely workman from the side track to join its five toy colleagues on the main track. The boy's kindness is moving, but only for a couple of seconds. Then his true intention is revealed, as he lets the trolley continue on the main track and crush all six workmen.

The early Michael would have approved of this. He is an architect of the human afterlife, an immortal being, a demon who perceives the world in nine dimensions. And yet, at first, his understanding of the trolley problem does not transcend that of a two-year-old human. When first presented with the dilemma in "The Trolley Problem," Michael states with confidence: "Well, obviously the dilemma is clear: how do you kill all six people?" He proposes a solution that allows

The Good Place and Philosophy, First Edition. Edited by Kimberly S. Engels.
© 2021 John Wiley & Sons, Inc. Published 2021 by John Wiley & Sons, Inc.

the agent to maximize harm in Foot's dilemma: a sharp blade reaching out of the trolley cabin will chop off the head of the sixth workman on the remote track, as we let the trolley continue and "smush our five main guys."

The child may be excused. After all, he's just playing with toys, and he doesn't understand the moral dilemma their positioning represents. But what is Michael's excuse? He is a fully developed rational being whose capacities seem, if anything, to exceed those of a human adult. How does *he* miss the point of the dilemma?

The Point of Human Ethics

One reason why Michael might have failed to see the point of Foot's dilemma is that no immortal being is likely to understand what it's like to live a finite life in which one will sooner or later cease to exist. It is not until "Existential Crisis" that Michael confronts the possibility of his own mortality. And we have to wait for the series finale, "Whenever You're Ready," to watch Michael living a fully human life, with all its limits. Being aware of our mortality certainly helps with understanding the ethics of life and death. It might help in more than one way, as we will see later.

Another reason for Michael's lack of comprehension is that he has spent his existence torturing those who end up in The Bad Place. In fact, that seems to be the whole point of his existence: to maximize human suffering in the afterlife. His design of the Good Place neighborhood is motivated by exactly that goal. For us, the death of any one workman is certainly bad and worth avoiding. Possibly the death of five is worse than the death of one. But for the early Michael, an end state in which none of the six workmen survive the trolley scenario is a "good" state, actually the "best" imaginable state. Michael's problem is not that he did not understand how to choose the appropriate means to achieve what is good. Instead, he simply applied another concept of "the good." He acts in accordance with values; they are just not the values of human ethics.

Chidi's rather traditional approach to teaching Michael is to make him write "people = good" over and over on the blackboard. As a result, Michael might learn some (very) basic human value theory. But the question of what we value isn't just important from the perspective of a torturer-demon. Our judgments about moral dilemmas may change dramatically depending on what we value. If all we consider is the disvalue of humans losing their lives, then it seems that we should always steer the trolley in the way that will allow the largest possible number of people to live. If this is all that matters, we find ourselves drawn to some version of "utilitarianism," a moral theory developed in particular by Jeremy Bentham (1748–1832) and John Stuart Mill (1806–1873). It combines "consequentialism," the idea that the rightness or wrongness of actions depends on the consequences or outcomes they produce or are expected to produce, with the idea that we should maximize utility, or how much good we do.

But one could also believe that there are things that are more important than allowing the largest number to live. Perhaps it is more important that we do not harm people even when we are benefitting others; perhaps we should not use other people as means to some end, not even for the "greater good." If we agree with this line of thought, then we may be more inclined to accept a non-consequentialist approach, such as the ethics of Immanuel Kant (1724–1804). We may even come to believe that, morally speaking, the numbers do not matter *at all* and that it would be the fairest approach to toss a coin to decide whether to save the smaller or the larger group of people.[3]

In a nutshell, *any* solution we may propose to a moral conflict like the trolley problem will be based on a certain idea about *what* we should value and *how* we should protect that value. It so happens that a torturer-demon, whose values are quite different from ours, may well believe that Foot's dilemma does not ask us what to do if we cannot save everyone, but that it asks us how to use the trolley in order to let none of the workmen get away.

Trolleys in *The Good Place*

Fortunately, everyone can change for the better. In line with what may be *The Good Place*'s most dominant moral theme, even a torturer-demon can learn human ethics. As we know, in Michael's virtuous development, the trolley problem plays a central role. First, however, old habits need to be overcome.

Michael's simulation of the dilemma in "The Trolley Problem" puts Chidi at the controls. We learn that the workmen aren't real, but that their pain is—Michael's attempt to create something that is not "just another thought experiment." We also learn that one Santa Claus is worth five William Shakespeares. But ultimately, Michael has just found another way of torturing the poor ethics professor. Michael only really begins to feel the grip of the trolley problem when the lives of his friends depend on him. When, in "Leap to Faith," he frames Vicky to save his friends, who are literally on the train tracks, he learns what it is like to make difficult decisions based on moral concern. Later, in "Rhonda, Diana, Jake, and Trent," Michael helps his human friends escape so they can present their case to the Judge. Here, he claims to have solved the trolley problem. The scenario "forces you to choose," Michael says, "between two versions of letting other people die; and the actual solution is very simple: sacrifice yourself!" He pushes Eleanor through the portal and stays behind to close it. Then he turns himself to face Shawn and his lackeys.

Michael's self-sacrifice represents the end state of the moral agent's virtuous development. It also draws our attention to an aspect of moral dilemmas that has largely been absent in the trolley problem discourse, and yet might be of considerable moral significance. Ever since its introduction into moral philosophy in the late 1960s, the trolley problem has spawned discussions about the conditions under which harming some people could be justified by saving the greater number. But deliberate self-sacrifice for the sake of others, or "moral heroism," has played no significant role in most of these debates. Presumably, this is so because the option of self-sacrifice is not available to the agent at the outset of the most prominent versions of the trolley problem. In fact, moral dilemmas are often construed so as to *exclude* the possibility of self-sacrifice, or to exclude it as an effective way of solving the particular conflict.

To illustrate this, let's consider two popular variations of Foot's trolley problem, both introduced by Judith Jarvis Thomson (1929-).[4] To continue Michael's work, let's place Chidi in the position of the moral agent. In the first scenario, call it "The Switch," Chidi is standing by the tracks when he sees a trolley hurtling towards five workmen. He can only save them if he pulls a lever next to him that will change the switch and lead the trolley to a side track occupied by a sixth workman. If he does so, the sixth workman will be killed but the five will live.

In the second scenario, call it "The Massive Man," Chidi is standing on a footbridge over a single track, right between the current position of the trolley and the five workmen further down the track. Next to Chidi stands Michael. Suppose that, being a demon, Michael's body mass is ten times greater than that of an average human adult. In particular, his body is massive enough to bring the trolley to a halt before it reaches the five further down the track. Michael is already leaning over the rail to see the trolley in the distance. If only Chidi would give him a push, so he would fall onto the tracks, the five workmen could be saved. (Let's assume that Chidi is strong enough to push even a massive demon like Michael over the rail. After all, in "Jeremy Bearimy," we catch sight of a surprisingly ripped ethics professor who seems to be working out regularly.) However, if Chidi pushes Michael off the footbridge, suppose that Michael would cease to exist or that whatever would happen to him is equivalent to the death of each workman.

In both scenarios, The Switch and The Massive Man, Chidi either cannot sacrifice himself or cannot do any good by sacrificing himself. He can leave the switch and sprint to the tracks, but even if he reaches it in time to jump in front of the trolley, it will only crush him before it crushes the five others. Similarly, he can jump off the footbridge, but his body mass will not be sufficient to bring the trolley to a halt. In all these popular versions of the trolley problem, Foot's original dilemma and Thomson's two variations of it, self-sacrifice is not an option, at least not an effective one.

So, is Michael simply violating the rules of the game when presenting self-sacrifice as the problem's definitive solution? Or is he refusing to play it altogether? Perhaps it is neither. Perhaps, what Michael shows us is that self-sacrifice has normative implications in moral dilemmas, *even when* it is *not* an option available to the agent.

Sacrifice Yourself!

One way to engage in moral philosophy is to begin with "common-sense morality," the intuitions we have on what is right or wrong in particular contexts of action, and then to try to explain diverging intuitions on the basis of general moral principles.

Empirical research suggests that moral philosophers have done a reasonably good job in predicting common moral intuitions about various types of trolley cases. Thomson's suspicion was that most of us will be inclined to say that, for the sake of saving five innocents, it is at least *permissible* to indirectly kill the one in The Switch, but *impermissible* to kill the one in The Massive Man. In fact, studies show that around 90 percent of respondents confronted with these scenarios agree on this evaluation.[5] Arguably, we should treat these results with caution. After all, for something to be morally right it takes more than just to match the opinion of the majority of people.

Still, we are left wondering why our intuitions about the wrongness of killing diverge so drastically across different cases where, on the face of it, outcome-related choices seem to be equivalent: it is the death of one versus the deaths of five.

Why do we deem it permissible to pull the lever and turn the trolley from five onto one, but impermissible to stop it by pushing the massive man on the tracks? One proposed explanation is the "doctrine of double effect," a complex moral principle that holds, in its most basic form, that an action that is performed in order to produce something good but that also would bring about a lesser harm is morally permissible *if* the harm occurs as an unintended side effect of the production of the good. For example, according to the doctrine of double effect, it is permissible for Chidi to pull the lever to redirect the trolley to the side track, if his intention is to save the five and if the death of the one is merely an unintended side effect. By contrast, if Chidi pushes Michael off the footbridge he seems to be saving the five *by* killing Michael. In this scenario, killing Michael is *a means*, not just an unintended side effect, of saving the five. Thus, if plausible, the doctrine of double effect might explain why it is permissible for Chidi to pull the lever but not permissible to push Michael off the bridge.

In a more recent paper, Thomson has revisited the minority view that the trolley problem might be a false problem after all because, contrary to common intuitions, it is just not true that we may choose to kill the one in The Switch.[6] Her argument gives explanatory force to the normative significance of self-sacrifice. Imagine that Chidi can throw the switch in two ways. If he pulls the lever to the right, the trolley will turn to the track occupied by one workman. If he pulls the lever to the left, it will redirect the trolley to a second side track occupied by Chidi himself. If he chooses to pull it to the left, there will not be enough time to get out of the way and the trolley will kill him. The moral dilemma, The Switch, has become "The Switch Trilemma." Chidi has three options now, though the outcome of each course of action seems undesirable.

Thomson asks her readers to agree that turning the trolley onto the one workman is not permissible in The Switch Trilemma. Saving the five would be a good deed on Chidi's part. But if he turned the trolley onto the one workman instead of turning it onto himself, he would "make the one workman pay the cost of his good deed because he doesn't feel like paying it himself."[7] That seems morally unacceptable.

Moreover, Thomson's suspicion is that our verdicts about the dilemma, The Switch, change once we consider the implications of The Switch Trilemma. To see how, suppose that Chidi *thinks* he can throw the lever either to the left or to the right, but then finds, upon testing it, that it is stuck and doesn't go to the right; he *cannot* turn the trolley onto himself. Chidi is relieved because he wouldn't have been willing to give his life anyway, and so he proceeds and turns the trolley onto the sixth workman. Is this morally acceptable? Thomson suspects that we might not think so. If Chidi would not be willing to pay the cost of his good deed himself, how could it be morally acceptable if he sacrifices someone else instead? And again, empirical studies support Thomson's presumption. Only just over one-third of respondents still think it is permissible to pull the switch in the dilemma case, *after previously* being presented with the trilemma.[8]

How can we explain these intuitions? As Thomson says, what seems to govern our intuitions *against* killing one to save five, in any given case, is "how drastic an assault on the one the agent has to make in order to bring about, thereby, that the five live."[9] The different intuitions about The Switch and The Massive Man could be explained by the fact that Chidi's assault on Michael seems much more drastic than his assault on the one workman, who just happens to be on the side track when Chidi diverts the trolley. A similar explanation might be given for the diverging intuitions regarding The Switch (considered on its own) and The Switch after considering The Switch Trilemma. Perhaps, The Switch Trilemma makes us think about what it would *mean* to make the ultimate sacrifice of one's life and helps us to show more empathy toward the sacrificed workman in The Switch. Again, the results of the empirical study are to be treated with caution as they do not tell us what is actually right or wrong. What Thomson's argument suggests, however, is that there is more to the question than whether we may sacrifice another individual for a morally good cause. If Chidi would not choose to kill himself to save five innocents, how could he "decently regard himself as entitled to choose to kill the one" instead?[10]

What Else the Massive Man Should Complain About

There is another worry about the disregard of self-sacrifice in trolley cases. The person sacrificed has usually been treated as an inactive subject to the choice of a morally responsible other: the agent. In this traditional fashion, I have introduced Chidi as the one who had to choose whether or not to sacrifice Michael in The Massive Man. But Chidi is not the only rational, moral agent on the footbridge. Michael is the other. Suppose that Michael has judged the situation, and has arrived at the initially disturbing insight that the only way to save the five workmen is for him to die. While Michael is leaning over the rail ready to let go and commit the ultimate sacrifice, Chidi, against his very nature, has made up his mind too, and has come to the same conclusion: that Michael should be sacrificed for the greater good. He takes action and pushes Michael over the rail.

Something has gone wrong here. How could it be up to Chidi to decide whether Michael should be sacrificed as long as Michael was conscious and capable of making this decision himself? It seems that by pushing Michael off the bridge Chidi interferes with Michael's moral agency. Imagine that, in "Rhonda, Diana, Jake, and Trent," it wasn't Michael who had pushed Eleanor through the portal after telling her that he intends to sacrifice himself, but that Eleanor, disregarding his decision, pushed him away from the portal to save herself and her human friends. Would that have been morally acceptable? After all, isn't it Michael's sacrifice, not Eleanor's, and thus a sacrifice that is *up to him* to make?

Another way to look at the issue is this. Suppose that utilitarianism holds that Michael should be sacrificed in The Massive Man. This way, one instead of five will cease to exist, and that is good; at least it is better than having to bewail the deaths of five. From the consequentialist perspective of utilitarianism, then, that the five workmen survive is an "agent-neutral" moral aim.[11] It is an aim that *everyone* has moral reason to try to achieve, as best they can. (Other moral aims may be "agent-relative," for example, the aim of caring for one's own children.) If saving the five is an agent-neutral moral aim, then both Chidi and Michael, who *are both capable* of achieving it, have reason to save the five. Therefore, if Michael is about to sacrifice himself to achieve that aim, he is acting on a stringent moral reason, a reason to save five innocent workmen. Supposedly, it is morally wrong to prevent someone from acting in the morally right way for the morally right reasons, without having a very good justification for one's interference. Chidi doesn't seem to have one. If he does not interfere, the common moral aim will still be achieved: the five will be saved. Thus, Chidi's interference appears morally unacceptable.

The worry that it is actually Michael's sacrifice, one that it is *up to him* to make, also spurs on one of the chief objections against utilitarianism, most closely associated with Bernard Williams (1929–2003). The so-called demandingness objection holds that once we are aware of its implications, utilitarianism seems too demanding a moral theory to be plausible. For it requires us to give up too much of our own happiness, well-being, and personal relationships. Just think of Doug Forcett, who judges each of his actions according to how much impersonal good they are expected to produce, and who finds his life stripped of any genuinely personal projects or concerns. (Let's not be bothered here by the fact that everything he does, he only seems to be doing because he expects that, this way, he will earn a seat on the train to The Good Place—arguably, a rather personal or even selfish concern.) When, in "Chidi Sees the Time-Knife," Michael pitches his concerns about the afterlife point system, a genuinely utilitarian system, to the Judge, he essentially formulates *The Good Place*'s version of the demandingness objection: "Life now is so complicated, it's impossible for anyone to be good enough for The Good Place." Not even Doug Forcett got in! In the final season, Chidi's reform of the afterlife system seeks to correct the shortcomings of the purely utilitarian system by shifting the focus to the virtuous development of one's moral character in the afterlife. As to the issue of self-sacrifice, a purely utilitarian view appears even *more* demanding once we understand that it might sometimes require us to sacrifice ourselves for the greater good. For if a utilitarian tells Chidi that he *must* push Michael off the footbridge to save five workmen, she seems to be committed to the view that Michael *must* jump.

Michael's Solution

Michael believes he has solved the trolley problem when he makes the choice to sacrifice himself in order to save his friends. While perhaps he does not solve the problem as traditionally presented, his decision to sacrifice himself still teaches us something meaningful about sacrifice and human ethics. Michael causes us to reflect on the original problem and whether the choice of sacrificing one to save many can ever be a moral choice we make for someone else. This, in turn, prompts us to consider the value of utilitarian ethics and whether it is ultimately too demanding of a standard to follow.

Notes

1   Philippa Foot, "The Problem of Abortion and the Doctrine of the Double Effect," *Oxford Review* 5 (1967), 5–15.
2   "A Two-Year-Old's Solution to the Trolley Problem," https://www. youtube.com/watch?v=-N_RZJUAQY4.

3   John Taurek, "Should the Numbers Count?" *Philosophy and Public Affairs* 6 (1977), 293–316.

4   Judith Jarvis Thomson, "The Trolley Problem," *The Yale Law Journal* 94 (1985), 1395–1415.

5   Marc Hauser, *Moral Minds* (New York: HarperCollins, 2006), 139.

6   Judith Jarvis Thomson, "Turning the Trolley," *Philosophy and Public Affairs* 36 (2008), 359–374.

7   Ibid., p. 369.

8   Ezio Di Nucci, "Self-Sacrifice and the Trolley Problem," *Philosophical Psychology* 26 (2013), 667.

9   Thomson, "Turning the Trolley," 374.

10   Ibid., 367–369.

11   Derek Parfit, *Reasons and Persons* (Oxford: Oxford University Press, 1984), 27.

Part IV
"HELP IS OTHER PEOPLE"

10

Some Memories You May Have Forgotten: Holding Space for Each Other When Memory Fails

Alison Reiheld

I'm scared.... What am I supposed to be doing right now? I don't remember. I'm having a hard time remembering.

—Eleanor ("Janet(s)")

On *The Good Place* we've seen Chidi, Eleanor, Jason, and Tahani lose their memories again and again. Each time, they reboot to an earlier version of themselves while Michael, Janet, and the demons retain their memories of their interactions with the "Soul Squad." Notably, in Seasons 2 and 3, Michael and Janet frequently remind the four intrepid humans of what has gone before. Eleanor frequently watches recordings of her and Chidi in love, often sharing this with him later on. In Season 3, Chidi does the same for Eleanor. Such reminders provide scaffolding for the characters' relationships in the present moment, a moment that may be stripped away in a flash.

It's easy to think that memory scaffolding belongs in the realms of science fiction and fantasy worlds like *The Good Place*. Yet in real life, people experience memory loss due to traumatic brain injuries or degenerative neurological conditions, and the folks with whom they are in relationships retain memories of those relationships. Because of Alzheimer's or other forms of age-related dementia, many of us must anticipate this as part of our own narrative arc. Given my family history, I expect this will be my fate if I live long enough.

Even without Alzheimer's or dementia, most of us are prone to "ordinary forgetting." *The Good Place* and careful philosophical reflection can help us think through memory loss, relationships, and making a place for each other as we live through the human condition. What do we owe to each other? How can we do right by each other when memory is so frail and yet so important to who we are, and who we are with each other?

Stories, Relationships, and the Moral Self in *The Good Place*

In Season 3, as part of an agreement with the Judge to see whether people are assessed too soon, the Soul Squad has been restored to their mortal timelines at the moment of their deaths, having forgotten everything they had learned in all the thousands of previous iterations of the Good Place neighborhood. This gives them an opportunity to learn to be better. But what happens when we begin to forget what we have learned?

With a bit of indirect pushing from Michael, the four humans come together again as part of an earthly near-death experience research project that Simone, a neuroscientist and Chidi's earthly girlfriend, is running with Chidi. Over time, Michael and Janet tell the reunited Soul Squad what has happened to them and what the consequences of failure would be.

In previous seasons, the characters prompted their own memories. At the end of Season 1, the four humans had their memories erased when they (re)discovered that the fake Good Place is fake. So, at the beginning of Season 2, Eleanor receives a note in her own handwriting that says, "Eleanor, find Chidi." This kind of "scaffolding" of relationships and self features prominently in Season 3 during the reboot on Earth. Eventually, the Soul Squad's lives are threatened by Bad Place demons. For their souls to survive, and to find out what has been happening with the point system that governs who gets into The Real Good Place, they must leave Earth. This destroys their bodies. Eventually, in the episode "Janet(s)," they enter a special dimension that Janet creates for them within herself. To occupy this dimension, they must each appear as Janet. Over time, this damages them. Their distress causes the dimension, and Janet herself, to come apart catastrophically.

Eleanor, trapped inside Janet, begins to forget who she is. Chidi, dressed as Chidi but looking like Janet, helps Eleanor remember. As he speaks, she cycles through the appearance of many people who are not her, mostly men of varying ages, races, and body types, beginning with a tall, muscular man wearing Eleanor's now-too-small sweater and a casual man bun.

ELEANOR-WEIGHTLIFTER:	I'm scared.
CHIDI-JANET:	I know.
ELEANOR-WEIGHTLIFTER:	What am I supposed to be doing right now? I don't remember.
ELEANOR-OLD MAN:	I'm having a hard time remembering.
CHIDI-JANET:	*pause* Right! Memories. You need to remember who you are. You're Eleanor Shellstrop from Phoenix, Arizona. Your favorite meal is shrimp scampi. You listed your emergency contact as Britney Spears as a longshot way of meeting her, and your favorite movie is that clip of John Travolta saying "Adele Dazeem." You flew halfway around the world because you wanted to be a better person and it was very brave. You're sharp. And you're strong. You make fun of me a lot. You once called me a human snooze button. But you also showed up in my classroom when I was drowning in despair and canned chili and you basically saved my life. You have very high self-esteem and a very low tolerance for men who wear sandals and your worst nightmare is someone saying something nice about you to your face. But too bad. Because I need to say it. Because you deserve it. Because … because …
ELEANOR [BRIEFLY HERSELF]:	Chidi … [she disappears again, cycling through other bodies to Janet] [Chidi-Janet kisses Eleanor-Janet. Eleanor-Janet becomes Eleanor. Chidi-Janet becomes Chidi. The dissolving dimension stabilizes.]
ELEANOR:	*relieved noises, pats her own face, smiles at Chidi* Nice work, bud.

This restores her, and thus Janet. But this also restores Chidi to himself.

It is critically important to realize that it is *not* the kiss that restores Eleanor; this is no Snow White or Sleeping Beauty. Rather, it is Chidi's deep and thorough knowledge of Eleanor, and his relationship with her, that does the work. By displaying and using his knowledge of Eleanor, Chidi reveals how much he cares. His knowledge leads to both her restoration and their kiss.

Significantly, Chidi's description of Eleanor includes moral content: about how she has acted and thus may act in the future, about her habits of action and judgment. In the tradition of virtue ethics, to say that someone is brave is to say they are virtuous. For Aristotle (384–322 BCE), to be brave means to find the perfect sweet spot between cowardice and rushing unthinkingly and unnecessarily into danger.[1] In that sweet spot of bravery, a person takes action despite being afraid, because the action will improve one's own life and the lives of others.

Chidi also tells Eleanor that she essentially saved his life with her actions. Thus, Chidi gives Eleanor a gift: he tells her not only small things about her identity but also important things she can hold onto that make it possible to know herself again more deeply. This is not an isolated occurrence. Throughout *The Good Place*, Chidi and Eleanor help each other develop and sustain their moral selves as well as their relationship.

Stories, Relationships, and the Moral Self in This Actual World

In real life too, we provide this kind of scaffolding for each other's identities, and to maintain our relationships. As a parent, I talk to my children about what they were like when they were too young to remember firsthand. I urge them to be their "best selves" when they have deviated from that, and remind them of times they were kind, fair, thoughtful, and able to control their anger or sadness.

We don't just use words, though. As a culture with access to photographs, we use images of ourselves and each other to remind us of what we have experienced. In the best memory care centers for people with dementia, residents record journals for themselves of what they most want to remember, in their own handwriting, so that they will trust it. Another common technique is the use of "memory walls" where pictures of loved ones through time are placed with their names, dates, and relationships to each other. Like the interactions in *The Good Place*, these scaffold our relationships and ourselves as surely as any ideal remembering would.

We all tell stories that structure our autobiographies and that help us to create and sustain our relationships with each other. Such stories can also create and sustain what Margaret Urban Walker calls "moral self-definition." Walker describes how a morally developed person can turn to her own personal history to "help her make a decision in the present moment that best reflects who she is and wants to be.... such stories are not entirely of the [person's] own making: the stories others tell about us can strongly define us as well."[2]

Stories matter.[3] They are fundamental to our sense of self, our sense of right and wrong, and our sense of the kind of people we are. Without someone to remember our narratives, or a place we can record them and retrieve them later, they don't exist. Stories certainly can't help us define ourselves and our place with each other if we cannot access them. Think of how important Michael's recordings of Chidi and Eleanor are, or the videotape from The Medium Place on which a scene of Chidi and Eleanor cuddling and expressing their love is preserved.

Indeed, Merlin Donald argues that symbolic technologies like writing and other recording methods allowed for a major leap in human evolution because "Symbols can be internal or external to the brain ... unlike most aspects of material culture, they are designed specifically to help us think, remember, and represent reality."[4] Let's get literal for a minute and look at that word "represent": to "re" present something, to present it again at a later time. We use memories and their preservation, in our minds or outside of them, to hold onto our stories. We then tell these stories to ourselves and to each other. We do all this even when our memory is working properly. But how *does* memory work?

What Is Memory?

In her book *Memory*, philosopher Mary Warnock (1924–2019) writes that common beliefs paint memory "as a 'storehouse', in which things that may come in handy later are put away: a kind of attic or junk room."[5] On this view, misremembering and forgetting are errors of recollection. This way of thinking about memory dominated for centuries and is reflected in public understandings of memory: "we tend to think of memories as snapshots from family albums that could be retrieved in precisely the same condition in which they were put away."[6]

However, scientists and psychologists who study memory now think that memories are heavily constructed at the time they are made (and so are not necessarily accurate records) and also reconstructed *and altered* by the process of recollection. Philosopher Susan Campbell suggests we should think of memory as an "appropriately relational capacity,"[7] about relations with other memories but also with other persons. When philosophers and neuropsychologists say memory is "constructed," they mean "subject to revision," to writing and rewriting. It turns out that remembering is a "creative, constructive process."[8]

Constructing Memories of What Really Matters

To understand memory as a construction, we must understand the three stages of individual memory: encoding, storage, and retrieval.

Encoding refers to how we pay attention to, process, and prepare experiences for storage in memory. In his autobiography, *Speak Memory*,[9] the great novelist Vladimir Nabokov reports that paying attention to butterflies and moths made him much better than others at both noticing and remembering such creatures. Nabokov recounts a conversation with a hiker who walked the same trail he did through what Nabokov recalls as swarms of butterflies. Upon reaching the bottom, Nabokov asks how many butterflies the other hiker had seen. "None," he replies. Similar instances in laboratory settings demonstrate that how well, and how much, we encode an experience is highly dependent on existing knowledge and on attention. What we pay attention to matters greatly, and so what we choose to pay attention to matters greatly.

In Eleanor's time on Earth, she doesn't much notice the suffering or needs of others, and so she doesn't remember who she's hurt. In a vicious cycle, she cannot care because she did not care. But in the Good Place neighborhood, she learns again and again to notice both the suffering of others and what might make them happy. In Season 3, Michael shows Eleanor a moment when Chidi fell in love with her, the time when, out of unthinking kindness, she offered to tell Michael that Chidi really wanted a puppy instead of the murderous owl that clawed Chidi's arm. In an earlier season, we see that in one version of the Good Place neighborhood, the reason Chidi falls in love with Eleanor is because of a moment in which he is about to need a tissue and she unthinkingly hands him one. The implication is clear: what we notice matters, morally. And we cannot remember what we do not notice.

The next stage of memory is storage, in which information is encoded and retained. Memory researchers Squire and Kandel posit that memories are stored better when the brain is accustomed to storing that kind of information, either through deliberate recollection and repeated re-encoding or through storing similar kinds of information on prior occasions.[10] This is why studying helps us learn.

Retrieval is the third stage of memory processing, occurring when a stored memory becomes consciously available. Retrieval can happen intentionally, when we strive to recall something we once committed to memory or when others remind us. But it can also happen unintentionally, as when memory is triggered by a smell or a word or a similarity between two memories. Memory construction can occur during encoding, storage, retrieval, or subsequent re-encoding: memory is writing and rewriting.

When Chidi restores Eleanor's sense of self, mentioning both their relationship and her virtuous behaviors, he is helping her write and even rewrite those memories. He is not merely reminding her: the fact that he noticed and admired these things about her will now be part of what she remembers, if she remembers.

Encoding, storage, and retrieval are generally agreed upon, but Squire and Kandel add "ordinary forgetting" to the list of normal memory processes. Ordinary forgetting is the "inevitable weakening of memories that were initially clear and full of detail.... In fact, it is not at all clear that we would be better off if we could remember everything easily."[11] Forgetting is not always a memory error. Some things ought to be forgotten. Others are simply fine to forget. Others, however, we cannot afford to lose.

The Ethics of Memory

So, what must be remembered? And how can we make space for memories and hold each other in that space? How would you feel if someone you care about, and who has claimed to care for you, forgot your birthday or a shared anniversary? Would you think they had done something morally wrong?

I believe that we can be blamed morally for forgetting information or events that are important to people with whom we are in relationships. It might be a birthday. It might be a promise to be home in time to take a kid to soccer practice. It might be a favorite food. Heck, it might be a *least* favorite food. Perhaps our loved one hates onions, so we choose recipes that don't include onions when we cook for them. When we care, we remember, and only by remembering can we act in ways that show we care. So we have obligations to remember, and to pay attention so that we can remember. We can fulfill our obligations to remember in many ways. We can store the information in our heads, write it down on paper, or put it into a device and have that device remind us of anniversaries or appointments. These are not lesser ways of fulfilling the obligation to remember. They get the job done, and that is what matters.

Now imagine that someone you care about, and who has claimed to care for you, doesn't just forget your birthday. They forget you. They forget that they ever loved you. How would you feel? Would you think they had done something morally wrong? Would you blame them?

This kind of complete forgetting happens with distressing frequency to the characters in *The Good Place*. In real life, it happens all too often as we or our loved ones experience memory loss through brain trauma, dementia, or even ordinary forgetting. If you think ordinary forgetting cannot cause this, consider the common experience of returning to your hometown and finding that others had very different memories of your relationships with them than you do. Or consider the experience of not being able to remember the names and appearances of all of the people you have ever been involved with romantically. Would you recognize them? How much should we blame ourselves or others for forgetting?

There are a few helpful rules for remembering rightly, based on considerations much like these.[12] In identifying such rules, we should take account of how what we remember is critically important for those with whom we are in relationships because it shows what we care about. But we must also account for the fact that memory is prone to error and that it can be taken from us at any time, and especially over time.

When we are thinking through our experiences, we should be aware that *how* we think about them will get encoded in our memory, as will how we rethink them later. We ought to be careful to think about our experiences in ways that treat others and ourselves fairly so that the memory isn't biased even though it might protect our self-image. We shouldn't just make ourselves into the good guys and turn other people into the bad guys. When we go over and over our past hurts, "rehearsing" them, we nurse grudges. We shouldn't do this because it's harmful to us as well as to other folks. But this doesn't mean we should forget wrongs done to us. After all, we might need to protect ourselves in the future from people who have harmed us in the past. The trick is in *how* we remember.

There is real value in deliberately creating positive accurate memories. One technique for this involves keeping a journal of one good thing that has happened each day so that negative memories don't dominate. This is not just good for mental health but also, I think, morally good. Nonetheless, if we have done morally wrong things, we should remember those too so that we can avoid repeating them and perhaps make up for them. We need to have an accurate sense of our moral self in all our terrible flaws and glittering facets. Finally, if we know we have problems with memory that could harm others, we need to behave accordingly. A doctor in the early stages of Alzheimer's should probably stop practicing medicine. A person who has learned they tend to remember things inaccurately should be very cautious before acting on their memories. And if you know you might forget something, then you really ought to leave yourself notes and reminders so that your difficulty with remembering doesn't harm yourself or others.

The kinds of memory prompts that Eleanor and the gang try to leave for themselves over time—"Find Chidi"—satisfy some of these moral rules. But beyond what we ought to do as individuals, we have to think hard about how we can use these rules to help each other remember rightly: to remember the positives as well as the negatives, to remind each other, to avoid grudges but not to simply forget wrongs done to us, to compensate for memory loss and for all the harms of memory loss. And sometimes, perhaps even to *not* remind each other of things that should be let go.

How we scaffold each other's identities and how we hold space for each other in the real world are ethical issues that have everything to do with memory and the stories we tell ourselves and each other. *The Good Place* can help us grapple with this. And it can help us to work through, for ourselves, what it means to hold space for each other through memory and stories.

Some Memories You May Have Forgotten

Season 3 comes to a close in "Pandemonium" and a deliberate choice to forget. For complicated reasons, Chidi has asked to have his memories of his ex-girlfriend Simone removed. Since these are intertwined with his memories of his relationship with Eleanor, he will lose those memories as well as much of the progress he has made in moral development. Before Chidi's memory is wiped, Michael plays a silent short film for him and Eleanor with scenes from their time together entitled *Some Memories You May Have Forgotten*. Michael intends it as a gift, but it is a gift only Eleanor will remember until one of the final episodes of the show, "The Answer," when Michael restores to Chidi all the memories of all his lives in a series of flashes. In one flash to the moments just before this final memory wipe, Michael helps Chidi reframe Chidi's memory of presenting a philosophical argument to his parents to prevent their divorce: "You made them remember: they loved each other. Sometimes people forget. You reminded them of what they already have." Chidi's boyhood act was not an example of the power of argument, so much as it was an example of the power of holding space for each other through memory and stories. What brings the characters from *The Good Place* together, what keeps them together, what makes them their selves and the selves they are with each other is, at least some of the time, the way they hold space for each other. It is one remembering for the other what the other has forgotten, or someone else holding space for them, their relationships, and their very selves.

We can do that for each other in the real world as well. In fact, we *do* do that for each other. Truly, we must hold space for each other. We must give each other memories we may have forgotten, and choose carefully and thoughtfully how we do so. We must remember rightly. And together. It's part of what we owe to each other.

Notes

1   Aristotle, *Nicomachean Ethics*, trans. David Ross (New York: Oxford University Press, 1998).
2   Hilde Lindemann Nelson, ed., *Stories and Their Limits: Narrative Approaches to Bioethics* (New York: Routledge, 1997), x–xi.
3   Rita Charon and Martha Montello, eds., *Stories Matter: The Role of Narrative in Medical Ethics* (New York: Routledge, 2002).
4   Merlin Donald, *A Mind So Rare: The Evolution of Human Consciousness* (New York: W.W. Norton & Company, 2001), 305.
5   Mary Warnock, *Memory* (London: Faber & Faber, 1987), 6.
6   Daniel. L. Schacter, *The Seven Sins of Memory: How the Mind Forgets and Remembers*
(Boston: Houghton Mifflin Company, 2001), 9.
7   Sue Campbell, *Relational Remembering: Rethinking the Memory Wars* (Lanham, MD: Rowman & Littlefield Publishers, 2003), 16.

8   Larry R. Squire and Eric R. Kandel, *Memory: From Mind to Molecules* (New York: Henry Holt and Company, 1999), 6.

9   Vladimir Nabokov, *Speak, Memory: An Autobiography Revisited* (New York: Vintage, 1989).

10 Larry R. Squire and Eric R. Kandel, *Memory: From Mind to Molecules* (New York: Henry Holt and Company, 1999).

11 Ibid., 75.

12 Alison Reiheld, "Rightly or for Ill: The Ethics of Individual Memory," *Kennedy Institute of Ethics Journal* 28 (2018), 377–410.

The Good Other

Steven A. Benko

Ethics: a comportment in which the other, who is strange and indifferent to you, who belongs neither to the order of your interest nor to your affections, at the same time matters to you.

—Emmanuel Levinas[1]

From beginning to end, the ethical vision of *The Good Place* is shaped by creator Mike Schur's reading of T.M. Scanlon's *What We Owe to Each Other*. When Schur announced that Season 4 would be the final season of *The Good Place*, he reiterated what he got from Scanlon's work and how it shaped the *ethos* of the show:

> It basically says if you're setting up a society, you should do it through a system where everyone has a vote and anybody can veto anybody else's idea. And if someone proposes an idea and you're a reasonable person and you don't reject that idea and no one objects, that's a good idea. That's the basic distillation of that book. But the larger sense of that book, to me, is that we owe things to each other. That you start from a position of owing things to other people and that your life should be led with that in mind all the time.... So, it's incumbent upon each person to provide that help, love and support for other people to the best of his or her ability.[2]

Schur's interpretation of Scanlon has shaped the moral arc of the characters: they have become better people because they have expanded their concern to include the interests and needs of others. Schur might be satisfied if he could inspire his audience to listen intently and agree to disagree more often. However, the moral arc of the characters on *The Good Place* goes further than this. The characters

The Good Place and Philosophy, First Edition. Edited by Kimberly S. Engels.

on *The Good Place* become better people not because they have figured out a system for getting along with each other. Rather, the moral journey of the characters on *The Good Place* changes them into fundamentally different people. These changes would not have occurred if they had not gone through inner transformations that reoriented their priorities away from themselves and toward the other.

Like Scanlon, the French philosopher Emmanuel Levinas (1906–1995) developed an ethics that begins with our obligations toward other people. Though they might not articulate it this way, both Scanlon and Levinas are concerned about selfishness: its origins, justifications, and how to correct for it. For Levinas, reorientation away from selfishness is an internal process where one's inner orientation matches one's outward behavior. The only reason that someone would give up their way of being in the world is because they realize that if they continue to be who they are, they will continue to harm those around them; this realization makes them change their behavior toward others. Rightly, the emphasis on the moral meaning and messaging of *The Good Place* has been in its deft use of philosophy to inspire the characters to become better people. But does the moral messaging of *The Good Place* inspire similar changes in the audience? If *The Good Place* is a commentary about morality and society, then we need to ask whether it effects changes in the audience through laughter.

Old Habits Die Hard (Not as Hard as Those People You Crushed with the Trolley, Though)

Chidi's summary of the different schools of ethical thought in the episode "Jeremy Bearimy" is accurate, even if the ending ("The true meaning of life, the actual ethical system that you should all follow is nihilism. The world is empty. There is no point to anything, and you're just gonna die") does not inspire one to play nice with others. Ethics is usually thought of as having the right intentions (Kant), producing the best outcomes (utilitarianism), or becoming the best possible version of yourself (Aristotle and virtue ethics). Levinas comes at ethics differently by starting with a fact of perception: the world we experience, including our experience of other people, contains more than we can possibly take in and comprehend: "From the outset, we think more than we can think. For me this is exemplary. The things that we have in our horizon always overflow their content."[3] The world exceeds human perception, so there is always a remainder—an excess—that is unaccounted for. But instead of trying to account for this excess, we leave it out of our understanding of the world and other people.

Levinas believes that individuals both cannot and do not want to account for this excess. It cannot be accounted for because there is too much to account for. More importantly, the individual does not want to account for it because doing so would disrupt the mental maps that make it possible to navigate the world and relationships in a familiar way. Every person has these mental maps, and they are all incomplete in different ways. That incompleteness extends to our knowledge of other people who are placed in the world in a way that is convenient and favorable to the individual. The world that the mind constructs is a world that each person enjoys inhabiting because it is familiar and predictable: if a person continues to experience themselves and the world in a familiar way, then their future will be like their past. The comfort and security that a person enjoys create their investment in continuing to see the world the way that they do. The way of seeing the world is a habit that dies hard. Quoting Pascal, Levinas likens the world-building activity of the mind to being in the sunlight. However, standing in the light inevitably leaves other people in the shade such that "by the fact of being there, I deprived someone of his vital space."[4]

On multiple occasions the metaphor of stealing the spotlight is used to describe the dynamic between Tahani and Kamilah. Tahani uses this language when she and Kamilah are being read their parents' last will and testament:

TAHANI: Well, what did they leave their second favorite child?
SOLICITOR: There's still quite a lot of money and property that goes to you. There is one issue, however. They have, um, spelled your name incorrectly in the will.
TAHANI: You've got to be kidding me.
SOLICITOR: IT SAYS, "WE BEQUEATH THE REST OF OUR ESTATE TO TAHINI." LIKE THE SAUCE.
TAHANI: You know what? I don't want the money. My sister can have it all. My whole life, I have lived in your shadow, but now I'm going to step out of it. I am going to reach heights of success and sophistication that you can only dream of.
KAMILAH: Your cardigan's on inside out.
TAHANI: I know! It's a new trend that I am starting. Just one example of how I'm going to step out of your shadow. ("Category 55 Emergency Doomsday Crisis")

That same language is used again in the title of Tahani's self-help book, *Get Out of the Spotlight*, although she does not mean it in the Levinasian sense. Rather, she wants people, specifically Kamilah, out of the spotlight so she can have it for herself. Even when she reaches The Real Good Place, Tahani is still preoccupied with her place in the spotlight. In the episode "Employee of the Bearimy," Tahani complains to Eleanor that she feels underused. Eleanor praises Tahani for being good at throwing parties, saying, "Look, if the roles were reversed and I had to throw a fancy party to save all of humanity, I promise we'd be screwed because I wouldn't know what salad fork to put next to the whatever spoon."[5] Tahani accepts Eleanor's compliment and promises that "if we ever get through this, I want to learn how to do something meaningful. A real skill. Something helpful and fulfilling." Tahani keeps her promise: in the series finale we see her cross items off an extensive to-do list. These included landing a triple axel, becoming a master woodworker (with help from Nick Offerman), spending one meaningful day with her parents, finishing reading *Infinite Jest*, and problematically objectifying Eleanor ("Whenever You're Ready"). Though it takes many Bearimys, Tahani overcomes the problem that animates *The Good Place*: the psychological and emotional investment in enjoying the world as we experience it and not feeling that the other is owed anything.

Levinasian ethics focuses on the encounter with other people and the response to that encounter. For Levinas, the act of preserving an understanding of the world or self is always done at the expense of other people. In order for the world to be familiar and not overwhelming, the nuance and details that make people and things in the world unique need to be reduced to broad themes. This is similar to stereotyping people or places in order to begin making sense of them. Some people are trash bags from Arizona; others are talking sweater vests; one is the dumbest person you have ever met; and yet another is "a self-obsessed socialite, a ridiculous giraffe, an absurd British aristocrat, a narcissistic attention seeker" ("Best Self"). Levinas's point is that people are more than the stereotypes or themes they have been reduced to.

The encounter with another person is a moment of decision when the individual has to decide if they want to continue to enjoy the world in the same familiar way, or if they want to give up the comfort that comes from familiarity and see the world from the perspective of the other person. Levinas is often accused of prescribing an impossible ethic. After all, seeing the world from the perspective of the other is more than agreeing to disagree about a certain state of affairs, and it is more than a temporary adoption of another perspective. In Levinasian language the necessary pivot is called substitution: the person encountering the other gives up their hold on their construction of their world—their space in the sunlight—so that the other can live not as a theme or stereotype. Levinas says this is the form our obligation and responsibility to others must take if we are to avoid violence against the other. Practically, this means that the individual not only has to give up the stereotypes and themes that shape their understanding of the other, but they have to give up the stereotypes and themes that shape their understanding of themselves. Anything short of substitution retains a residual of the pre-encounter themes, attitudes, biases, and stereotypes that would allow for the preservation of a familiar and comfortable way of being in the world.

I Want to Become the Person I Pretended to Be

The obstacle to substitution has already been mentioned: enjoyment (Levinas calls it *jouissance*). Enjoyment is the momentum that comes from living in a familiar world and the ability to perpetuate that familiarity. One's enjoyment of the world is threatened when the excess that is obscured by themes and stereotypes bubbles to the surface or erupts from below, calling into question the terms, ideas, and attitudes that shape and contour the world. Enjoyment tempts us, but the ethical move is to pivot toward the other, away from enjoyment, substituting self-understanding for the understanding of the other. Tahani and Kamilah are who they are because of the way their parents pitted them against each other. As children and then adults, Kamilah enjoyed her parents' attention and praise both in the sense that it made her feel good and because it gave her a sense of self. In turn, Tahani developed a sense of self that was fueled by both her feelings of inadequacy and her need to deprive others of being in the sunlight she desperately craved. This not only became Tahani's world, but how the whole world saw her. In an interview for *International Sophisticate* magazine, after being told that they wanted Kamilah for the cover but were turned down, Tahani suffered this moment: "But first, another question about Kamilah. Don't you think she and I would be friends? We have a lot in common, we are both Capricorn, and we're both only children. I'm sorry, I forgot about you" ("Team Cockroach"). The title of the article turned out to be "Tahani Al-Jamil: Not Just Kamilah's Sister."

Tahani dies trying to pull down a statue of Kamilah, screaming, "I'll bring you down! Come down to the ground where you belong!" ("Team Cockroach"). She realizes who she truly is when she has this conversation with Michael:

TAHANI: I died in Cleveland?
MICHAEL: I don't think that should be your biggest takeaway from that story.
TAHANI: Is that really all I cared about? Just outshining my sister and gaining praise and acclaim? I mean, I did gain praise and acclaim. You know, I dare say on some occasions, more praise and acclaim than my sister, Kamilah, so. Oh. Oh, I see. Oh, God.
MICHAEL: Oh, come on, now. It's not all bad. Imagine you're me and you're designing a torture chamber for people who think that they belong in the Good Place. I mean, you were perfect.
TAHANI: But I've always wanted to be perfect at something. I just never thought it would be the perfect stooge. I want to do it. I want to become the person I pretended to be. ("Team Cockroach")

Though she does not enjoy the competition with her sister in the sense that she derives no emotional pleasure from it, she nevertheless enjoys it in the sense that it shapes her sense of self and allows her to make sense of the world and interactions with others.

The hardest thing Tahani could ever admit is that Kamilah suffered from the way she was treated by her parents. Tahani saw Kamilah as their favorite. They tell Tahani that the 5.2 million pounds she has raised at her art auction fundraiser was "very middle thermometer" and that her public failure is their public failure ("Category 55 Emergency Doomsday Scenario"). They shame her into including a lunch with Kamilah as part of the auction, at which point Tahani introduces her sister by saying, "Take it away from me! Sorry, I mean take it away, Kamilah!" ("Category 55 Emergency Doomsday Scenario"). Her father then bids 5 million pounds for lunch with his own daughter. Never seeing the toll that the rivalry took on Kamilah, Tahani could not allow herself to see Kamilah as just as alone as she was. Opening herself up to the possibility that Kamilah suffered too, she allows Kamilah to be more than the theme Tahani reduced her to. Tahani makes an ethical move when she pivots away from her own enjoyment of the world and tries to reconcile with her sister. After being saved by Michael and learning about the afterlife in "Jeremy Bearimy," she sets herself on a new course. She travels to Budapest to mend her relationship with Kamilah and put her on the path to The Good Place. Tahani's enjoyment of her sense of self had denied Kamilah any opportunity to express her own sadness, frustration, or alienation (which she chose to do through art). Tahani's inner transformation occurs when she opens herself to the possibility that Kamilah is as much of a victim of their parents as she is. Tahani's moment of clarity comes when she sees Kamilah's paintings as a metaphor for the dynamic created by their parents (which is different from Jason's interpretations of the paintings).

Their joint rejection of their parents (the biggest wankers ever) is a rejection of their inheritance of the way that their parents enjoyed being in the world. When Tahani confronts Kamilah about the truth of their parents, it is an accusation against them: their parents had no justification for being the way that they were. For Levinas the appearance of the other, in this case Kamilah's suffering, challenges the individual to respond to the way the other suffers by being reduced to a theme or stereotype. In Budapest, Tahani has to admit her part in continuing her rivalry with Kamilah and take responsibility for the pain she has caused. So when Lawrence Burns writes that "I can look at my situation from the perspective of the disparity between my enjoyment and the claims of the other," and that "this disparity makes me responsible, i.e. conscious of the injustice suffered by the other," in this case it means that Tahani had to realize that though Kamilah's experiences of their parents were different, she still suffered and still felt alienated and alone (as indicated by the paintings).[6] Put more simply, the other asks, "Why are you entitled to enjoy the world the way that you do?" and Tahani's realization is that because her parents had no right to enjoy the world the way that they did, then she had no right either. Nobody does. She needed to cede her place in the spotlight and let Kamilah's suffering come to the fore.[7] When Tahani could admit to herself that she does not have a natural or inevitable right to enjoy the world the way that she does (no one does), she could satisfy her responsibility to her sister.

Reunited in The Good Place, Tahani and Kamilah await the arrival of their parents. Upon their arrival, they embrace their daughters and apologize profusely for pitting them against each other. The audience is treated to a montage of the Al-Jamil family doing so many normal things (including enjoying a family movie night watching *Home Alone*) that it eventually becomes boring. The 1,000,000 flowers and stuffed teddy bears meant to serve as another apology for how they treated Tahani and Kamilah fall flat. The possibility that their apologies will go on forever, because they can go on forever, robs them of their gravitas and meaning. The obligation to the other, which Levinas says is infinite, is only meaningful if it occurs within the finitude of a natural human life. Being able to choose otherwise than the other, the decision to commit to the other must occur within the awareness of those limits. Waqas and Manisha Al-Jamil cede their place in the sunlight to their daughters, and it eventually becomes meaningless. Echoing the larger theme of *The Good Place*, inspired by Todd May's *Death: The Art of Living*—that finitude restores the meaning to life that an endless life, filled with endless possibilities, makes impossible— it is clear that ceding one's place in the sunlight is only meaningful when there is a sunset on the horizon.

Pobody's Nerfect!

Tahani's moral journey is difficult and ego-bruising. Each step forward is accompanied by the realization that even if moral progress has been made, there is the wound that comes from recognizing that work had to be done and the frustration that there is still more work to do. This is evidence of how entrenched enjoyment is. Levinas was always reminding his readers that the good is more important than enjoyment: "I'm not saying at all that this is done with cheerfulness, that it's no problem ... the responsibility for the other is the good. It's not pleasant, it is good."[8] Is there a way, though, to make the good pleasant? Mike Schur and the writers may not be trying to be moralistic in a show about morality, but they are trying to make a show that makes the audience laugh. *The Good Place* generates laughter through clever puns ("Sushi and the Banshees" or "Knish from a Rose"), sight gags (Chidi being chased by bees, though not with teeth), and non sequiturs (Jason on oranges: "They don't make sense. Apples, you eat their clothes. But oranges you don't?"; from "Rhonda, Diana, Jake, and Trent"). None of these efforts at humor have any sort of moral force. So, is there a way for the audience to laugh better? Is there ethical laughter? The ethical laughter in *The Good Place* comes from the generosity in realizing that morality is not a destination. It is a journey, and the good person is the person who is trying to be good. To put this in the language of *The Good Place*, "Pobody's nerfect!" ("What's My Motivation").

Laughter can be ethical when the variation on the theme disrupts the laugher's enjoyment and gets them to see the topic of the joke otherwise. Unethical laughter is laughter that reimposes a theme or stereotype back on the world. Ethical laughter treats the moment of incongruity as a moment of transcendence and openness to the other. The laugher makes this ethical move when they welcome the surprise of the joke. Brian Bergen-Aurand writes,

> Jokes show me the other side of things, prompt me toward other ways of looking at things, things I have come to take for granted, things I thought were only digressions. And, in gaining a different angle or shot of something, in looking at them differently, I am opened to different points of viewing the situation. Jokes slow me down and speed me up. They displace me, and in doing so, they replace me.[9]

Eleanor's attempt to make amends to the residents of the neighborhood is derailed by their lingering animosity. After they list all the harms they suffered because of her (crashing into a turkey carcass, falling into a sinkhole, and having their dog kicked into the sun), the best that Eleanor can do is point to (what she thinks is) their shared, flawed humanity. When the other residents laugh at Eleanor's malapropism, the audience sees (what they think are) the best people responding to her vulnerability with laughter that shows that they understand what it means to be flawed and vulnerable. This is a self-critical laughter that can be a pivot away from how one enjoys one's self and the world. As Robert Bernasconi points out, laughing at oneself is a response to the other that is the beginning of the pivot away from selfish enjoyment of one's self and world:

> Our own shameful laughter at ourselves, open[s] us up for responsibility … the laughter that interrupts our pathetic self-aggrandizement, the self-righteousness of those who take themselves too seriously.… There is not only the laughter directed at us that shames us and accuses us. There is also the laughter that draws us toward our responsibility and our intimate connections with others. Sometimes the first form of laughter turns into the other, and instead of merely being laughed at we join in the laughter.[10]

Laughers who do not take themselves seriously are not so firmly entrenched in their enjoyment of themselves and the world that they would refuse to cede the spotlight to another. They are not entrenched in their enjoyment because they recognize that taking their enjoyment too seriously is how others are denied what they are owed. There is a possibility, then, for laughter to be a form of responsibility and for the responsibility owed to the other to be pleasant, at least in the end. That possibility is realized when one becomes open to the possibility of truths other than one's own. Eleanor and the other main characters demonstrate this trait when they celebrate each other's flaws. Having flaws defines what it means to be human, which is why they gift Michael with a human starter kit (including a Dr. Oz diet book because humans are such suckers).

Conclusion: The Good Other

The "pobody's nerfect" attitude—that nobody is perfect, so people should be accepted for their flaws if they are trying to be a better person—becomes the flaw in the system discovered in Season 3: the world is too complex for anyone to be good, let alone perfect. Moral improvement is possible, though, if one tries. In the world of *The Good Place*, trying looks like ceding one's place in the sun so that the others can be themselves. The difference between Levinas and Scanlon, then, is that for Levinas responsibility is an ongoing commitment to try to become for the other, which requires more than respecting someone's disagreement. For Levinas, the responsibility for the other is manifested in actions that point to a changed inner emotional state. Contrary to Scanlon, on *The Good Place* the responsibility for the other is not met in agreement or in respecting disagreement. It is met in the willingness to cede one's place to the other. This willingness comes from the realization that any enjoyment of the world or self is always temporary. What the audience sees on *The Good Place* is that if the temporary nature of our enjoyment is met with laughter instead of angst and frustration, then there is the possibility for moral improvement and a better community. Ultimately, the characters on *The Good Place* are showing that we meet our responsibilities to others by constantly trying to become good people.

Notes

1 Emmanuel Levinas, quoted in *Is It Righteous To Be? Interviews with Emmanuel Levinas*, ed. Jill Robbins (Stanford, CA: Stanford University Press, 2001), 48.

2 Lesley Goldberg, "*The Good Place* to End with Season 4 on NBC (Exclusive)," *The Hollywood Reporter*, June 7, 2019.

3 Levinas, quoted in Robbins, *Is It Righteous To Be?*, 159.

4 Ibid., 128.

5 Thank you to Katie Benko for pointing out this connection.

6 Lawrence Burns, "Identifying Concrete Ethical Demands in the Face of the Abstract Other: Emmanual Levinas's Pragmatic Ethics," *Philosophy and Social Criticism* 34 (2008), 324.

7 Ibid., 325.

8 Levinas, quoted in Robbins, *Is It Righteous To Be?*, 46–47.

9 Brian Bergen-Aurand, "Knock, Knock/Who's There?/Here I Am, Exposed ..." in *Comedy Begins with Our Simplest Gestures: Levinas, Ethics, and Humor*, ed. Brian Bergen-Aurand (Pittsburgh, PA: Duquesne University Press, 2017), 87.

10 Robert Bernasconi, "You've Got to Laugh," in Bergen-Aurand, *Comedy Begins with Our Simplest Gestures*, 32.

Not Knowing Your Place: A Tale of Two Women

Leslie A. Aarons

It was the best of times, it was the worst of times, it was the age of wisdom, it was the age of foolishness, it was the epoch of belief, it was the epoch of incredulity, it was the season of Light, it was the season of Darkness, it was the spring of hope, it was the winter of despair, we had everything before us, we had nothing before us, we were all going direct to Heaven, we were all going direct the other way.

—Charles Dickens, *A Tale of Two Cities*

Eleanor Shellstrop and Tahani Al-Jamil are polar opposites—or are they? As a result of childhood mistreatment, both women are skewed and stymied in their moral development, landing them in "The Good Place." Clearly, there is a correlation between one's ability to be a good person and one's psychological well-being, but how is this psychological well-being affected by one's gender? With a little help from the philosopher Luce Irigaray, Eleanor and Tahani can answer this question.

"You're Okay, Eleanor. You're in The Good Place."

Eleanor has died, and she is told that she's made it into the equivalent of heaven. From the very first scene of *The Good Place*, monumental duplicity is at work. Everything is contrived and everyone is lying, both to themselves and to one another. This deception extends to the viewing audience, as our expectations are upended by revelations about the characters and the plot. Just nine minutes into the first episode, we learn there's been a cosmic case of mistaken identity, and

The Good Place and Philosophy, First Edition. Edited by Kimberly S. Engels.
© 2021 John Wiley & Sons, Inc. Published 2021 by John Wiley & Sons, Inc.

Eleanor doesn't actually belong in The Good Place. Cloaked well by her cute, wide-eyed persona, Eleanor manipulates and deceives her soulmate Chidi Anagonye into pledging his fidelity to her in their first minutes together. Then she discloses to him, "There's been a big mistake. I'm not supposed to be here" ("Everything Is Fine").

The case of mistaken identity is verified when Eleanor is shown what are supposed to be memories from her life, and it turns out that they are not hers. Now, hopelessly trapped by his coerced pledge of allegiance, Chidi is complicit in a colossal clusterfork. "Because those aren't my memories. I wasn't a lawyer. I never went to the Ukraine." But the memories are not actually the most compelling evidence that Eleanor doesn't belong in The Good Place.

Eleanor was a foulmouthed, angry woman in her relatively brief life. To say that she lacked a moral compass would be an understatement. From the first episode, she laments her misfortune of having narcissistic parents, and the hardship that it caused her. Abandoned both psychologically and physically by her parents, she grew up trying to compensate by belittling and abusing others in an attempt to soothe her painful insecurities. Eleanor describes her parents as extremely self-centered, tending exclusively to their own ever-elusive happiness. In a rare moment of self-reflection (because she was drunk), she confides to Chidi, "My parents were divorced when I was a kid. They were both crummy people, so they're probably in The Bad Place" ("Everything Is Fine").

Eleanor is insecure about her own moral inadequacies and lashes out at anyone who she perceives as more virtuous than her. *The Good Place* has a good time with that. In her earthly life, Eleanor flouted conventions and had no sense of social or personal responsibility. For example, she takes a little too much pleasure in patronizing a known sexual predator's coffee shop, and she never misses an opportunity to berate an unassuming environmental activist. Needless to say, if even Florence Nightingale didn't qualify for entrance to The Good Place, Eleanor Shellstrop shouldn't have a chance in hell to be there.

"Take It Away from Me! Sorry, I Mean Take It Away, Kamilah."

Mercilessly compelled to compete against her sister for her parents' attention and admiration, Tahani Al-Jamil achieves fame and fortune but not morality and happiness. Despite securing sponsors like the

Rolls-Royce Group and raising £5.2 million at an auction she was running for the Great Britain Children's Defence Fund, Tahani's parents belittled her efforts: "Tahani! This auction threatens to be an embarrassing failure.... Your public failure is our public failure" ("What We Owe to Each Other").

When her mother declares, "You know what has to be done," Tahani is deflated and silently acquiesces. We learn what that means when Tahani introduces her sister Kamilah as an addition to the auction's docket. Kamilah declares that she will donate a lunch date with none other than herself. "The bidding shall commence at £3 million." As Tahani sits next to her father, he eagerly makes the first bid of £5 million.

Her parents' blatant favoritism of Kamilah causes Tahani a lifetime of suffering, which no amount of her own success will allay. Dealing with deep-rooted insecurity and envy, Tahani compensates by inflating herself. As Eleanor put it, "Tahani, what a condescending bench" ("Everything Is Fine"). We are never quite sure whether Tahani's stories of intrigue with (and as) the rich and famous are actually true, or delusions of grandeur. But we can empathize with her after witnessing the unremitting psychological abuse inflicted by her parents. Of course, there's a reason that she is in "The Good Place," and there's a good chance that her exaggerated narcissism has something to do with it.

Irigaray and Woman as Other

The Good Place raises the issue of how to determine whether a person is ethical or not. For thousands of years philosophers have theorized about ethics, and most societies' mores and systems of justice are founded on the principles established by these time-honored philosophical theories. Plato (428–348 BCE), Aristotle (384–322 BCE), Immanuel Kant (1724–1804), and John Stuart Mill (1806–1873) have been highly influential in Western society. Guess what they all have in common? That's right, they were all men. So, we should wonder whether their ethical guidelines really apply to *all members* of society. Luce Irigaray (1930–), a contemporary French feminist philosopher, argues that they do not.

Irigaray has dedicated her career to critiquing Western ideology, arguing that Western culture is inherently unethical due to its exploitive and dismissive treatment of women. For literally thousands of years, men have been granted social and political freedoms and rights that women were not. According to Irigaray, this has been made possible by a long-standing bias established and reproduced by men that defines the "male" subject not simply as one sex among two, but as the standard by which the female subject is judged—always falling short. As philosopher Simone de Beauvoir (1908–1986) wrote in her seminal book, *The Second Sex*: "She is defined and differentiated with reference to man and not he with reference to her; she is the incidental, the inessential opposed to the essential. He is the Subject, he is the Absolute—she is the Other."[1]

Like Beauvoir, Irigaray argues that there is only one identifiable "subject" in the history of Western thought—Man. A subject, as opposed to an object, is one who acts, a "doer." Adding an intriguing psychoanalytic critique of this historical bias, Irigaray argues that the cultural and political ethics of Western society is founded on sexual *indifference*: "Further, she has no 'proper' name. And her sexual organ, which is not *one* organ, is counted as *none*."[2] Irigaray asserts that the feminine subject is simultaneously subsumed and marginalized in this patriarchal or "phallogocentric"[3] order. According to Irigaray, we exist in a culture that perpetuates a male-dominated attitude, which objectifies and exploits women: "Mother, virgin, prostitute: these are the social roles imposed on women.... Neither as mother nor as virgin nor as prostitute has woman any right to her own pleasure."[4] Irigaray elucidates how the roles and dominant values, established by men, have objectified and silenced women and reduced them to commodities to be exchanged among men.[5] "And there you have it, Gentlemen, that is why your daughters are dumb."[6]

For Irigaray, and for most feminist thinkers, the problem is male *exclusivity*. Ethical systems have pondered what it means to be a good person in male-dominated society. If the feminine subject could wrestle herself free from this domain, what would her conception(s) of happiness be? If she were a celestial architect, how would she design The Good Place? Seeming to address this question, Irigaray says, "I think we must not merely instigate a return to the *cosmic*, but also ask ourselves why we have been held back from becoming *divine women*."[7] As we'll see, Irigaray's philosophy can help us to psychoanalyze Tahani and Eleanor, and maybe even discover a path to The Real Good Place.

"My Whole Life I've Tried to Be Extraordinary, but It Has Never Seemed to Be Enough."

Their parents mercilessly pitted Tahani and Kamilah against each other, blatantly favoring Kamilah, and perpetuating a deep-seated sibling rivalry. Tahani was cast as the black sheep of the family, and despite her impressive social and professional achievements, she was never commended or even acknowledged by her parents. Despite her privileged, worldly experiences, Tahani comes off as pretentious and inauthentic. She brags about sensational accomplishments and engagements, leaving her companions and the viewing audience to wonder how much of it is true.

In "Unwanted Houseguest," Tahani is distraught with being second-to-last in Michael's ranked list of residents in the Good Place neighborhood. Determined to raise her ranking, she schemes ways to make herself more beneficent than ever. Disobeying Michael's strict order for residents to remain in their homes due to the "Category 55 Emergency Doomsday Crisis," Tahani greets Michael and Janet with a freshly baked batch of donut holes to lighten the devastating mood. As usual, Tahani's awkward attempt to artificially inflate her importance is completely ineffective. Upon Michael reviving her, Tahani asks, "Did I fix the sinkhole? Am I a heroine?" Michael responds, "No you did something catastrophically stupid and we had to knock you unconscious."

Tahani's attempts to appear successful, charitable, and helpful fail to improve her ranking in "The Good Place," just as she failed in her earthly life to get the acknowledgment she so desperately wanted. Tahani doesn't realize that this game is impossible for her to win. She should listen to Irigaray, who says, "Women, stop trying. You have been taught that you were property, private or public, belonging to one man or all. To family, tribe, State, even a Republic. That therein lay your pleasure.… If you disobeyed, you were the cause of your own unhappiness."[8]

Even after their death, Tahani's parents continue to deride her by misspelling her name in their will, as Tahini—like the sauce ("Category 55 Emergency Doomsday Crisis"). But why is Tahani so obsessed with acclaim and recognition? The competition for it never ends. She's dead, and she still suffers from tremendous feelings of insecurity and self-loathing, as she ineffectively attempts to fill a bottomless void of rejection. Tahani has so much that her inability to recognize it is tragic. Seemingly describing Tahani, Irigaray writes, "Meanwhile, her shining raiment, her gleaming skin conceal the disaster within, hide all that devours and rends her body … at least as far as the eye can see; the striking makeup … cover up the fact that she is torn to pieces."[9]

Irigaray argues that in Western culture, male desire is the only desire that is validated and can be actualized. Woman, for her part, merely supports this symbolic/social process: "She functions as a *hole* … in the elaboration of imaginary and symbolic processes. But this fault, this deficiency, this 'hole,' inevitably affords woman too few figurations, images, or representations by which to represent herself."[10]

Perhaps Tahani's self-loathing is not ultimately her parents' fault. The culpability lies in the *culture* in which she lived. Tahani is fantastically fortunate and fabulously gorgeous. Judging from the assets in their will, her family were billionaires. With such wealth and beauty came great prestige and opportunity within the most elite social circles. The world was her forking oyster! Healthy and wealthy, the culture kept her from being truly wise—and thus the true Good Place eluded her.

… Coming from a Place Where Penis Envy Is a Thing

Both Eleanor and Tahani struggle with significant feelings of inadequacy, compelling them to commit enough ethical infractions to land them in "The Good Place." Although Tahani and Eleanor come from divergent social stations, they share a common legacy of familial abuse that deeply affected their sense of self-worth, causing them to relentlessly exploit and abuse others in their attempts to gain a positive self-image. In their misdirected attempts to find happiness, they became lost souls.

Eleanor has serious "abandonment issues" that she blamed on her parents, using them as an excuse for her unethical behavior throughout much of the series. In "…Someone Like Me as a Member," the "Fake Eleanor" is having dinner at the Good Plates restaurant with Trevor the Demon, Chidi, and the "Real Eleanor." Trevor taunts "Fake Eleanor" for thinking that she could pull off pretending to be "Real Eleanor," who was über-ethical in her lifetime. The two Eleanors have a critically insightful exchange:

FAKE ELEANOR: Whatever, it's easy when you're just born perfect. My parents were both dirt bags who split up when I was eight.

REAL ELEANOR: I don't mean to eavesdrop, but did you say your parents got a divorce?

FAKE ELEANOR: Yeah, and that kind of thing really changes a person. I mean, that trauma ... it can explain away a lot of behavior.

REAL ELEANOR: Oh of course.

FAKE ELEANOR: Your parents are still together, I guess.

It's clear that "Fake Eleanor" has convinced herself that her ethical indiscretions are justified because of her past. But then "Real Eleanor" annihilates her pretext by telling a story of how she never knew her birth parents. As the story goes, she was found as an infant, abandoned in an empty fish tank at a train station in Bangladesh. She was adopted by the Shellstrops, but then they died when she was *four*. "Anyway, orphanage burned down, yadda, yadda. yadda." But as it turns out, like so many other scenarios in *The Good Place*, this is a ruse. The "Real Eleanor" is actually a cunning demon from The Bad Place, who is there under Michael's command to torture the humans. And she actually winds up being a really bad character, mutinying against Michael, making him look virtuous by comparison.

Deciphering who is good or bad is complicated. Perhaps the real problem is with our ethical system itself, which is unsurprisingly lopsided, warped—perverted by one sex dictating the rules for all, as every influential ethical theory was written and enacted by men. As a result, these dominant philosophies perpetually commit two unavoidable errors: first, they wrongly assume that male-centered principles can be suitably generalized to everyone. Second, many of these theories diminish or preclude women's capacity to become ethical, autonomous subjects. "Because the order that lays down the law to us is of the male sex.... Social and cultural acceptance of sexual difference has not yet been achieved and this can be the only goal of a movement for women's liberation."[11]

Why Haven't You Forkers Invented a Medium Place?

In order to protect the quality of life for members of a society, it is important to regard everyone's rights and responsibilities equally. The moral fabric of a society would swiftly unravel if people were able to justify lying, cheating, and stealing by arguing that they had suffered some kind of abuse. A victim of a crime doesn't suffer any less because the perpetrator came from a broken home. But unfortunately, our standard of ethics is not adequate and fair for all individuals of society.

Irigaray and other feminist philosophers have critiqued time-honored ethical theories and highlighted rampant misogyny. Canonical male ethicists have had plenty of unfavorable things to say about women and what they are like. Without being consulted themselves, women have been factored into ethical systems that are supposed to be "universal" but are actually gender-specific, giving the masculine subject the complete upper hand, and the feminine subject (all puns intended) the shaft. Aristotle, for example, quite famously asserted that women are inferior to men, and are incapable of the rational thought necessary to develop into autonomous ethical agents. In his book *Politics*,[12] Aristotle states, "Again, as between the sexes, the male is by nature superior and the female inferior, the male ruler and the female subject."[13] Aristotle is not alone in this hierarchical thinking. The Western tradition repeatedly describes ethical action as requiring reason and objectivity, and it describes women as lacking in these regards. Irigaray writes, "Thus abandoned in her weakness, deformed and formless, the 'female' is said to desire the 'male' as ugly desires beautiful."[14] This leaves us wondering, should Eleanor even bother trying to become an ethical person? And if so, what kind of ethical principles should she strive to live by?

"Surprise Idiots! You're All in The Bad Place."

As we've seen, our ethical standards are skewed and inequitable, because contributions from half of humanity have been excluded. Suffering is bad; that's why The Real Bad Place had appropriate things in it like ferocious four-headed flying bears and food that turned into spiders in your mouth. Yet humans continue to inflict great suffering upon all life on Earth in the name of progress, convenience, and profit—the most popular aims of Western societies: "But wealth must be understood to mean the accumulation of goods through exploitation, and to be the outcome of one sex's submission to the other.... The race of men have always put property before life.... The society of men is built upon the possession of goods."[15]

Both Tahani and Eleanor had such traditional ambitions, and therein may lie their problem. It appears that their character flaws were prompted by the culture in which they lived. Tahani, for example, was a victim of her own success. In "The Book of Dougs" the humans find themselves in The Real Good Place, where the aromas are reminiscent of each person's favorite smell on Earth. What Tahani smelled was indicative of her life's pursuit: "To me it smells like a curtain closing between first class and economy." And we all know that curtain always closed behind her. Wealth, power, and prestige remain enviable goals in our capitalist society. What's the problem with that? Well, you need not be an ethical person in order to achieve these ends. Actually, it may enhance your chances of success if you're willing to be unethical. If there is a Real Good Place, it would have to offer the opportunity and the motivation to reevaluate what your highest values ought to be, and these considerations must be receptive to and inclusive of the ideas of its diverse residents. We catch a glimmer of hope of this in "Employee of the Bearimy."

Eleanor and Tahani seem to have a shared existential epiphany. By the end of this episode they gain important insights about themselves and each other. In the progress of their afterlife soul-searching, they discover strengths that they never realized they had, as well as a bonding friendship and sincere appreciation for each other.

ELEANOR: That was insane, but—we got through it ... together.
TAHANI: No we didn't. You got through it. I almost ruined it a hundred times. From now on, I'm just going to stick to throwing parties, 'cause it's the only thing I'm good at.

As Tahani is mired in self-pity, Eleanor uncharacteristically responds to her with deep insight and care. "Your parties aren't pointless. They're opportunities for them to bond and form friendships. You know, the *thing we need them to do so we're not tortured forever*!" Grateful, Tahani realizes the political prowess of her party planning. And with this, they have become more virtuous individuals.

As *The Good Place* aptly depicts, the line between good and evil is a "bench" to decipher. The show dramatically reminds us that in our lives we are constantly confronted by ethical dilemmas that challenge us to make choices, and all we have for guidance are flawed, often conflicting ideals that we pick up along the way. If there really is a Good Place in the hereafter, it would be fair for it to be a merit-based destination where people have earned the right to be there because they lived an ethical life. *The Good Place* also shows us that becoming an ethical person is not just about the individual. Rather, it requires an *egalitarian* community effort if we are to ever get it right. We still have a lot of choices to make and dilemmas to solve. Whether we ultimately deserve a utopia or dystopia for our efforts, only time will tell.

Notes

1   Simone de Beauvoir, *The Second Sex*, trans. H.M. Parshley (New York: Alfred A. Knopf, 1976), xvi.

2   Luce Irigaray, *This Sex Which Is Not One*, trans. Catherine Porter (Ithaca, NY: Cornell University Press, 1985), 26.

3   The term "phallogocentric" was coined by Jacques Derrida to capture the Western emphasis on the masculine form. Irigaray recognizes that Freudian (psychoanalytic) theory, too, was blatantly preoccupied with the phallus: "Freud brought to light something that had been operative all along though it remained implicit, hidden, unknown: *the sexual indifference that underlies the truth of any science, the logic of every discourse*"; ibid., 69.

4   Ibid., 186–187.

5   Ibid., 86.

6   Ibid., 112.

7   Luce Irigaray, *Sexes and Genealogies*, trans. Gillian C. Gill (New York: Columbia University Press, 1987), 60.

8   Irigaray, *This Sex Which Is Not One*, 203.

9   Ibid., 228.

10   Luce Irigaray, *Speculum of the Other Woman*, trans. Gillian C. Gill (New York: Cornell University Press, 1985), 71.

11   Irigaray, *Sexes and Genealogies*, 192–193.

12   Aristotle, *Aristotle's Politics* (Oxford: Clarendon Press, 1905).

13   Ibid., 1254b13–1254b14.

14   Irigaray, *Speculum of the Other Woman*, 167.

15   Irigaray, *Sexes and Genealogies*, 194.

Part V

"ABSURDITY NEEDS TO BE CONFRONTED"

13

Marginal Comforts Keep Us in Hell

Jake Jackson

In Jean-Paul Sartre's (1905–1980) play *No Exit,* the inspiration for *The Good Place,* a character exhaustedly exclaims, "Hell is—other people!"[1] In both the play and the sitcom, condemned characters are pitted against each other in a share-economy of torture. On *The Good Place,* the characters' attempts to find "marginal comforts" worsen their suffering by lulling them into a false sense of security and keeping them from fully resisting or rebelling against their situation.

Bad Faith and Bad Place

In the initial design of the fake Good Place neighborhood, demons hide in plain sight and play at being happy while the four real humans remain unhappy. This is another way in which "Hell is Other People" in The Good Place: Hell is other people who are happy (or seem happy) when you are not. In response, the characters flee into the bad faith of marginal comforts, like frozen yogurt. In heaven there should be no calories or feelings of guilt, yet frozen yogurt, a "guilt-free" comfort food, is abundant. As Michael says, "there's something so human about taking something great and ruining it a little so you can have more" ("What We Owe to Each Other").

This paper was presented at the 2018 meeting of the North American Sartre Society in a plenary session featuring Michael Schur and Todd May.

The Good Place and Philosophy, First Edition. Edited by Kimberly S. Engels.
© 2021 John Wiley & Sons, Inc. Published 2021 by John Wiley & Sons, Inc.

As Sartre sees it, all individuals are "condemned to freedom." In other words, one's freedom is a heavy burden and unavoidable. Nonetheless, humans try to escape their freedom. In bad faith (*mauvaise foi*), one lies to oneself regarding the conditions of one's own freedom, thus attempting to avoid responsibility. The human condition is such that a person is free in their decisions but also constrained by circumstances. Bad faith can be a denial of either of these facets of the human condition. In bad faith, one either claims that one is free to choose without limitation or conversely that one is so constrained by circumstances that one cannot choose freely.[2] On *The Good Place*, the four humans often do not recognize the limitations on their freedom, as they put themselves into precarious circumstances that do not directly result from the diabolical design of the neighborhood. And routinely they deceive themselves by saying that things are not so bad.

Bad faith itself is not necessarily "bad" in the sense of immoral, but it does undermine one's sense of freedom and keeps one from living authentically and resisting oppression. By contrast, existential authenticity is a matter of being self-aware and confronting limitations. In The Bad Place, seeking marginal comforts is an easy escape into thinking that the world is magical or that everything is going to be alright even though one does nothing to fix the situation. Sartre writes, "One puts oneself in bad faith as one goes to sleep and one is in bad faith as one dreams."[3] That is, bad faith is an escape from the drudgery of life, and in the case of *The Good Place*, an escape from demonic torture.

Everything Is Fine!

Despite Mindy St. Claire's bitter horniness and frustrated cocaine addiction in The Medium Place, Eleanor seeks marginal comfort there. The Medium Place is comforting at least in the sense that it provides a temporary and incomplete respite. It's also where Eleanor discovers her past love affairs with Chidi and takes comfort in the thought that she could fall in love like that again.

The episode "Team Cockroach" provides one of the most telling examples of seeking marginal comforts in vain. At this point in the saga, the Good Place neighborhood has been revealed to be an experimental version of The Bad Place. Yet after teaming up to work with Michael in secret so that Vicky's regime change is none the wiser,

Tahani walks right into an obvious trap. Michael explicitly tells Tahani that, as a form of torture, Vicky will task her to throw a birthday party that will inevitably be outclassed by another party. Despite being told that this is a trap, Tahani takes up her old living vow "to make every event too much" and ends up investing tremendous energy into a party that is immediately outclassed. A larger crowd attend the other party where they get to hang out with unicorns and other more magical and impressive things. Tahani is crushed by her vain efforts to achieve comfort by being the center of attention.

Michael and Janet comfort themselves in different, failing ways. Once Michael and Janet join "Team Cockroach" for their own survival, they become more and more human-like in their capacity to suffer. As a result they try to avoid that suffering in any way they can. In "Existential Crisis," Michael confronts the possibility of his own "death" by way of "retirement," a nasty and torturous process that would terminate him. Chidi asks Michael to imagine what it would be like for him to no longer exist while others go on living and existing without him. Michael responds, "So you're saying, I would be.... No.... Me?" and then wails and collapses into an existential crisis. Chidi insists to Eleanor that it is a *good* thing for Michael to experience the groundlessness and fear and anguish of confronting his own death. Chidi then tries to guide Michael into realizing his future potential non-existence authentically.

Despite Chidi's efforts, Michael slides into an unproductive midlife crisis in which he pierces his ear, dresses casually, gets a sports car, and makes Janet play the role of a ditzy blonde girlfriend (albeit not a girl) who is too young for him. In doing this, Michael inauthentically follows the *script* of a midlife crisis.

Janet likewise gets lost in the bad faith of marginal comforts by making Derek, who exists merely to please her. Predictably, Janet immediately tires of Derek. She has created a dependent yet autonomous being that she cannot control and cannot enjoy. Derek is a failed experiment. He is loud, uncouth, improperly designed, and a danger to blowing the cover of everyone else who is silently resisting the neighborhood's design.

For his part, Jason (when he is masked as Jianyu) has some success in making his marginal comforts *work* for him. Creating his own budhole, a place where he can hang out with his buds (albeit without buds at first), Jason throws himself into a little world of passing pleasures.

Chidi, the Serious Man

Chidi is a perfect example of Simone de Beauvoir's (1908–1986) conception of the Serious Man.[4] For Beauvoir, the Serious Man is the person who reacts to the conditions of his freedom by setting up strict rules and projecting them out into the world. Unlike the authentic existentialist who knows she is projecting rules, the Serious Man pretends that these rules are objective. Seriousness is thus a form of bad faith; the adherence to rules and the formulation of rules are ways to deny one's freedom.

By insisting on teaching moral philosophy after death just as he did in life, Chidi finds marginal comfort in adherence to order amid chaos. Again and again he becomes frustrated by his pupils. Eleanor begins as a poor and rebellious student; Jason is a foolish slacker who doesn't get it; Tahani is too swept up in herself; and in the second season, Michael eventually joins in as the student who believes he knows much more than the professor. These are not model students, and Chidi does not adjust well to them. Rather, he is rigid and inflexible, experiencing not comfort but anxiety. Unsurprisingly, he gets a stomachache.

The Serious Man is in a delicate position. He seeks comfort in the stability of rules, but that stability is always threatened by new or chaotic elements. When the Serious Man finally confronts the arbitrariness of his rules, he collapses into nihilism. This is precisely what happens to Chidi in the third season, when he learns about the shape of time as the cursive form of the words "Jeremy Bearimy."[5] When he realizes that all the rules and morals he has put up for himself across his life have doomed him to The Bad Place, and that knowledge of this fact has now precluded his actions from ever being counted toward residency in the true Good Place, Chidi loses all sense of reason and lapses into a nihilistic funk.

Growing unstable, Chidi yells at a stranger, strips in public, makes and consumes too much marshmallow chili, and berates his students for asking about exams. Chidi's breakdown into nihilism is not a full collapse, though. Once again he is lying to himself about his actual conditions and beliefs. Even when he says he is utterly convinced that the world is meaningless and that his life is ruined beyond repair, Chidi still takes comfort in philosophizing, both to his students and also to strangers. When he is approached by a man who asks him, "Do you want to see God?" Chidi replies, "God is dead. God remains dead. And we have killed Him. Who will wipe this blood off us? What festivals of atonement, what sacred games shall we have to invent?!

Friedrich Nietzsche, 1882" ("Jeremy Bearimy"). What is significant here is not Chidi's breakdown and recitation of the Mad Man Speech from *The Gay Science*, but that he still *gives a citation*. While he is clearly anguished and has frightened the other man away (although what drug dealer on a college campus hasn't heard "God is dead"?), Chidi's strict adherence to the tradition of quoting and attributing shows that even his foray into nihilism isn't a full departure from his position as a very Serious academic. Beauvoir writes:

> That is why the serious man's life loses all meaning if he finds himself cut off from his ends. Ordinarily, he does not put all his eggs into one basket, but if it happens that a failure or old age ruins all his justifications, then, unless there is a conversion, which is always possible, he no longer has any relief except his flight; ruined, dishonored, this important personage is now only a "has-been."[6]

Chidi immediately and thoroughly devolves into this "has-been" upon learning that all of his formulations and attempts at being a good person have not only failed but can never be redeemed. Even with the collapse of reason and meaning, Chidi projects the rules and regulations that still make whatever sense they can for him in a meaningless cruel world. Even his nihilism is altogether serious. While he may be cooking a vile and disgusting stomachache-inducing meal (though honestly I'm interested in trying it), he still is doing it performatively under the auspices of being a professor in a lecture hall, a performance that still brings him some comfort.

When asked by his students if Peeps chili will be on the final, Chidi returns to lecture mode, telling students about three major ethical theories: virtue theory, consequentialism, and deontology. He gives an honest, clear, and lucid lecture on the main points of these theories, but only to set up the punchline:

> But here's the thing, my little chili-babies, all three of those theories are hot stinky cat dookie. The true meaning of life, the actual ethical system that you should follow, is *nihilism*. The world is *empty*. There is no point to anything, and you're just gonna die. So do whatever. And now, I'm going to eat my marshmallow candy chili in silence, and you all can jump up your own butts. ("Jeremy Bearimy")

Comical, yes, but still following the format for a philosophy lecture. The "true" or unserious nihilist would never have returned to class. Chidi always seeks comfort in the rules of the classroom and his position as a lecturer. Anything else would fill him with anxiety and fear of making a decision.

A Turn toward Authenticity and against Comfort

People will justify the worst and most hellish marriages, jobs, and living situations, if they can find small marginal comforts that keep them stable. Seemingly, people confuse Nietzsche's claim that "If you have your *why* for life, you can get by with almost any *how*"[7] for just finding the "silver lining to every storm cloud" and not finding some deeper, life-sustaining purpose. Being comfortable is not a "why" in life, and it's really just a good way to hurt oneself all the more. Finding marginal comfort in a terrible situation does not fix the terribleness of the situation. Appealing to one's marginal comforts and trying to be positive in the face of The Bad Place are ultimately self-defeating and all the worse for our characters. It *resists* resistance and embraces complacency. In the face of adversity, suffering, oppression, and hell, perhaps it's best not to let oneself get comfortable.

It is, ironically, Chidi who makes a fundamentally radical move toward being authentic in "Pandemonium." Although he has altogether avoided making decisions or commitments, when faced with having to pretend that he doesn't know Simone, he chooses to wipe his own memory and start again in order to avoid compromising the new Good Place experiment. He takes this action, knowing that he won't be in love with Eleanor and that it will cause her pain, but also knowing that it is the right thing to do.

This is a definitive move, and it is a clear choice that Chidi makes without panicking, without letting the fork in the garbage disposal take over his life. It is a sacrifice in which he knows he will suffer again in his reboot, but he chooses it anyway. He sacrifices his love for Eleanor, fleeing whatever marginal comforts in keeping his identity intact, in order to do the right thing. This is his first authentic choice that we have seen him make. He is no longer lying to himself. He is still afraid of what the future may bring, but he enters the nothingness of not knowing who he is and detaches himself from his friends. This is a moment of hope, because he knows that the others will take care of him. He is able to trust himself and others in knowing this is best, overcoming his previous self-imposed sufferings of choice anxiety. Sartre believes that any coward can become a hero by stepping up and acting,[8] and Chidi steps up and acts. He rejects marginal comforts and casts himself into the unknown, finally confident in what is the best course of action. Once his memories are restored to him in the final season, he remains resolute, no longer questioning his decisions.

Welcome! Not Everything Is Fine!

But as much as marginal comforts provide for complacency, too much comfort and guaranteed pleasure can undermine what it means to be human. Suffering, to some extent, appears to give and shape meaning in our lives. In the final episodes when the four humans, Michael, and Janet are each allowed into The Real Good Place, they meet disappointment. All of the residents of The Good Place have been stagnating for centuries. While hell has been tacky, heaven has been even tackier. When Chidi meets Hypatia, the famed ancient philosopher, he is instantly disappointed immediately by how forgetful she is. The lack of suffering and the lack of the absurdity of death keep the residents of The Good Place from being able to do new and interesting things. Hypatia desires something that is meaningful, but instead the hedonism of The Good Place kills her sense of reason and curiosity.

This reminds us of novelist and philosopher Albert Camus's idea that not only is life absurd and seemingly meaningless, but that we must authentically respond to that absurdity and suffering in order to make our lives happy.[9] The happiness that is so freely given by The Good Place is ultimately meaningless and not enough for its inhabitants. Instead, Chidi and the others redesign The Good Place entirely, giving residents another chance at death, another chance at the unknown that also has a meaningful endpoint. Whereas Camus argues that the only philosophical question is suicide, whether life is worth living,[10] the final iteration of The Good Place allows for its inhabitants to choose a meaningful point to move on once their afterlife has hit its peak. While escaping suffering can lead individuals to cling to marginal comforts, the absence of suffering cheapens comfort altogether.

Notes

1   Jean-Paul Sartre, *No Exit*, in *No Exit and Three Other Plays*, trans. S. Gilbert (New York: Random House, 1989), 45. Michael Schur talks about *No Exit* being the inspiration for the basic story of the show on the podcast *The Good Place: The Podcast*.

2   Jean-Paul Sartre, *Being and Nothingness*, trans. H. Barnes, (New York: Random House, 1956), 102–103.

3   Ibid., 113.

4   For an in-depth discussion of Chidi as Beauvoir's Serious Man, see Matthew P. Meyer, "From Indecision to Ambiguity: Simone de Beauvoir and Chidi's Moral Growth," Chapter 16, this volume.

5   There's an unintended Sartrean Easter Egg in this scene, where Michael identifies that the dot over the "i" in "Jeremy Bearimy" are moments outside of time, such as Tuesdays and July, where in Sartre's novel *Nausea* there is a journal entry that states, "Tuesday: Nothing. Existed." In a conversation at the 2018 North American Sartre Society plenary session on *The Good Place*, Michael Schur admitted that he wasn't aware of this line in *Nausea* but clearly agrees with the (in)significance of Tuesdays.

6   Simone de Beauvior, *The Ethics of Ambiguity*, trans. Bernard Fretchman (New York: Philosophical Library, 1948), 55.

7   Friedrich Nietzsche, *Twilight of the Idols*, trans. R. Holt (Indianapolis, IN: Hackett, 1997), 6.

8   Jean-Paul Sartre, *Existentialism Is a Humanism*, trans. C. Macomber (New Haven, CT: Yale University Press, 2007).

9   Albert Camus, *The Myth of Sisyphus*, trans. J. O'Brien (New York: Random House, 1983).

10 Ibid, 3.

14

"I Would Refuse to Be a God if It Were Offered to Me": Architects and Existentialism in *The Good Place*

Kimberly S. Engels

"To experience oneself, to take risks, to discover oneself by discovering the world, to change while changing things, what better is there? I would refuse to be a god if it were offered to me."[1] In this line, Jean-Paul Sartre (1905–1980) rejoices in the complexity and the marvel of being a mortal human: the ability to change, to become different, and the inherent risk in doing so. Rejecting an eternal, unchanging soul or essence, he praises the beauty of the human experience and definitively declares his preference for a temporary life of change and transformation over an eternity of certainty.

In *The Good Place*, Michael is an immortal demon called an architect, who takes on the ambitious task of designing a neighborhood that will prompt condemned humans Eleanor, Chidi, Tahani, and Jason to unknowingly torture each other (a move straight from Sartre's *No Exit* playbook). When his experimental neighborhood fails and he risks being sentenced to an eternal punishment called retirement, Michael changes course and decides to try to get himself and the humans into The Real Good Place, befriending the very humans he is supposed to be torturing. Along the way, Michael undergoes an existential transformation as his new friends try to teach him to be ethical through the study of moral philosophy. The possibility of becoming good reveals

This paper was presented at the 2018 meeting of the North American Sartre Society in a plenary session featuring Michael Schur and Todd May.

that Michael has more in common with the humans than he realizes. We see Michael, an immortal demon who is supposed to be eternally evil, attempting to transcend his current essence through his choice, and become worthy of The Real Good Place. As part of this transformation, he risks the comfort and certainty of immortality for the chance of change, improvement, and helping his friends.

The Silent Indifference of an Empty Universe

Sartre's existentialism is characterized by his rejection of a pre-given human essence as well as his focus on the power of individual freedom. In Sartre's view, there is no divine creator, no final judge, and no supernatural moral fabric holding everything together. Since there is no creator who designed a human blueprint, we get to design ourselves through our choices. Some people find this view pessimistic, because there is no one "looking out for us," so to speak. The universe is indifferent to us. But Sartre thinks his philosophy is inherently optimistic, because if we get rid of the blueprint, humans are free to create our own futures and give our lives our own purposes.[2] No pre-given destiny or eternal self restricts us.

Sartre argues that every person builds their essence through a choice of "project." The existential project is an ongoing image we have of ourselves that we use to structure our beliefs, choices, and behavior. The project unites our conscious behavior and experience into a teleological whole, and this is what constitutes our essence or "self." The ends we pursue are used to organize the objects of our experience, and we give meaning to the objects of our perception based on our project. Sartre writes,

> In fact, it is this original choice which originally creates all causes and all motives which can guide us to partial actions; it is this which arranges the world with its meaning, its instrumental-complexes, and its coefficient of adversity.[3]

We do not choose a project based on prior motives or conscious states. Rather, our motives, actions, and conscious states are a product of our chosen project. Sartre says that the project

> [E]xpresses the finite choice which [the human being] has made of himself. But henceforth what makes his person known to him is the future and not the past; he chooses to learn what he is by means of ends toward which he projects himself.[4]

For example, my existential project consists of being a philosophy professor and writer. When I go about my daily experience, the choices I make, the possibilities I affirm or deny are made in light of my project as a philosophy professor. I use this image or goal of self to structure my conscious experience into a coherent whole. However, I can never coincide with my essence in the way an object coincides with its essence. For example, a rock is a rock and cannot be anything else. Human beings, by contrast, are always separated from our essences to the extent that we can reflect on them and potentially change them. I can, at any time, decide to give up being a philosophy professor and pursue a new project.

To have a true change in project, though, one must go through a rupture in the initial project and then direct oneself toward a new set of ends. This happens "by an abrupt metamorphosis of my initial project – i.e. by another choice of myself and of my ends. Moreover this modification is always possible."[5] When you make a choice in the world to direct yourself toward a new future and new set of ends, you break from your old project and enter a new one.

A key aspect of our existential situation that influences our choice of project is our relationships with others, which Sartre calls "being for others." As he says, "Being-for-others is a constant fact of my human reality, and I grasp it with its factual necessity in every thought, however slight, which I form concerning myself."[6] This means that our essence, or the self that we build, is always created while taking other people into consideration. Michael's existential transformation is steeped in his relationships with others. He transforms as a reaction to his initial goal of torturing the humans, his new goal of helping them get to The Good Place, and his further expanded goal of dismantling an unfair system of judgment that has sentenced everyone from the past 521 years to The Bad Place. Through all of this, his relationships with the four humans and his AI companion Janet are key to his own transformation.

Michael is supposed to be eternally bad. But after a twist of fate, he takes on a new project and decides he wants to be good. In Sartrean terms, we must wonder: can demonic architects transcend themselves?

Existential Crisis

It is revealed in the final episode of Season 1 that the characters have not been occupying The Good Place at all, but have really been in The Bad Place all along. We learn that Michael, who is first presented to us as an angelic architect of The Good Place, is actually a demonic architect of The Bad Place, who designed the "neighborhood" with the intention of getting the four humans to torture each other. The beginning of Season 2 shows Michael trying repeatedly to get it just right. In a quasi-Nietzschean eternal return of the same, he makes attempt after attempt to get his plan to succeed. After it fails 802 times, Michael changes course: he suggests the humans pretend that they are still deceived into thinking they are in The Good Place, while he works on getting them all into The Real Good Place. Eleanor makes Michael a deal: they will agree to the plan, but Michael must take Chidi's ethics class and learn to truly be good. Michael accepts the offer, though perhaps just to buy himself time, and it turns out to be the first step of his existential journey ("Team Cockroach").

After a few ethics lessons, Michael doesn't seem to make much progress. Chidi hypothesizes why: Michael is immortal and cannot face consequences, throwing the whole basis for moral philosophy out the window. Chidi aims to get Michael into the "human mindset" that acknowledges that life has an end, and therefore, that our actions have meaning. When Chidi asks Michael if he could "die," the architect says, well, kind of: he could "retire."

> It's an extreme form of punishment. We call it "The Eternal Shriek." My soul will be disintegrated, and each molecule will be placed on the surface of a different burning sun. And then my essence will be scooped out of my body with a flaming ladle and poured over hot diamonds, and then what's left of my body will be endlessly beaten with a titanium rod ("Existential Crisis").

When Chidi prompts him to think about his retirement, Michael is disturbed and perplexed that he would no longer exist: "You're saying that I would be ... no ... me?" This realization sparks an existential crisis for the demon. As Chidi explains the experience, "It's a sort of anguish people go through when they contemplate the silent indifference of our empty universe." Indeed, this very human understanding is the first step needed for Michael to embark on a journey of human change and transformation. Sartre would agree that our immediate reaction to our situation of being wholly responsible for ourselves in an indifferent creator-less universe is often one of horror and turning away—an anguish at the fact that we are thrown into a meaningless world that we will pass away from. On the positive side, however, because human life comes to an end, things matter—the projects we build, and the selves we choose to be, matter. For Michael to have a true existential rupture he will have to not only realize this, but embrace it.

Like many humans, Michael's existential crisis transitions into a midlife crisis, as he cruises onto the scene in a convertible with his secretary "Jeanette," showing off his new tattoo. Michael admits he is trying to distract himself, keeping himself moving so he can't start thinking. Thinking, after all, reminds him of the empty universe, the possibility of his death, and the fact that there are stakes. Luckily, Michael has friends. To get him to snap out of it, Eleanor tells Michael that he is having a very human experience: "All humans are aware of death. So we're all just a little bit sad. All the time. That's just the deal." Michael responds that seems like a crappy deal. Eleanor acknowledges this is true, but adds, "We don't get offered any other ones." She helps Michael see it is okay to be a little bit sad about the prospect of mortality, and Michael thanks Eleanor for pulling him out of his existential funk. More importantly, he is now ready to learn about ethics: he has entered the proper human mindset to understand why our actions matter.

So Michael continues ethics lessons with Chidi. There are bumps along the way as Michael admits to intentionally torturing Chidi during the trolley problem exercise, making Chidi relive the simulation over and over knowing it causes him mental anguish. Eleanor gets Michael to admit that he did this as a form of lashing out because he felt insecure about not understanding human ethics, even getting Michael to apologize to Chidi ("Trolley Problem"). With these conversations and experiences, Michael learns more about being a human and more about the possibility that he could change and become better.

Despite this progress, Michael still ponders whether he should murder Derek, Janet's rebound booty-call, to avoid being exposed. When Chidi reminds him that this would be morally wrong, Michael points out that murdering Derek will make their lives easier, and so that makes it okay. Clearly, Michael still doesn't fully get it, though he has made progress. To Michael's credit, when Eleanor suggests he simply reboot all of them to solve the Derek/Janet/Tahani/Jason romantic entanglement, he refuses. Michael believes they have made too much progress to erase ("Derek"). Faced with the choice of erasing his friends' memories, he instead chooses the harder path, the one he thinks will be ultimately more fulfilling. We also see that he has grown to value his friendships and relationships and does not want to lose them. This already represents a significant change in Michael's chosen ends, as he is no longer motivated solely by self-interest.

Michael later has a heart-to-heart with Eleanor, revealing to her that his entire design of the fake Good Place relied on his assumption that she would always give up. However, surprisingly each time, she never stopped trying to become a better person. Eleanor admits that this is because Chidi has changed her. In all 802 reboots, Chidi never ceased to help Eleanor—he chose to help her every time ("Derek"). Michael thus realizes that Chidi makes Eleanor want to change and be a better person. It's one of the benefits of being human: being able to change and become better because of your relationships with others.

You're All in The Bad Place

Despite Michael's improvement, things come to a head when his fake progress reports about torturing the humans earn him a promotion with his Bad Place crew. Michael announces to the neighborhood that they are in The Bad Place, and that the humans will be sent for some traditional torture going forward. The four humans are left pondering whether Michael has defected and abandoned their plan, choosing self-interest over the ethical path. Eleanor, however, has trouble believing that Michael would betray them after all they have been through.

When they throw a party to celebrate the destruction of the old neighborhood, Michael "roasts" the humans, hurling insults at them that make everyone, including the viewer, wonder if Michael has chosen to resort back to his pre-given, evil essence, and reject the progress of his existential journey. Eleanor is convinced that Michael is merely putting on a show for the other demons, but begins to doubt herself as Michael's insults get crueler and he seems to be enjoying the jokes. Maybe Michael could not transcend his evil essence after all?

Thankfully, Eleanor realizes that Michael's roast contains within it a secret escape plan. When the train full of demons rolls away, Michael bursts into tears at the sight of the four humans on the track. "You guys are my friends and I was so scared for you!" ("Leap to Faith"). Michael cared about his friends so much that he was willing to take a risk to save them. In discovering the world, he discovers himself: he realizes he can reject his essence as a demon and build his own project with his own set of ends. He has taken on a noble goal beyond self-preservation.

In "Best Self," Michael is forced to admit to his human friends that he has failed to figure out a way to get them all into The Real Good Place. Nonetheless, Chidi, Tahani, Eleanor, and Jason name Michael an "Honorary Human" for going above and beyond and doing more to attempt to be ethical than the average person. In "Rhonda, Diana, Jake, and Trent," a plan is made to talk to the Judge herself, but first the crew must make their way through The Bad Place headquarters to obtain the badges needed to access the Judge's portal. Michael gets the badges, but the humans are eventually exposed and must make a run for it. When they get to the Judge's portal, Chidi, Jason, and Tahani go through. Just Eleanor and Michael are left, and Michael realizes he is one badge short. As Shawn and the other demons approach, Michael realizes it is him or Eleanor. "Hey, you know what," he says,

> I just solved the Trolley Problem.
> Remember the thought experiment where you can either plow into a group of people or you can turn and hit one person? I solved it.
> See, the Trolley Problem forces you to choose between two versions of letting other people die. The actual solution is very simple: You sacrifice yourself.

Giving Eleanor the final badge, he pushes her through the portal and turns to face the wrath of his fellow demons.

With this action, Michael has an existential rupture, a metamorphosis of his ends, and a new choice of self. By sacrificing himself to save his friends, Michael risks being "retired." But he has discovered that there are things that matter more than self-preservation: saving his friends. He has truly engaged in an ethical transformation and learned that his actions have meaning, and that he can give meaning to his life and to the world through his free choices. Michael has made his own independent value judgment: he chooses to value the certainty of his friends' escape over the possibility of his own. He also takes a leap into the unknown, as he is now caught by the Bad Place demons. What will happen to him? It's okay not to know. It's okay to take a risk. It's the most human thing he can do. With this action, Michael is truly rejecting the certainty of immortality for the possibility of transformation.

In a plenary session of the 2018 North American Sartre Society conference, show creator Michael Schur commented, "The moment he shoves Eleanor through the portal, he gives her the pin, he says I've solved the Trolley Problem and sacrifices himself, the existential rupture, at that point we in the writers' room thought about it like, 'He's all in. At this point he's all in with the humans.'" By transforming himself over the course of his journey with his friends, Michael has learned the true beauty of rejecting an eternal, pre-given essence in favor of a life of meaning, risk, and change. His path with his human friends has shaped him, and now he is shaping his world and choosing a new set of possibilities. In the moment he risked his own life to save his friends, becoming different in the process, Michael exemplifies Sartre's fondness for being human over being a god.

Snowplowing Circumstances

In Season 3, the demon makes more progress and continues to pursue his new existential project. Michael's conscious experience is now organized around a new goal: to get his friends into The Real Good Place. His actions thus make sense in light of this new goal. In "Snowplowing Circumstances," Michael consistently intervenes to make sure that the four humans meet up in the real world. He doesn't see this as cheating. Rather, he recognizes that sometimes you need a little push in the right direction because your situation can have a drastic effect on the actions you choose. Small changes in circumstance can put you on a different path and can have a radical effect on your project—and your overall point total. For example, meeting Chidi makes Eleanor want to be better, but she needs a little push to get there.

Due to Michael's actions, the Soul Squad are able to meet and bond over a scientific study for those who have had near-death experiences. Michael is never far even while the humans work together, showing how much his current project now revolves around his human friends and their fates. Even though they cannot remember him, he still cares and refuses to give up on them. Truly, an unreciprocated friendship is one of the most obvious displays of genuine affection and concern toward others.

Michael's transformation does not stop there. He realizes there is a bigger problem when he learns that even the do-gooder Doug Forcett is headed for The Bad Place. In response, Michael gets the system accountant to admit that no one has made it into The Good Place for over 521 years. Michael recognizes this as unjust—the whole system must be off. This genuine concern for people is a product of his new project. At first Michael thinks The Bad Place must be tampering with the points system, but then realizes the problem is more complex (and grave): modern life is so complicated that the points system is no longer a reliable measure of who is good and who is bad (if it ever was) ("The Book of Dougs").

Michael now wants to fix the system, not just for the sake of his four friends, but for a sense of ultimate justice and fairness for all people. Michael's circle of moral concern has widened from thinking just of himself, to caring deeply about the fates of his four friends, to caring about the fate of all humans and a sense of ultimate justice. His deal with the Judge to set up a new neighborhood at the end of Season 3 shows that his focus has shifted from caring just about his four friends to fixing a social problem. At the end of "The Book of Dougs" he prepares to enter the Interdimensional Hole of Pancakes (IHOP), which he describes as the "most dangerous place in the universe." Asked why he is taking this bold action, Michael answers decisively, "to save humanity." The determination with which he states his goal cannot be overstated. Michael's project is now clearly directed at this new, noble end.

Critics charged Sartre's existentialist worldview with pessimism due to his argument that human life has no meaning or purpose other than that which we choose to give it. But Michael exemplifies the fundamental optimism contained within this philosophical world-view. Michael had an essence, a goal, a purpose, a function: a torturer of humans. Through assuming a human mindset, he goes on a human journey in which he transcends himself. He chooses a noble project in the world and orients himself toward this end, immersing his entire being into the project and putting his own physical well-being on the line multiple times. Michael wants to show that the system for judging humans is unfair and can be better: like him, like humans, like the world, the points system must change as human civilization and human situations have changed. Michael's personal transformation contains within it the possibility for initiating long-term social change. In the existentialist worldview nothing is inherent, even the points system. If it is not facilitating the possibility of meaningful human projects, it too must change. In changing himself, Michael is motivated to change things.

In "Pandemonium" Michael has another crisis, though it is not the result of contemplating his own mortality or the indifference of the universe. Rather, his anguish is triggered by Shawn's revelation that if his experimental neighborhood fails, his friends will be tortured forever by a demon who looks like him. The thought that his human friends may think he has betrayed them is overwhelming for Michael. While his initial existential crisis was triggered by contemplating only himself, this crisis is a result of a fear of a breakdown of his new relationships. What is unbearable to him is not the fear of his own retirement, but the fear that his friends will not only be tortured, but also think he has betrayed them.

In Season 4, Michael continues his quest to save humanity by participating in the experimental Medium Place neighborhood and negotiating with the Judge. One of the season's pivotal moments comes when Michael must convince Shawn to agree to his new system of judgment in order to prevent the Judge from wiping out and restarting Earth. Michael takes a risk in telling Shawn that he is out of ideas ("You've Changed, Man"). When Michael is made the caretaker of The Good Place and the committee resigns, Michael has the courage to make some much-needed changes to the structure of The Good Place itself ("Patty"). In the series finale, Michael is finally rewarded in his quest to experience being a human. He is told that there is an element of risk in doing so, as he will have to pass the same tests as every other human in order to enter The Good Place. But Michael has decided it is a risk worth taking ("Whenever You're Ready").

I Would Refuse to Be a God

"To experience oneself, to take risks, to discover oneself by discovering the world, to change while changing things, what better is there? I would refuse to be a god if it were offered to me."[7] Throughout the course of four seasons, Michael decides that the project of an eternal certainty is less preferable than a possibly limited lifetime of risk, change, and transformation. In discovering his new possibilities alongside his friends, he discovers new dimensions of himself. As he seeks to change the circumstances of his friends, and later the fate of all humanity, he too becomes different through this task. The silent indifference of the empty universe means that we get to be the voice we listen to. Perhaps the universe doesn't care, but humans—and demons—do.

Notes

1 Jean-Paul Sartre, "L'Engagement de Mallarme," *Obliques* 18–19 (1952), 187, translator unknown.
2 Jean Paul Sartre, *Existentialism Is a Humanism* (New Haven, CT: Yale University Press, 2007), 22–23.
3 Jean-Paul Sartre, *Being and Nothingness: An Essay on Phenomenological Ontology*, trans. Hazel Barnes (New York: Washington Square Press, 1953), 465.
4 Ibid., 468.
5 Ibid., 464.
6 Ibid., 373.
7 Sartre, "L'Engagement de Mallarme," 187.

Part VI

"SEARCHING FOR MEANING IS PHILOSOPHICAL SUICIDE"

15
Death, Meaning, and Existential Crises

Kiki Berk

What do the following things have in common: a demon lying on a couch in the fetal position, a philosophy professor making marshmallow chili in front of his class, and a selfish girl handing out leaflets for the environment? First, they're all hilarious scenes from *The Good Place*. Second, each depicts a character—Michael, Chidi, and Eleanor—responding to an existential crisis. These existential crises differ in a number of ways, but they have one thing in common: they're confrontations with death that call into question the meaning of life. In particular, they all raise the following questions: what's the relationship between death and the meaning of life? Does death deprive life of meaning? Or does death make life more meaningful? Let's try to answer these questions by exploring these three existential crises through a philosophical lens. Hopefully, we can do so without experiencing any of the horror, angst, or shock that the three characters do. But I make no promises. Continue reading at your own risk!

"So You're Saying That I Would Be ... *No ... Me*?"

Imagine your long-awaited, well-deserved retirement. Did you picture your essence being scooped out of your body with a flaming ladle, and every molecule in your body being placed on the surface of a different sun? No, because you're not a demon. However, demons who screw up can expect this kind of treatment. So, when Chidi asks Michael to think about his "retirement," this is what he has in mind: "Everyone else is here. But you? Poof. Gone. Nothingness. Inky black void. Done" ("Existential Crisis"). In other words: *dead*. Michael goes very quickly from Zen-like calm ("Okay, I'll think about that..."), to shocked realization ("So, you're saying that I would be ... *no* ... *me?*"), to falling on Chidi's lap with an expression of pure horror on his face (think Edvard Munch's *The Scream*). Michael is having an existential crisis.

But what *is* an existential crisis? Chidi describes it as "a sort of anguish people go through when they contemplate the silent indifference of our empty universe." Existential crises come in different flavors, but they're typically evoked by confrontations with mortality and accompanied by feelings of existential angst. Have you ever been hit by the realization that you're going to die and then suddenly felt paralyzed by fear? That's an existential crisis—albeit on a much smaller scale than the one Michael has in this episode.

It's important to distinguish between *existential angst* and *fear of dying*. Existential angst (or anguish, as Chidi calls it) isn't an emotional response to an actual threat. It isn't the feeling caused by peering into a gaping sinkhole or being chased by a giant flying cocktail shrimp. It isn't even about dying *per se* or the pain that dying so often involves. There's no direct threat to Michael's life during his existential crisis; he's sitting on a comfortable couch in Chidi's philosophy classroom. And even though the process of demonic retirement doesn't sound particularly appealing, Michael doesn't seem to be worried about being painfully torn apart and burnt molecule for molecule. Rather, Michael's angst is caused by the mere contemplation of there being "no me," as he puts it. Indeed, existential angst has been described by philosophers as the horror of annihilation (Simone de Beauvoir)[1] and the horror of non-being (Karl Jaspers).[2]

It's also important to distinguish between *existential crises* and *midlife crises*. After the scene on Chidi's couch, Michael disappears and comes back accompanied by a blonde, sexy "Jeanette." He's driving a red convertible, wearing a white suit, and sporting a new tattoo and ear piercing. These are all stereotypical signs of a midlife crisis. But while such crises often involve an awareness of our ever-closer approaching demise, they also typically involve feelings of missing out, regret, and dissatisfaction.[3] None of the latter apply to Michael, so he's not really having a midlife crisis. What's happening is that Michael has managed to temporarily repress his existential angst by being in denial about his mortality. But it's not very long before this strategy fails: "Can't stop moving. If I stop moving, I'll start thinking. And if I start thinking, I'll start thinking about things I don't want to think about—like death. Oops. I'm thinking about it now. Yep, thinking about death again."

"Searching for Meaning Is Philosophical Suicide"

As we've seen, contemplating our non-existence can evoke angst. But should it? Is being dead really a bad thing? It might be bad for the loved ones who are left behind. But if there's no afterlife, then what's so bad about being dead for the person who dies? After all, there won't be anything it's like to be dead. If death is complete annihilation, then it won't feel good; but it won't feel bad, either. It won't feel like anything at all! This argument against the badness of death was first given by the Greek philosopher Epicurus (341–270 BCE). In his words: "Death, therefore, the most awful of evils, is nothing to us, seeing that, when we are, death is not come, and, when death is come, we are not."[4] Accordingly, while fear of death might be natural, it isn't rational.

Some philosophers are convinced by Epicurus. Others argue that death doesn't have to be like anything in order for it to be bad. According to these philosophers, we're not afraid of death because of any definite qualities that it has but because of all the good things in life we'll miss out on after we die. In short, the problem with death is not that being dead *hurts* us but that being dead *deprives* us.[5] And if that's true, then death is something to feel bad about after all.

I'm tempted to agree with the "deprivation theory," as it's called. Isn't the reason we don't want to die that we don't want to miss out on more frozen yogurt (or better: ice cream!), cocktail shrimp, and episodes of *The Good Place*? But Epicurus has a reply: when, exactly, will I be deprived of these things? Not while I'm alive, surely, for while I'm alive I can still enjoy them. And I won't be deprived of them after I die, either, for then I won't exist, and only things that exist can have properties—like being deprived. Because these are the only two times I can be deprived of anything—either before or after I die—it seems like death can't be a deprivation after all. And yet, I find it very hard to shake the feeling that my death will be bad for me precisely because it will deprive me of so many good things. It's hard to say who's right: Epicurus or the deprivationists.

Regardless of who's right, death presents us with another worry. If we die, and death is the end, then does anything we do really matter? As Michael puts it: "How does anyone *do* anything when you understand the fleeting nature of existence?" That's a good question. Can things be meaningful if they don't last forever? Some philosophers think not. According to them, if everything ends, and there's no God and no afterlife, then there's no point in doing anything, and life is meaningless. The French philosopher Albert Camus (1913–1960) famously said that death makes our lives "absurd." He compares our lives to that of Sisyphus, who's condemned by the gods to roll a boulder up a hill, only to watch it roll back down again, at which point he has to roll it back up the hill—again and again, for eternity. Just as endlessly rolling a rock up a hill doesn't amount to anything, neither do our lives—if death is the end. (This explains why Chidi says, "Gotta go grab some Camus!" when Michael starts having his existential crisis.)

So, is life meaningless if it doesn't last forever? Surprisingly, most philosophers don't think so. Sure, it's disappointing that our actions and our lives don't really amount to anything in the end (after all, the sun will eventually explode, all but guaranteeing this conclusion), but things that are temporary can still be meaningful. For example, a friendship you had in college can still mean a lot to you even if it didn't last past graduation. And if that's true about relationships, then why not about life? In the end, there just don't seem to be any good reasons to think that life is meaningful only if it lasts forever.

"Let Me Just Get into the Mindset of a Human"

But even if life isn't rendered meaningless by death, wouldn't it be *more* meaningful if it lasted forever? This question is especially interesting in Michael's case, since demons can live forever if they're good at their jobs (of torturing people!) and don't get in trouble with their bosses. Immortality is clearly desirable, isn't it?

The English philosopher Bernard Williams (1929–2003) argues in his classic paper "The Makropulos Case: Reflections on the Tedium of Immortality" (1973) that immortality would *not* be a good thing.[6] Why not? Well, for one thing, Williams argues, an endless life would become so excruciatingly and unbearably boring that all of us would want "out" at some point. This is exactly what happens in *The Good Place*. When the four humans, Michael, and Janet finally make it to The Real Good Place, they soon realize it's a disaster. As long-term inhabitant Patty (formerly Hypatia of Alexandria) explains: "'Cause you get here and you realize that anything's possible, and you do everything, and then you're done. But you still have infinity left.

This place kills fun, and passion, and excitement, and love, till all you have left are milkshakes" ("Patty"). Michael's solution, based on an idea from Eleanor, is to create a door that exits the afterlife. Step through the door, and *poof*—you no longer exist (except, perhaps, as a ball of energy that returns to Earth to help people do the right thing, but we'll ignore that possibility here). Having the option to go through this door and annihilate oneself allows a person to enjoy the afterlife while it lasts. It works for Patty: "I've been dreaming of ending the ennui of this eternal existence for a long time, but now I think I'll stick around for a while." Many inhabitants of The Real Good Place— including (spoiler alert!) Jason, Chidi, and Eleanor—ultimately choose to go through this door ("Whenever You're Ready"). Thus, the show clearly sides with Williams on the undesirability of immortality.

But not all philosophers agree. Contemporary philosopher John Martin Fischer, for example, argues that some things continue to be good no matter how many times you have them—like coffee, sex, and whisky. So, an immortal life would keep being enjoyable because of these "repeatable pleasures."[7] But it's hard to know if Fischer is right. For one thing, it's difficult to imagine what it would really be like to live forever. And for another, it might just depend on one's personality. Perhaps some people would get excruciatingly bored after a thousand (or a million, or a billion) years, while others would be happy living forever. Who knows?

But boredom is just one potential problem with immortality. Another argument against the desirability of immortality is that our choices lose their weight and significance in a life that lasts forever. In a mortal life, it really matters which career you pursue, whom you choose to marry, and where you decide to live, because you make these choices only so many times. But if you live forever, then you can have an endless number of careers, loves, and hometowns. And in that case, it doesn't really matter what you choose at any given time. What's the importance of a particular job if you've had a hundred before? What's the value of falling in love for the thousandth time? And why should the place you live matter if it's just one of hundreds— or thousands? There's time for everything in an immortal life, so it doesn't really matter what you do, now or later. And if none of your choices really matter, then life as a whole seems to become meaning-less. So, perhaps death isn't such a bad thing after all. Perhaps it's only because we die that life has any meaning to begin with. Chidi makes this point explicitly in the final episode of the show ("mortality offers meaning to our lives," he says), and the rest of this episode tries to drive this point home ("Whenever You're Ready"). The idea that death makes life meaningful seems to be one of the major moral lessons of *The Good Place*.

This idea also appears to be what motivates Chidi to try to get Michael to think about his "retirement" in the first place. Since Michael is immortal, he can't understand why humans take their lives, their actions, and their ethics so seriously. As Chidi explains, "Maybe the reason Michael can't latch onto the ideas is because he's immortal... Before I can teach Michael to be good, I have to force him to think about what we used to think about: that life has an end, and therefore our actions have meaning" ("Existential Crisis"). It works, too. Michael eventually comes out of his crisis, with Chidi's and Eleanor's help, and he even goes on to become an ethical person as a result. He becomes so ethical, in fact, that he's willing to sacrifice his own life for those of the four humans at the end of Season 2 ("Rhonda, Diana, Jake, and Trent"). Michael's existential crisis clearly changed him for the better.

"I'm Gonna Eat All This Chili and/or Die Trying"

Have you ever taken a philosophy course? Did your professor spend an entire class making a giant pot of chili with Peeps and M&Ms and then announce, "I'm gonna eat all this chili and/or die trying"? Sadly, your philosophy class probably wasn't that fun—or weird.

As funny as this scene from "Jeremy Bearimy" is, however, Chidi's not laughing. He's having an existential crisis. Earlier that morning he found out that he's going back to The Bad Place, and there's nothing he can do about it. In his own words (to Michael): "So, to sum up: there is a heaven and hell; we've been to hell; and now, no matter how good we are—for the rest of our lives—we're going back to hell." Completely disillusioned, Chidi wanders off, first through a park where he tells a stranger that "God is dead. God remains dead, and we have killed him. Who will wipe this blood off us? Friedrich Nietzsche, 1882." (Needless to say, the stranger is scared away: "I was just trying to sell you some drugs, and you made it weird!") Chidi is so depressed that he doesn't even bother moving out of the way when the park's sprinklers turn on. He simply takes off his shirt and wanders into a grocery store, where he spends $880 and gives his credit card and car keys to the cashier. Finally, he ends up in his philosophy class, wearing a tiny pink t-shirt and cooking chili with all the random ingredients he just bought at the grocery store.

As fun as this class sounds, one of his students insists on learning something. "All right, nerd," Chidi says, and proceeds to give a lesson on *nihilism*. Nihilism (more specifically, *moral* nihilism) is the view that there aren't any moral values. In other words, according to this view, nothing is right or wrong. Moral nihilists give different reasons for thinking this, but one of them is that right and wrong depend on God, and God doesn't exist. "God is dead," as Nietzsche said.[8]

Why think that moral values depend on God? First, because moral values don't seem to be part of nature, so they must have a supernatural origin if they exist at all. Second, because even if right and wrong do exist, they matter only if we're rewarded or punished in the afterlife for being good or bad on Earth. As Dostoyevsky said in *The Brothers Karamazov*: "If there's no immortality of the soul, then there's no virtue, and everything is lawful."[9] Chidi makes essentially the same point in his lecture: "My little chili babies, ... the true meaning of life, the actual ethical system that you should all follow is nihilism. The world is empty. There is no point to anything, and you're just gonna die. So do whatever."

Is Chidi—speaking like a true moral nihilist—correct? Do moral values depend on the existence of God? I don't think so. A completely naturalistic worldview doesn't rule out the existence of moral values. Sure, they're odd, but so are numbers, concepts, meanings, and other values—like beauty. The fact that conscious beings like humans (and many animals) have interests and can experience pain gives us a very good reason not to harm them. Harming them is wrong, and you shouldn't do it—even if there's no punishment for doing so. By the same token, helping other conscious beings is good—even if there's no reward. And this, of course, is precisely what the "Soul Squad" decides at the end of the episode. Even though they're eternally damned, and there's absolutely nothing they can do about it, they're going to help other people anyway. Why? Because it's the right thing to do.

"I'm Gonna Teach You the Meaning of Life"

Is doing good the *only* thing worth doing? Helping other people is certainly a good way to make your life meaningful. And for your life to be meaningful, virtue might even be necessary. But is it sufficient? Is there more to meaning in life than being a virtuous person?

Virtue is undoubtedly valuable in itself, but other things might be as well: achievements, autonomy, happiness, knowledge, and love—to name just a few. Perhaps filling your life with these things also makes your life meaningful, in which case there are many things worth doing, in addition to helping others, for example: maintaining friendships, having children, reading books, swimming in the ocean, making music, and learning about philosophy.

But is doing these kinds of things *really* enough to make our lives meaningful? Is human-made meaning *real* meaning?

Naturalists about meaning think so. Naturalists (about meaning) think that individual human lives can still be meaningful even if the human species wasn't created for a purpose. But not everyone agrees. *Supernaturalists* (about meaning) and *nihilists* (again, about meaning) hold a different view. Supernaturalists think that life can be meaningful only if it was created for a purpose. In the absence of that, any meaning we create is just that: created, made-up, fake. (Lucky for them, supernaturalists also believe in God, so they still believe that life is meaningful.) Nihilists agree with supernaturalists that meaning depends upon the existence of God, but they conclude that life is meaningless, since there is no God. Who's right? The naturalists, or the supernaturalists and nihilists? Does meaning depend on God, or doesn't it?

The Good Place seems to weigh in on the side of naturalism. At the end of the episode, Eleanor gets Chidi out of his funk by proposing that they help other people. Why? Not because God exists, or because they'll be rewarded in the afterlife (remember: they're damned to The Bad Place no matter what they do). They decide to be good by helping others because they think it will make their lives meaningful. And that's exactly what naturalists think.

"Holy Crap! I Just Almost Died"

Since it was Eleanor who talked Michael and Chidi out of their existential crises, you might think that she would be spared one of her own. But she isn't. While bending over to pick up a dropped bottle of "Lonely Gal Margarita Mix for One," Eleanor nearly dies from being run over by an out-of-control column of shopping carts. (This is at the end of Season 2, of course. In Season 1, she was hit by the shopping carts and swept out into the street, where she was killed by a mobile billboard truck advertising an erectile dysfunction pill.) Eleanor's close encounter with death makes her seriously reconsider how she's living her life. And while her experience differs significantly from Michael's and Chidi's, it still counts, I think, as an existential crisis. Why? Because it's a confrontation with mortality accompanied by a profound feeling, not of horror (like Michael) or angst (like Chidi), but of *shock*. This feeling of shock makes her reflect on her mortality, which, in turn, changes her perspective on life. In her own words: "My name is Eleanor Shellstrop, and I think I might be a monster. I'm rude, I'm selfish, I cyberbullied Ryan Lochte until he quit Instagram, but something happened to me today, and from now on, I'm gonna try to become a better, kinder, more generous person" ("Somewhere Else").

As a result of her existential crisis, Eleanor decides that she wants to try to be a better person instead of a "selfish ass." She quits her telemarketing job selling fake medicine, apologizes to the environmentalist guy who saved her life, and even joins his team to help the environment. She tries to eat vegetarian, tells her roommate the truth about the humiliating t-shirts that she sold on the internet, and leaves her insurance information after bumping a stranger's car. All of this makes sense because, as we've already seen, helping other people is a good way of making your life more meaningful. And virtue is valuable even if we die, God doesn't exist, and there's no afterlife.

But is it *really*? After some backlash, Eleanor is ready to give up: "I've been nothing but good for, like, six months, and all I have to show for it is this crummy apartment, a lawsuit, a loose caboose, and an overdrawn bank account. Being good is for suckers. What do you even get out of it?" ("Somewhere Else"). In other words: *Why be good?* We've already seen the answer that virtue is valuable for its own sake, but Eleanor gets three more answers in this episode.

The first answer, from the "twerpy twerp from the environmentalist place," is that being good gives you "a feeling of fulfillment in your soul." This makes Eleanor puke in her mouth a little bit: "Gross. That's the grossest sentence I've ever heard, okay?" But then she has a heart-to-heart with Michael (who looks suspiciously like the bartender in *Cheers*), who gives her a second answer:

> You know, I had a friend that said whenever she was doing something bad, she'd hear this little voice in her head, distant little voice, saying, "Oh, come on now. You know this is wrong." And then when she started doing good things, that voice went away. It was a relief… She's a little rough around the edges, but she was also a really good person, when she tried. See, I think that little voice was her conscience, trying to guide her in the right direction.

As Eleanor gets up to leave and asks what she owes him for the drinks, Michael says: "The real question, Eleanor, is what do we owe to each other?" The third answer Eleanor finds to her "Why be good?"

question is in a three-hour YouTube lecture from Chidi, who says: "I argue that we choose to be good because of our bonds with other people and our innate desire to treat them with dignity. Simply put, we are not in this alone." Plenty of reasons, then, to be good and to make our lives more meaningful by doing so.

"We're All Just Corpses Who Haven't Yet Begun to Decay"

The underlying message of all three existential crises in *The Good Place* is that the key to a meaningful life is to be a morally good person. Through his existential crisis, Michael learns what it is like to be human, which enables him to learn human ethics. He actually starts caring for his friends and becomes a better person. The only thing that gets Chidi out of his nihilist funk is Eleanor's idea of helping other people even though their own fates are sealed. And Eleanor herself decides that she wants to be a better person after her close encounter with death. It's important to keep in mind, however, that there are other ways of making one's life meaningful. Mozart and Einstein had meaningful lives, but they were focused on beauty and knowledge rather than on virtue. And you certainly don't have to be Mother Teresa, Mozart, or Einstein to have a meaningful life. Ordinary people like you and me can live meaningful lives by actively engaging in projects of worth, which is how contemporary philosopher Susan Wolf defines a meaningful life.[10]

In closing, let's consider one last question: are existential crises good or bad? They certainly can be bad, but the three existential crises in *The Good Place* are undoubtedly good. Michael, Chidi, and Eleanor all benefit from their existential crises. In all three cases, the crises provide the characters with the perspective and motivation to make their lives more meaningful. So, existential crises can be helpful in this way. And happily, you don't need to have a full-blown crisis to get this effect (though you would be in good company). Awareness of your own mortality, which you can get in a more benign form, can make you spend your time better, get your priorities straight, stop taking things (and people) for granted, do what you really want to do (rather than what is expected of you), and live more authentically. In this spirit, I will leave you to contemplate Michael's observation, hopefully without horror, angst, or shock, but rather as a reason to go out and do something meaningful: "We're all just corpses who haven't yet begun to decay" ("Existential Crisis"). Think about it.

Notes

1   Simone de Beauvoir writes, "This annihilation filled me with such horror," in *La Force de l'âge* (Paris: Librairie Gallimard, 1960). Translated as *Prime of Life*, trans. Peter Green (London: Andre Deutsch and Weidenfeld and Nicolson, 1963), 474.

2   Karl Jaspers writes, "Yet none can lift the horror from the mere thought of not being," in *Philosophie* (Berlin: Springer,1932). Translated as *Philosophy*, trans. E. B. Ashton (Chicago: University of Chicago Press, 1969–1971), 197.

3   See Kieran Setiya's *Midlife: A Philosophical Guide* (Princeton, NJ: Princeton University Press, 2017) for an accessible, therapeutic, and state-of-the-art philosophical account of the midlife crisis.

4   Epicurus, *Letter to Menoeceus*, in *Stoic and Epicurean*, trans. Robert Drew Hicks (New York: C. Scribner's Sons, 1910), 169.

5   For a classic discussion of the Deprivation Theory, see Thomas Nagel's "Death," *Nous* 4 (1970), 73–80.

6   Bernard Williams, "The Makropulos Case: Reflections on the Tedium of Immortality," in *Problems of the Self* (Cambridge: Cambridge University Press, 1973), 82–100.

7   John Martin Fischer, "Why Immortality Is Not So Bad," *International Journal of Philosophical Studies* 2 (1994), 257–270.

8   Friedrich Nietzsche, *Die fröhliche Wissenschaft* (Chemnitz: E. Schmeitzner, 1882). Translated as *The Gay Science*, trans. W. Kaufman (New York: Random House, 1974), 181.

9   Fyodor Dostoyevsky, Братья Карамазовы (Moscow: The Russian Messenger, 1880). Translated as *The Brothers Karamazov*, trans. C. Garnett (Auckland, NZ: The Floating Press, 2009), 150.

10 Susan Wolf, "Happiness and Meaning: Two Aspects of the Good Life," *Social Philosophy and Policy* 14 (1997), 207–225.

16

From Indecision to Ambiguity: Simone de Beauvoir and Chidi's Moral Growth

Matthew P. Meyer

Chidi Anogonye has difficulty making decisions. In fact, that may be his defining characteristic, and it is the one that ultimately led to his demise on Earth. But Chidi is not stupid. If anything, his indecisiveness could be attributed to too much intelligence and not enough "gut" feeling, as the latter often accompanies a kind of brute confidence born of ignorance. That said, there is one mistaken assumption upon which all his indecision-related misery is based: that there is only *one* right answer to every moral quandary, and that if he only thinks through every possible outcome, he *will* arrive at it.

The idea that there is *one* right answer to ethical quandaries and that we *can* arrive at them flies in the face of everything we learned—or should have learned—from the existentialists. Let's briefly review the tenets of that theory. One, we will all die (check: they're all dead in The Good Place). Death is a result of the fact that we are all born at some time, in some place, to some people (we learn where each of the characters is born, and to whom). We speak some language (check, though I keep forgetting that Chidi is speaking French). We are embodied (check). All these aspects of our factual being amount to an undeniable *finitude*, that is, a limitedness to our being. More importantly, this finitude means a limitedness to our *knowledge*. The possibility of a human taking on a *universal* point of view becomes impossible upon this recognition. If we cannot take on a universal point of view, then *every* decision we make must include some degree

The Good Place and Philosophy, First Edition. Edited by Kimberly S. Engels.

of uncertainty. Furthermore, existentialists argue that our freedom entails responsibility. Since we can choose, we *must* choose. Under this way of seeing things, even indecision is a choice (not to make a choice). For that reason, if a person avoids making a difficult decision, they are said to be fleeing their responsibility. The mindset of pretending that one *doesn't have a choice* is called *bad faith* because it entails pretending that we have no choice. In other words, it involves lying to ourselves about our own possible choices. However, Chidi's problem isn't that he pretends he doesn't have a choice. Rather he has a problem with the uncertainty of it all.

Chidi doesn't like uncertainty, and it's his belief in the possibility of certain right decisions that is really his Waterloo. As he tells Eleanor in the very first episode ("Everything Is Fine"): "I have spent my entire life in search of fundamental truths about the universe, and now we can actually find them together as soulmates."

The belief in "fundamental truths" entails a belief in "objective values," that is, values that exist outside of the frame of human thinking. Simone de Beauvoir calls such a belief "the spirit of seriousness." The reason she calls it "seriousness" is complicated, but think of it as the attitude that one might hold when one thinks of *grave* events; this isn't just play, or imagination, it's serious! There are two claims that are implicitly being made by the serious person. The first, pertaining to reality, or what philosophers call "ontology," is that objective values do exist. By "objective value" philosophers usually mean a value that is universal. For example, if telling the truth were an objective value, then lying would always be wrong (even if it were for a good reason, like hiding a refugee who is sought for deportation or imprisonment). These values, then, are supposed to guide our decisions. In Chidi's discussion of "fundamental truths" it's clear that Chidi believes in objective values. The second implicit claim of the serious person is that we *can actually know* what these objective values are (if you're wondering, this is what philosophers call an "epistemological" claim). Again, this is clearly Chidi's position in his remark to Eleanor.

Chidi, then, most certainly begins the series as a *serious* person. This being the case, we must first connect how the spirit of seriousness ties into Chidi's indecisiveness. Next, we will suggest why anyone—and not just Chidi, and he is certainly not the first, the last, nor the worst—would become a serious person. After that, we'll take a look at the meaning of nihilism—the exact opposite of seriousness—in the famous "Peeps chili" incident in "Jeremy Bearimy." Lastly, I'll suggest that Chidi overcomes his spirit of seriousness and accepts the ambiguity of responsibility through his decision to reboot himself in "Pandemonium."

Chidi's Indecision as *Seriousness*

As suggested in this chapter, Chidi's indecisiveness arises out of the combination of three assumptions: (1) there is a right answer to every ethical situation; (2) we can know what that is; and (3) doing anything other than that would not only be bad, but also wrong. According to Beauvoir, a person would unconsciously take such a position to shirk the responsibility of making a choice and the consequences of that choice. The serious man "forces himself to submerge his freedom in the content which [he] accepts from society. He loses himself in the object [or objective value] *in order to* annihilate his subjectivity."[1] As we said, individual choice—here "subjectivity"—involves responsibility. By choosing to believe in objective values—just believing in what society tells us is true—that are beyond individual choice, the serious person is fleeing from their individual responsibility. Imagine someone asks me, "Why did you not leave a tip for the barista?" and my answer was "Because my parents told me not to; they said baristas get paid enough." There I am deferring to the belief of someone else, my parents, to justify my action. As you might imagine, this happens with social norms, sacred texts, eccentric positions of our friends and family, and so on. Anytime I cannot justify a decision I have made based on my own "internal" reasons, I am either operating thoughtlessly or in a "serious" way. To Chidi's credit, he appears to be much more thoughtful than the average member of society. But he does seem to count himself among a "society" of philosophers, each of whom believes that they found that answer to ethics.

Remember, Chidi's belief that there exists a right answer to each decision is the same as saying that "there are" objective values, values that exist beyond individual knowledge and beyond the individual situation, such as that lying is always wrong. The serious person imagines that values are absolute and are never subject to the conditions in which they arise, namely, the decision of human beings in a particular situation.[2] Chidi is terrified of everything having to do with taking responsibility for his own choices. This is why he can't decide on which soup to order, which muffin to eat, which speech to give at the wedding, and which bar to choose (the moment before the air conditioner falls on him and kills him) ("Chidi's Choice"). His unwillingness to "own" his choice is probably also behind his 3600-page book manuscript, which Michael says is unreadable because of its second-guessing of its own positions, as well as unwillingness to serve as editor: "Obviously I like to write. But I don't like deadlines. I prefer to take my time with things" ("Tahani Al-Jamil"). Again, Beauvoir's picture of the serious person is relevant: "The thing that matters to the serious man is not so much the nature of the object which he prefers to himself, but rather the fact of being able to lose himself in it."[3] For Chidi, the lack of deadlines—or page limits!—allows him to lose himself and his choices in his own writing without ever having to make a deadline or an editing decision. But all of these are relatively small matters.

Chidi's real fear of choosing comes to the fore when he must choose his love interest in the episode "Chidi's Choice." While there is not much at stake here ethically, outside of hurting two people's feelings—oh, and maybe Eleanor going to The Bad Place, so I guess that's big—Chidi still cannot decide. Here is the conversation between Michael and Chidi on the subject:

CHIDI: I'm sorry, choices are hard for me when I am under pressure.

MICHAEL: I know that buddy, but we're short on time here and it's kind of important for Eleanor.

CHIDI: Right, which is why I can't take this lightly. What if I screw up?

MICHAEL: Listen, I don't need the Chidi who once had a panic attack during Rock-Paper-Scissors because there were, and I quote 'just too many variables.' I needed the Chidi who stormed in here to tell me to stop Eleanor's train without thinking of the consequences.

CHIDI: Oh boy, now I am nervous about that decision.

MICHAEL: Retroactively? I mean how do you even …

CHIDI: I don't know.

Beauvoir hits the nail on the head once again with regard to Chidi's seriousness: "he will be constantly upset by the uncontrollable course of events."[4] Chidi is, after all, Professor Stomachache!

If Beauvoir has tapped into the human subconscious as accurately as I think she has, then Chidi is indecisive because he is afraid of his own freedom. But why would one be afraid of one's own freedom? Because being free to choose highlights the fundamentally individual aspect of our being. And our individuality highlights our fundamental aloneness—our own mortality. One of the outcomes of indecision is a "decision" toward inaction that makes things worse. But the other possibility here is that eventually, the root of one's indecision—namely, hope for a clearly evident, "correct" answer to an ethical situation, or to life itself—will be exposed as impossible. All of this comes to the fore for Chidi in the amazing episode entitled "Jeremy Bearimy."

Chidi's Nihilistic Chili

In "Jeremy Bearimy" one of Chidi's prized fundamental truths—that time is linear—is exposed as incorrect. In fact, we are told, time in the afterlife travels in an almost inarticulable way, save for that the pattern resembles the name "Jeremy Bearimy" written out in cursive. This realization leads Chidi down a rabbit hole of doubt, such that he begins to doubt the purpose of life altogether. A hilarious segment follows. First, we see Chidi walking through a sprinkler and getting soaked; then taking off his shirt; then going to the grocery store; then being told he must wear a shirt in the grocery store; then picking out a random one that says "Who What Where When Wine"; then purchasing over $800 dollars in groceries, including chili beans, Peeps, and M&Ms; and then proceeding to assemble the chili in his philosophy classroom. When asked by a student if he can teach them something because exams are next week, Chidi first explains the three major ethical systems (virtue ethics, deontology, and utilitarianism) that help us to determine what to do with our lives. After explaining these, Chidi says:

> But here's the thing, my little chili babies, all three of those theories are hot stinky cat dookie. *The true meaning of life, the actual ethical system that you should all follow is nihilism.* The world is empty, there is no point to anything, and you are just going to die. So do whatever. And now, I am going to eat my marshmallow candy chili in silence and you all can jump up your own butts. (Emphasis added)

In this monologue, Chidi's implicit belief in objective norms and a clear purpose to life is exposed, but only after it was shown to be incorrect. By admitting that nihilism is true, Chidi is admitting that there are no *objective* values (not that there are *no values* at all). For Chidi, this realization is devastating. Beauvoir predicts this collapse perfectly as one possible outcome of the serious person whose ideals have been defeated: "The failure of the serious sometimes brings about a radical disorder. Conscious of being unable to be anything, [the person] then decides to be nothing. We shall call this attitude nihilistic."[5] In other words, Chidi explicitly states in his reaction to being shown that time isn't linear that "the world is empty, there is no point to anything, and you are just going to die." In Chidi's reaction we see the connection between a lack of objective values inherent in the universe, a fear of his own freedom (in opting for nihilism), and a fear of mortality.

Luckily, just in the way that nihilism is a possible response to failed seriousness, it too has possible outcomes, at least one of which is positive. In *The Good Place* we might look to Eleanor in "Jeremy Bearimy" for inspiration here as well. Her response to the fact that she is doomed is to double-down on goodness and form the Soul Squad. Now, really, Beauvoir has an explanation for this as well, which we get to further in this chapter. But for now, it's worth pointing out that the idea that a response to "life *having* no purpose" must be violent and negative is rather adolescent and short-sighted. And while it takes Chidi a little while to come around (not that he really did anything violent), he does wind up agreeing with Eleanor's position and joining the Soul Squad.

Beauvoir points out that while there can be destructive or "negative" responses to nihilistic thinking, there can also be positive ones. A person can choose to embrace their newly confronted freedom to help others.[6] I don't want to put the cart before the horse, but this is what Chidi will be doing in the final episode of Season 3, "Pandemonium." For the time being, let's point out that Chidi's nihilistic attitude in "Jeremy Bearimy" is not entirely unfounded, but rather arises out of a sort of "half-baked" confrontation with reality. As Beauvoir points out, "The nihilistic attitude manifests a certain truth. In this attitude one experiences the ambiguity of the human condition."[7] As we will see in this chapter, ambiguity does not mean "meaninglessness." Quite the opposite: it means that human beings see meaning in things whether we want to or not. Even in a nihilistic collapse, we can still order a cup of coffee, or know where to find our sock drawer. What ambiguity gets at is the shiftiness of meaning; a sweater that means the world to me today, I might donate in six months. A person who is my best friend now might be persona non grata five years from now.

It turns out that in this middle period between the search for fundamental truths that exist independent of himself, and a sense of self-given purpose, Chidi is just adjusting to a misplaced sense of meaning. For the serious person, meaning exists *in the world* as an actual thing that can be lost or found. For the subjective individual and existential-ist, meaning is not found, it is made, or even *won*. For the nihilist, there is no meaning. The nihilist is partially correct. As Beauvoir points out, "The nihilist is right in thinking that the world *possesses* no justification and that he himself *is* nothing. But he forgets *that it is up to him* to justify the world and to make himself exist validly."[8] In this "between" realm, Chidi is *forgetting* that *he* has always given the world meaning, no matter where he mistakenly located it. So Chidi must confront his nihilism (and thank god Eleanor saves him before he eats the chili!) and *decide* to save souls.

There are only a handful of possible reactions to nihilism. One pos-sible reaction to this nihilism is to become an "adventurer," a person who acts just for the sake of acting. The adventurer wants to accumu-late experiences, mainly so she can say she has done so. Skydiving today, the Eiffel tower tomorrow. The adventurer uses his or her own freedom with no regard for "purpose," and so to that end remains somewhat nihilistic. While their acknowledgment of the universe hav-ing no purpose does not result in their paralysis, it does result in their own self-centeredness.[9]

Another, and preferable, possibility for returning from nihilism is for a person to "extend [her own freedom] by means of freedom of others." Such a person is "genuinely free."[10] For Beauvoir, the "free" person takes responsibility not only for her own evaluations, but also for using her choices toward "liberating"—making *more* free—her-self and others. Admittedly, this does seem to make freedom an objec-tive value for Beauvoir. However, because the very essence of freedom is its openness, its possibilities, this is not the same as the serious attitude that holds that there is one right answer to how to live. To be clear, for Beauvoir, whether we have freedom is not a metaphysical question, that is, a question of whether "freedom exists in the world at all," but rather an *existential* question: is this slave-wage laborer free? Is this person living under an authoritarian regime free? Are marginalized and oppressed people as free as I am? In other words, we must secure freedom for ourselves *and others* through our choices.

Reboot: Chidi's Positive Ambiguity

Beauvoir also makes a distinction between absurdity—that which has no meaning—and *ambiguity*—that which has no *fixed* meaning.[11] The latter, says Beauvoir, must be constantly "won," that is, made to be relevant to multiple people. Chidi, being a philosopher, is constantly trying to "win" someone's understanding and agreement, be it Eleanor's or the group's. Ironically, for most of the series he seems not willing to acknowledge the fluidity of his own positions, and his own values. Again, even if we can imagine one "right" answer to an ethical problem, there would be no way that we as mortals could ever know it.

Case in point is the counteractivity of unintended consequences. Consider one exchange from "The Book of Dougs." Here Chidi and Tahani are trying to see how points are assigned to actions. It occurs to Chidi that the real difference between a Doug in 1534 who brought roses to his grandmother and the Doug who did the same in 2009 is the *unintended* consequences. In the first case (1534), Doug picked the roses from the garden himself; in the second case (2009), Doug *lost* points:

> Because he ordered roses using a cell phone that was made in a sweatshop. The flowers were grown with toxic pesticides, picked by exploited migrant workers, delivered from thousands of miles away, which created a massive carbon footprint, and his money went to a billionaire racist CEO who sends his female employees pictures of his genitals. Whoo!

This serves to prove Chidi's position *in part*. To the extent that in the universe of *The Good Place* heaven and hell (aka "The Good Place" and "The Bad Place") actually *do* keep track of points attached to actions, one *could* argue that "there is an absolute and numerical answer to the best thing to do in any scenario" (if you Google "Jeremy Bentham," this comes oddly close to his version of utilitarianism). But the unfairness of the point system also serves to prove Beauvoir's point: given how complicated the world actually is, it would be impossible for a real human to actually *know* or figure out the right thing to do. For instance, Doug Forcett tried his whole life to do this, and look how that worked out for him.

What's more, in spite of the "sureness" of The Good Place's system, both Michael and the gang have the instinct that the points system is unfair. From what "ground" could they possibly contradict The Good Place's *absolute* value numerical system? From the ground of freedom. That is, there is an unfairness in assigning points to consequences that are virtually impossible to know. While this is not curtailing anyone's freedom per se, it is assuming a kind of knowledge that is all but impossible for human beings, thereby locking them into "evil" actions.

And given the variability of consequences, and the butterfly effect, taking ownership of those consequences becomes nearly impossible— or at the very least it becomes profoundly unfair to expect someone to take ownership of them. Here's where Beauvoir wins the day again: the group *decides* that they must *convince* The Good Place that the points system is unfair. The good news? They agree to look into it. The bad news? It will take 400 years to form the committee....

Pandemonium, or Not?

To see Chidi's growth by the end of Season 3, we must jump ahead a couple of episodes to the finale, "Pandemonium." Here we see that The Bad Place has cleverly tricked The Good Place and the gang into making their experiment—to show that humans can change for the better—doubly difficult by making the four subjects of the experiment related, in some way, to the original four. Tahani's charge is an internet troll who made her online life a living hell. And Chidi's charge is Simone, his ex-girlfriend from Earth. While the arrangement is made that *her* memory of Chidi will be erased, he will still remember her, and he becomes deathly (does that adjective work in The Good Place?) afraid that he will blow his cover and hence the entire experiment. Talking to Michael, Chidi and Eleanor explain:

CHIDI: Look, this isn't just me getting awkward around my ex. This is that if I get awkward around my ex, everyone gets tortured for-ever.

ELEANOR: If there were any other choice, we'd choose it.

However, for Chidi's memory to be erased prior to the point of his ex-girlfriend, he must also be made to forget *all* of what has happened with Eleanor and the rest of the gang. Here is where Chidi shows moral growth in the way of existentialism, methinks. For Beauvoir, existence and freedom are inextricably linked. This is why people who deny their own freedom are lying to themselves.[12] Any desire to *exist* is a desire *to be free*. We want to exist as beings who are—within rea-son—capable of deciding our own fates (when we are not pretending that we are not free). The converse is also true: the desire to *be free* is also the desire *to exist*. It may be obvious, but we cannot have any possibilities to do anything if we do not first exist. But there is one more important component here. If I am only desiring my freedom for my own sake, or worse yet, acting in a way that limits the freedom of others, I am not actually living up to my potential *to be free*. I am, in some ways, betraying the very notion of freedom as something that has to be lived and fostered. The reformed nihilist then, as Beauvoir is getting at, would do well to foster not only her own freedom, but also the freedom of others. This is an affirmation of both freedom and existence. For this reason, it's entirely possible for one to maximize her own freedom by sacrificing herself for the sake of others. This is exactly what Chidi is doing in "Pandemonium."

By sacrificing his own recent and cherished memories, Chidi is affirming not just his own freedom, but the freedom and potential "pleasure" of every existing human being. Beauvoir argues that the sacrifice of the hero is not a *renunciation* of the self and its freedom, but instead an affirmation of the future, and the freedom others can find in it.[13] Chidi argues:

> It won't be okay, which is why you *need to* erase my memory and reboot me.
> ...
> If we don't wipe my memory, I will, one way or the other, ruin the experiment. ("Pandemonium," emphasis added)

Chidi follows one of Beauvoir's favorite principles of existentialism: "Do what one must, come what may." In order to understand both Chidi's and Beauvoir's meaning of "must" we have to move away from an understanding of right and wrong as existing *in the world*, independent of human thought and assessment. The only "things" that *exist* in the world are human beings themselves. Instead, we must understand "must" and "need to" in terms of the pressing necessity of the person making the free choice to preserve the freedom of others. That is why existential ethics—an ethics of *ambiguity*—can be more demanding than other ethical systems (including the ones Chidi reviews in "Jeremy Bearimy"). It calls upon us to listen to and *act* upon our conscience—as opposed to waiting to find the correct answer out there. This is the real value of understanding ambiguity: it is not that it prevents us from deciding. Rather, it is only through realizing the power of *deciding for himself* that Chidi shows the power of ambiguity and escapes his paralytic indecision.

Getting to "The Answer"

Indeed, the hypothesis that Chidi's paralytic focus on certainty ("paralysis by analysis") is due to this desire for an "answer" is confirmed in Season 4, Episode 9 ("The Answer"). In a conversation with Jason, in the midst of his being rebooted, Chidi again introspects: "I just don't think I'll ever be the kind of person who just acts. I mean, I can't just open a door and walk through without knowing what's on the other side." Or when he says to Tahani: "I can't make a decision unless I'm sure I'm right."

But Chidi's "aha" moment comes in a conversation with Michael, after Chidi was forced to decide who his soulmate is.

MICHAEL: Turns out life isn't a puzzle that can just be solved one time and it's done. You wake up every day and you solve it again. Terribly inefficient.

CHIDI: Wow, what a time to learn.

Chidi then asks Janet for a pen and paper. Later we find he wrote: "There is no answer. Eleanor is the answer" ("The Answer").

It's difficult to imagine a more beautifully ambiguous idea. There is no one answer to most questions: what is the purpose of the universe? Who is my soul mate? But we create (or select) an answer for ourselves: Eleanor is Chidi's answer, because he chose it. Here we have excellent advice for couples as well. The answer to who our soulmate is—and Michael had previously confirmed to Chidi that soulmates probably don't even exist—is not one that is found in the confirmation of a certain answer, but instead in the assertion of a commitment. Eleanor is Chidi's answer because he makes it so, and he will wake up every day and have to "solve the puzzle"—make the commitment—again. And so Chidi and Michael teach us all a valuable lesson. We will be miserable, guilt-ridden, immobilized messes as long as we continue to hold that there is something out there, something out there that we cannot know, and that we won't be happy until we find it. But, as Chidi eventually works out, here's the thing about this complicated life of ours: there are not answers to be found, only answers to be chosen.

Notes

1   Simone de Beauvoir, *The Ethics of Ambiguity*, trans. Bernard Frechtman (Secaucus, NJ: Citadel Press, 1980), 45, emphasis added.

2   According to Beauvoir, "The serious man gets rid of his freedom by claiming to subordinate it to values which would be unconditioned," 46.

3   Ibid., 47.

4   Ibid., 51.

5   Ibid., 52.

6   Ibid., 55.

7   Ibid., 57.

8   Ibid., 57, emphasis added.

9   Ibid., 58–59.

10 Ibid., 60–61.

11 In her own words: "To declare that existence is absurd is to deny that it can ever be given a meaning; to say that it is ambiguous is to assert that its meaning is never fixed, that that it must be constantly won," 129.

12 Consider what Beauvoir says about the connection between freedom and existence: "there is a concrete bond between freedom and existence; to will man free is to will there to *be* being, it is to will the disclosure of being in the joy of existence; in order for the idea of liberation to a concrete meaning, the joy of existence must be asserted in each one, at every instant; the movement toward freedom assumes its real, flesh and blood in the world by thickening into pleasure, into happiness," 135.

13 Ibid., 106–107.

Beyond Good and Evil Places: Eternal Return of the Superhuman

James Lawler

"It's a warped version of Nietzsche's Eternal Recurrence," Chidi comments, having just learned that his life in "The Good Place" has been repeated 802 times after his fatal encounter with an air conditioner ("Dance, Dance Revolution"). Chidi's remark takes us to Friedrich Nietzsche's (1844–1900) famous book *The Gay Science*, where he asks the reader:

> What if some day or night a demon were to steal after you into your loneliest loneliness and say to you: "This life as you now live it and have lived it, you will have to live once more and innumerable times more; and there will be nothing new in it …" Would you not throw yourself down and gnash your teeth and curse the demon who spoke thus?[1]

Nietzsche's words are generally interpreted as proposing a test of a person's love of life. Those who would gnash their teeth and curse their fate at the thought of repeating the same life over and over again do not really love their lives. The person who passes the test, however, would say to the demon, "You are a god and never have I heard anything more divine." This person's life is so complete that she would be happy to relive it an infinite number of times. We should presumably aspire to having such an outlook, to live our lives as if they would be endlessly repeated.

The problem with this interpretation is that it is indeed a demon who proposes eternal return of the same life, *not* a god. *The Good Place* seemingly agrees, for the powers that would decree an eternal sameness are demonic, evil beings. What Nietzsche's demonic thought

The Good Place and Philosophy, First Edition. Edited by Kimberly S. Engels.

experiment calls a good life would actually be a life of self-satisfied complacency. It would involve a repetitiveness of pathetic, unproductive actions occurring over and over. We would be like hamsters turning on a wheel in the same place while thinking they are going forward. Isn't there more to a good life?

Aim for the Stars, for the Superhuman

In Nietzsche's philosophical novel, *Thus Spoke Zarathustra*, the central character is the prophet Zarathustra, also called Zoroaster, the founder of the Zoroastrian religion who lived over 2500 years ago. Zarathustra is still alive in Nietzsche's nineteenth-century Germany, or perhaps he has come back to life at least one more time, like the characters in *The Good Place*. But he has not come back to repeat his old life once more. He has come back to change the message he once taught about the final triumph of good over evil at the end of history. He is trying to outdo his old teachings and his old self.

Zarathustra calls individuals who live complacent, self-satisfied lives— lives they would be happy to live over and over again—the last humans. Warning his audience against such a possibility, Zarathustra says:

> Alas! The time will come when the human will no longer shoot the arrow of its yearning over beyond the human, and the string of its bow will have forgotten how to whirr!
>
> I say to you, one must still have chaos within, in order to give birth to a dancing star. I say to you, you still have chaos within you.
>
> Alas! The time will come when the human will give birth to no more stars. Alas! There will come the time of the most despicable human, who is no longer able to despise itself.
>
> Behold! I show you *the last human*.
>
> "What is love? What is creation? What is yearning? What is a star?"— thus asks the last human and then blinks.
>
> For the earth has now become small, and upon it hops the last human, who makes everything small. Its race is as inexterminable as the ground-flea. The last man lives the longest.
>
> "We have contrived happiness"—say the last humans, and they blink.[2]

The last humans are the ones who would be pleased at the demon's message. They have made happy lives for themselves—contented little lives, involving no awareness of a chaos within themselves, with no aspirations to something greater than themselves. Zarathustra calls this something greater that the last humans are missing the Superhuman. This is the target of the human who shoots "the arrow of its yearning over beyond the human."

Since George Bernard Shaw wrote his play *Man and Superman*, Nietzsche's term "Übermensch," literally "Overhuman," has come into English as "Superman." But it's not about a super *man*, or a superior human being, but rather a being who is superior to humans in general. Nietzsche's Superhuman is the next stage of evolution after the stage of humanity.

In defense of this idea, Zarathustra appeals to evolution. There is the evolution from primitive forms of life to more developed forms, from worm to ape to human. Should we think that humans are the end of the line? Are we so proud of our humanity that we can think of nothing better? Thinking that we are at the end of the line, the end of evolution or of history, is the kind of thinking that characterizes the last humans. But we *can* think of something better. The film *2001: A Space Odyssey* literally begins with apes overcoming themselves to become human—to the sound of Richard Strauss's musical composition titled *Thus Spoke Zarathustra*. The film ends with the rebirth of a space traveler as a "Star Child" on a moon of the planet Jupiter. Zarathustra is the prophet of the yearning for going beyond our merely human selves to which our current pop culture, with its X-Men and Marvel superheroes, appeals. *The Good Place* is an important component of this culture. Its main moral message is that human beings should aspire to go beyond themselves.

Demons Too Can Go beyond Themselves

The Archdemon Michael of *The Good Place* (not to be confused with the Archangel Michael of Christian teaching that he at first pretends to be) is put in charge of torturing humans whose lives fail to meet the standard required for getting into The Good Place—the place Christians call heaven. This standard is based on a point system in which all actions gain or lose points. All four characters selected for Michael's experiment—Eleanor, Chidi, Tahani, and Jason—have failed to achieve the requisite number of points for getting into The Real Good Place, and so they all wind up in The Bad Place—something like the Christian hell. Michael decides that it would be more interesting and more fun for the demons themselves to get the humans to torture each other. Endlessly smashing people with hammers, gouging out their eyes, and roasting them in volcanoes of fire can get pretty boring for the tormentors.

Michael's main idea is to put extreme opposite personalities together—egotistical, mind-in-the-gutter Eleanor with the selfless moral philosopher Chidi, the sophisticated world traveler Tahani with the simple-minded local boy Jason. The demon tells them they are in "The Good Place," and so have the soulmates that they have always yearned for and that their good lives on Earth have merited. But Michael's experiment is ruined by his subjects. The plan is for them to repeat endlessly the self-inflicted torture that their personalities would logically dictate, but they repeatedly foil Michael's scheme. They constantly become better than they were, and they learn to despise the narrowness of their previous lives. To Michael's surprise, the four *become* soulmates and friends as they help each other, and help other humans, to become better. Indeed, they eventually are able to recruit Michael himself to join their "Soul Squad." Zarathustra would say they are on the evolutionary path toward the Superhuman.

Eleanor Really Is Better than Others

On learning that she does not belong in what she believes is The Good Place, Eleanor thinks she is at least good enough for some kind of Medium Place. Her high school motto, after all, was "You're not better than me." This does not mean that she thinks she is a good person. Eleanor was always aware of the deficiencies of her behavior. In "Derek," she tells Chidi:

> Whenever I would do something on earth there would be a tiny voice in the back of my head saying, "Eleanor, don't grab that hand full of olives from the salad bar. You didn't pay for that. Or, Eleanor don't spit those olive pits on the grocery store floor. That's not cool. Or, Eleanor, that old man, he just slipped on your olive pit and he fell down. Don't use the fact that everyone is distracted to go back and steal more olives."

The meaning of Eleanor's high school yearbook motto is conveyed in a flashback to her arrival at a new high school in which she receives invitations to join various cliques. Fed up with others trying to get her to join them, she stands on top of a table in the cafeteria and announces: "I don't want to be a part of whatever group you've formed, because they're all equally lame." The title of the episode, "Someone Like Me as a Member," offers insight into what she means. Eleanor would not want to belong to any group that would have someone like her as a member. Implicitly following Zarathustra's notion that human beings are more ape than any ape, Eleanor not only despises others around her, she also despises herself. This is what sets her apart from others. She would not belong to any group that pretends to be better than others, as the various groups in her high school all claim to be. She really is better than others, paradoxically, because she knows she is *not* really a good person—contrary to what all the others falsely think about themselves.

When Eleanor comes to the end of her study of Nietzsche's philosophy, she tells Chidi: "I'm going to miss Nietzsche. I spent a lot of my life thinking I was better than everyone else, and he showed me why I was right" ("The Worst Possible Use of Free Will"). Zarathustra argues that by thinking they are the height of evolution, by looking down on the ape and also on other human beings who are not like them, humans are worse than the ape. Moved by an inner urge to become better, some apes have gone beyond themselves in giving rise to human beings. But as long as human beings think they are at the pinnacle of evolution, or living at the end of history, they are worse than apes, and even worse than worms. In despising others around her who believe in their superiority, while despising herself for failing to listen to the little voice within her, Eleanor is open to Zarathustra's teaching.

Eleanor failed to achieve the points required for getting into The Good Place, but she is not alone in that failure. It turns out that no one had gotten to The Good Place in over 500 years. Perhaps not coincidently, 500 years is the span of Western capitalist culture that has produced contemporary "globalization"—drawing the whole world into one orbit. For 500 years Western culture claimed to have achieved the highest possible civilization, and so to be the pinnacle of history. By thinking they are the end of evolution and human history, modern humans are in danger of giving birth to the last humans, whom Zarathustra compares to fleas. Unlike worms and apes, fleas do not aim at overcoming themselves. They are parasites who live by sucking the blood of their hosts. Fleas are like so many humans who derive their sense of superiority from looking down on others.

The Good Place according to Zarathustra is not the heaven that is depicted in many religions—a place where souls can settle down after gaining enough points in their lives to merit a great reward, and so never have to achieve anything more ever again. Chidi's idea of heaven is to float down a river with a bottle of wine and a book of French poetry. Eleanor's idea is to eat all the shrimp she wants, and fly in the sky. But how long can anyone be happy with endlessly repeating such fantasies? At the end of Season 4, we learn that The Real Good Place consists precisely in such fantasy fulfillment, and it turns out to be a crashing bore. The Real Good Place according to Zarathustra would be a world whose inhabitants strive to outdo themselves, as certain worms and apes have already done, but which modern humans are in danger of abandoning.

The Problem of Getting to The Good Place

This view of Eleanor's paradoxical superiority to others is contradicted by Simone, the neuroscientist. Simone is working with Chidi to investigate the physiological and moral implications of people who have nearly died. In their scientific and philosophical investigation, Chidi and Simone wrongly call this close encounter with death a "near-death experience." True NDEs are experiences in which individuals physically die, experience leaving their bodies, and then come back to life again. Such NDEs occur for our four heroes, since they do in fact leave their bodies and then come back to life again—and again, and again, hundreds of times. It is a warped form of Nietzsche's Eternal Return, says Chidi. But perhaps it is the true meaning of Eternal Return according to Zarathustra, since all four are using their cycles of lives to constantly overcome themselves, aiming at the coming of the Superhuman.

Simone does not believe in any kind of afterlife. As a neuroscientist, she believes that consciousness is nothing more than the functioning brain, and so consciousness could not survive the cessation of brain activity at death. The premise of *The Good Place*, however, is that souls do in fact survive the death of their bodies, and so Simone and her science are wrong about this crucial question. Chidi has to break up with Simone because he knows that there is an afterlife. He also knows about the point system necessary to avoid the tortures of The Bad Place for all eternity. The dilemma is that once people know what the system is, they will begin to do good things for the sake of the eternal reward and to avoid eternal punishment, and not because they are good in themselves. As an atheist, Simone's chances of getting to

The Good Place are much better than if she has this knowledge. Her motivation for doing good things will be pure, and not corrupted by the goal of getting to The Good Place. Here is a paradox of an afterlife of rewards and punishments. Believers are damned. Only nonbelievers can be saved.

(In Season 4 ["A Girl from Arizona," Parts 1 and 2], Simone finds herself in "The Good Place," having survived her death after all. Sticking to her philosophical/materialist guns, she doesn't believe what she witnesses. She thinks she must be hallucinating as an effect of her dying brain, and puts this theory into practice by pushing others around, including into swimming pools. She reevaluates her position when Chidi accuses her of committing the philosophical sin of solipsism, that very unscientific belief that everything the individual experiences is the product of the individual's consciousness. For the solipsist there would be no independent things to know, including the brain itself!)

Me versus Us

In "The Snowplow," Eleanor naively thinks that Simone, as a scientist, must have true knowledge, and goes to her for advice. Eleanor wants to know why she got so angry and walked out on the others. Simone replies:

> As humans evolve, the first big problem we have to overcome is me versus us, learning to sacrifice the little individual freedom for the group, like sharing food and resources so we don't starve and get eaten by tigers. Things like that.... The next problem to overcome is us versus them, trying to see other groups different from us as equals. That one we're still struggling with. That's why we have racism and nationalism.... What's interesting about you is I don't think you ever got passed the me versus us stage.... Have you ever been part of a group that you've really cared about?

We note that Simone's account of human history has no place for going beyond the present stage. Her highest ideal is a human equality that overcomes racism and nationalism. She argues that good human beings belong to groups, but unlike the groups that exist in Eleanor's high school, human groups should recognize that no group, no nation or race or any other similar grouping, is superior to any other. The groups that believe this are nevertheless superior to the groups that don't. Simone is a humanist, believing that nothing is better than a human being. Eleanor, however, has not even made it to the group stage of history.

This criticism hits home with Eleanor, who thinks she must have been determined by her upbringing in a loveless family, making her unlovable and incapable of loving others. In "The Worst Possible Use of Free Will," Michael tries to disabuse her of this notion by showing her that in one of the 802 afterlife reboots, she and Chidi fell in love: "So you get it, right?... You liked him, he liked you. You did nice things for each other. Your lack of parental affection did not make you numb to love, blah, blah, blah." In this exchange, Eleanor is convinced by the deterministic account of life, where people lack the free will to make decisions that are truly their own.[3] Determinism seems to follow from taking a scientific perspective—scientific explanations, after all, consist in explaining events by their causes. To say that someone acts on the basis of free will, rather than as part of a causal chain, seems to defy science. According to the definition of determinism that Eleanor reads from a philosophy book: "Determinism is the theory that we have no control over our own actions. Everything we do happens because of some external force which exists outside of our control." She tells Michael, "I didn't *choose* to fall in love with Chidi, because some all-knowing demon, you, brought us together and scripted our lives."

Michael provides a refutation of this perspective by showing Eleanor how she constantly defied his expectations, culminating in her standing up before the neighbors in the Good Place neighborhood and taking responsibility for the actions that she believed were destroying the harmony that was supposed to prevail there. She did this despite her belief that she would be damned to eternal torture as a result. "I tried to script your whole afterlife. I devised a fifteen mil-lion point plan to torture you." Michael concludes, "You made choices I never saw coming. I call that free will.... I put you and Chidi in close proximity because I needed you to drive each other crazy. But I never intended for you to fall in love."

Eleanor eventually *does* listen to the little voice within her, the voice of her conscience. It's this inner voice, connected with a longing to go beyond ourselves, that Zarathustra calls "the will to power." Living beings do not evolve because outside forces compel them to evolve, as deterministic science argues, but because they sense an inner chaos and choose to follow an inner urge to expand their power over themselves. It is this choice to go beyond themselves that propelled certain worms and apes, and that ought to propel us to want to go beyond mere humanity.

The End of History?

In arguing against Eleanor's deterministic account of her life, Michael is implicitly disagreeing with Simone's diagnosis of Eleanor's problem. Simone has her own theory of superiority. Those who are engaged in the struggle for human equality are superior to those who think their group is better than others. But those who belong to groups are superior to individualists, such as Eleanor, who do not belong to groups, who take a stand against such belonging.

Zarathustra also proposes a theory of human history that includes a stage of animal-like humans foraging on their own, a stage involving identification with groups that think they are superior to each other, and a stage in which human equality becomes the dominant value. Though it hasn't been achieved, we seem to have entered the epoch of the pursuit of equality as an ideal. The US Declaration of Independence proclaims: "All men are created equal." The UN Universal Declaration of Human Rights begins: "Whereas recognition of the inherent dignity and of the equal and inalienable rights of all members of the human family …"[4] These declarations are translations in secular terms of the teaching of Jesus that all human beings, men and women of all races, are children of one God, and so should love one another. In the name of Christianity, however, Western nations have colonized the rest of the world, beginning the phase of history that today we call "globalization." In the past 500 years the Western nations that proclaim the teaching of human equality in their religion have betrayed it in their practices. The US Constitution of 1787 legitimized slavery and deprived women of the right to vote. The top 1% in the United States today has more wealth than the bottom 90%. Some beneficiaries of the world system have more wealth than entire nations. And so, because of this hypocrisy erected into a world order, during the whole time of this Western egalitarian idealism no one has gotten to The Good Place.

Most would agree we should be consistent with our commitment to human equality. But then what? With no great goal beyond our humanity, we are in danger of becoming parasitical last men and women, taking satisfaction from our superiority to previous human groupings, but going nowhere ourselves.

If Zarathustra is right, there is a greater possibility for humanity than completing the stage of equality at which we currently find ourselves. There is the stage of overcoming humanity itself, the stage of aiming at Superhumanity. Zarathustra asks us seriously to question the theory of evolution—from worm to ape to human. Does it make sense to think that it all stops with us humans?

If not, then there is room in the theory of history for a new stage, the stage of going beyond egalitarian humanism. This is the stage of individualists who, like Eleanor, despise belonging to groups that think they are better than others. This includes the group of egalitarians of Western societies, including Simone, who for the last 500 years have thought that with their science and technologies, their moral and political ideals, they have essentially reached the end of history.

Beyond Good and Evil Places

Eleanor longs to belong to a group that is different from those of her high school cliques. She finds this group in her Soul Squad, composed of misfits like herself, Chidi, Tahani, and Jason, including the demon Michael and the Informational Assistant Janet. This group is different from the other groups in that it recognizes its deficiencies, seeks to become better than what it was before, and inspires others to do the same. Indeed, this group has gone beyond the Good and Bad Places and their broken promise of a life without struggle. Chidi longs to float down a river, read poetry, and sip wine—forever enjoying the reward for his high point score. But he eventually learns that this goal is not only impossible but demeaning.

In "Jeremy Bearimy," Chidi meets a drug dealer who promises a shortcut to such a heaven, asking, "Want to talk to God?" Chidi replies:

> God is dead. God remains dead and we have killed him. Who will wipe this blood off of us? What festivals of atonement, what sacred games shall we have to invent?" Friedrich Nietzsche, 1882.[5]

Chidi quotes from Nietzsche's *The Gay Science*, with its demonic thought experiment about eternal sameness, which is the goal of most religions. At the end of Season 4, we learn that The Real Good Place, the heaven of religions, consists precisely in such sameness. The eternal repetition of the individual's wish fulfillment turns everyone into a "happiness zombie." Zarathustra provides the answer to the death of a goal that humanity has long cherished, the goal of eternal bliss in an unearthly afterlife, and so of never having to struggle and strive again. The alternative is a new goal, in which we human beings strive to overcome ourselves, aiming at the stars, aiming at the Superhuman.

In Season 4 Chidi has gone through one more reboot, as well as an intense review of his more than 800 afterlife lifetimes. The effect has been a deepened confidence in himself. "You're cool, confident Chidi now," Eleanor tells him ("Mondays, Am I Right?"). Chidi has become a new person. He no longer oscillates between abstract logical possibilities, and acts confidently on his certainty that his love for Eleanor is real and true. He still has goals to realize: answering the deepest philosophical questions, "Why?" and "How?" ("Patty"). Why is there something rather than nothing? How did the universe come into being? There is a third question, however, whose answer Chidi implicitly knows: "What for?" What is the purpose of life? Nietzsche's Zarathustra supplies the answer that underlies most of *The Good Place*: endless self-development, eternal overcoming of oneself.

However, in "Whenever You're Ready," the bittersweet final episode, Chidi gives up his quest as mere rational superficiality, and seeks a mystical solution to all questions in the nothingness of Buddhist Nirvana, in the disappearance of the little wave that he sees himself as being in an unknowable infinite sea. But this is essentially no different from the self-complacency of Zarathustra's "last men," epitomized by Michael's final words after he has become a little human himself: "Take it sleazy." Zarathustra teaches that we must despise and overcome the littleness of our ordinary human goals, and become a sea ourselves. "Behold I teach you this Overhuman. It is this sea, in this can your great despising submerge itself."[6] Thus spoke Zarathustra.

Notes

1 Friedrich Nietzsche, *The Gay Science*, trans. Walter Kaufmann (New York: Vintage Books, 1974), #341, 273.
2 Friedrich Nietzsche, *Thus Spoke Zarathustra*, trans. Graham Parkes (New York: Oxford University Press, 2005), Prologue #5, 15.
3 For a detailed discussion of free will and determinism, see Joshua Tepley, "What's the Use of Free Will?" Chapter 23, this volume.
4 United Nations, "Declaration of Human Rights," https://www.un.org/en/udhrbook/pdf/udhr_booklet_en_web.pdf.
5 Chidi cites Nietzsche, *The Gay Science*, #125, p. 181.
6 Nietzsche, *Thus Spoke Zarathustra*, Prologue, #3, 12.

Part VII

"THE DALAI LAMA
TEXTED ME THAT"

18

Conceptions of the Afterlife: *The Good Place* and Religious Tradition

Michael McGowan

The Good Place is based on the idea of an afterlife. But how does it work? What's the metaphysical machinery of the show? Presumably, Eleanor, Chidi, Tahani, and Jason have immaterial essences that manifest themselves in recognizable ways after their bodies die. We can call these disembodied essences "souls," or "minds," or "spirits," or whatever. After we die, at least on the show, our souls go places and do things.

Speculation regarding the afterlife is well-trodden territory in the history of Western philosophy. Plato (428–348 BCE), for example, offers several afterlife teachings. In Plato's *Phaedo*, *Gorgias*, and the *Republic*, the character of Socrates tells stories of people who die, get sorted, and, based on the quality of their lives, get sent to a good place as a reward for their virtue or to a bad place as punishment for their vices.

But Plato wrote well over two thousand years ago, and myths are not nearly as persuasive as they used to be. Many thinkers today believe the physical, material, natural world is all that exists. If there's no immaterial world, there's no need to take the idea of God or an afterlife seriously. When your body dies, it's all over. Atheist philosophers may still take death seriously, but only as a way to measure the quality of their lives. This is the approach taken by the show's philosophical consultant and guest in the series finale ("Whenever You're Ready"), Todd May. In his book *Death*, May writes, "For the record, I am an atheist (which is why I don't believe in an afterlife)."[1] Conceptions of the afterlife today are almost exclusively the domain of the world's great religious traditions.

Why Religion, and Which One?

Making sense of *The Good Place* from the perspective of traditional religion is a bit tricky. Within the first five minutes of the pilot, Michael tells Eleanor that the afterlife does not neatly map onto any of the world's religions, which were all only "a little bit right ... about five percent." Even if we accept that Michael's sole purpose during the first season was to deceive and torment the Soul Squad, there are indications that he was not lying to her about the metaphysics of the show and its relation to the world's religions. After Michael's moral conversion, for example, they visit Doug Forcett because he got it 92% right, implying that the world's religions got it wrong.

Even if the show permits a religious interpretation, it challenges the one that may come most naturally to Western viewers. When everyday Americans and Europeans think about the category of "religion," most imagine the Abrahamic faiths of Judaism, Christianity, and Islam. The writers of *The Good Place* are certainly aware of the ways in which these monotheistic traditions understand the afterlife. When Chidi enters his colleague's lecture hall in "The Eternal Shriek" to reluctantly receive his red boots, Chidi's colleague has given a lecture on "eschatology," the study of the "last things," and the blackboard is replete with Jewish and Christian understandings of the apocalypse and what happens after we die.

However, none of the Abrahamic faiths really fits the world of *The Good Place* for several reasons. Whereas the entire show is predicated on the existence of an afterlife, the Hebrew Bible (aka the Old Testament) simply does not discuss an afterlife much. When it does, the authors use the Hebrew word *sheol*. Scholars are divided on what the ancient word means, and the Hebrew Bible suggests that it is a destination for both good and bad people alike with no concern for the moral quality of one's life.[2] Nor is the Soul Squad's experience Christian. It is certainly true that Christians believe in an afterlife, which usually takes the form of rewards doled out in a good place (heaven) and punishments in a bad place (hell) in response to living and/or believing rightly. It is also true that the afterlife is discussed in the New Testament (especially in the Johannine literature[3]). But the show has no discussion of central Christian theological doctrines of atonement, forgiveness of sins, or eschatology beyond what was written on Chidi's colleague's blackboard. Finally, although *The Good Place* and Islam both emphasize the value of living well, there is no discussion of central Muslim concepts like Jinn, Shirk, or the Day of

Days/Judgment/Reckoning. Nor do members of the Soul Squad lie in wait, unconscious in their graves until the physical resurrection on the Day of Judgment, as in Islamic teaching.[4]

Asian Religions and *The Good Place*

Rather than reflecting the Abrahamic religious traditions, the metaphysics of *The Good Place* share similarities with the Asian (aka Eastern) religions of Hinduism and Buddhism. Hinduism is the predominant religion in India, the third largest religion in the world by numbers (over 1 billion adherents), and one of the world's oldest religious traditions. Buddhism is an offshoot of Hinduism that now has over half a billion followers, and it is growing quickly through "mindfulness" movements in Western countries. Although both "Hinduism" and "Buddhism" are convenient categories that cover a variety of religious beliefs and rituals, we can speak of some family resemblances that permit us to posit three interrelated concepts that situate *The Good Place* among them: time, karma, and reincarnation.

First, in *The Good Place*, time works like it does in the Asian religious traditions. In the Abrahamic faiths time moves linearly from the pre-existence of souls to incarnation and life, to death, and to an afterlife, but in *The Good Place*, time does not move in a straight line at all. Comedically, this is shown through "Jeremy Bearimy," the warped timeline introduced in the episode of same name. Time in *The Good Place* is cyclical, folds in on itself, meanders, and circles back. Some moments even exist fragmented from the rest of the timeline altogether. Sometimes the "i" in "Bearimy" represents "Tuesdays, and also July … [or occasionally] the moment when nothing never occurs." At the end of Season 3, Chidi finally accepts the timelessness of reality, saying, "Time means nothing." He and Eleanor make plans to "chill out" in that timeless space together, forever. In the series finale, "Bearimy" becomes the unit by which time itself is measured (which, one could argue, undermines the claim that the Bearimy is itself nonlinear, but I digress).

In Asian religions, time also acts in nonlinear ways. While not as meandering as the Bearimy timeline, in Asian religions time is cyclical for individuals who live, die, and are reborn, and also for worlds, galaxies, and universes. Not only does time operate cyclically, but it also slows down to the point of not really passing at all. According to an ancient Indian story,

The Himalayas ... are made of solid granite. Once every thousand years a bird flies over them with a silk scarf in its beak, brushing their peaks with its scarf. When by this process the Himalayas have been worn away, one day of a cosmic cycle will have elapsed.[5]

Billions of years are compressed into one day of a cosmic cycle for Hinduism. What's more, there have been billions of cosmic days before the current one, and there will be billions of days after. Somewhat similarly, for the Soul Squad, three hundred years can pass in an instant, and they are given an opportunity to make different choices.

This brings us to the next similarity with the Asian religions, the method for sorting the good people from bad. In the pilot, Michael tells the community about the "Point System." He explains:

[D]uring your time on earth, every one of your actions had a positive or a negative value, depending on how much good or bad that action put into the universe.... Every single thing you did had an effect that rippled out over time and ultimately created some amount of good or bad.... When your time on earth has ended, we calculate the total value of your life using our perfectly accurate measuring system. Only the people with the very highest scores, the true cream of the crop, get to come here, to the Good Place.... You are here because you lived one of the very best lives that could be lived.

When the Soul Squad reaches the Accounting Department, they are told that an action is judged and assigned a point value based on "use of resources, the intentions behind it, its effects on others." The point value is then checked by 3 billion other accountants who always get the same score for the action, and then it's official. "The math is cold, objective, and airtight," says Neil ("Janet(s)").

The idea that earthly actions have consequences for the afterlife mirrors the notion of *karma*, "the moral law of cause and effect"[6] believed by both Hindus and Buddhists. The doctrine of *karma* states that one reaps what one sows, both now and in the future. Present suffering is attributable to past wrongs, and future suffering is attributable to present wrongs. In "Flying," Eleanor steals shrimp and wakes up the following day to find shrimp swimming through the sky.

According to Huston Smith (1919–2016), if *karma* is metaphysically true, then this entails the truth of two other principles: first, a strong commitment to personal responsibility; and, second, that concepts like "luck," "chance," and "accident" are fabrications designed by morally weak people to delude themselves from the painful truth that they are, in fact, morally weak.[7] This is not fatalism (the view that we have a fate we can't escape no matter what), however, because although one is dealt a certain hand, one has freedom to play that hand as one pleases. The will may be influenced, but it is not controlled by the law of *karma*. The table was set for the Soul Squad in the world of *The Good Place,* but no one controlled their choices once they got there. Michael takes great pains to demonstrate the reality of human choices to Eleanor in "The Worst Possible Use of Free Will," when he shows her clips from past afterlives to help her realize that although she had been influenced, her choices were not scripted.

These two ideas—(1) the nonlinear nature of time and (2) the law of *karma*—create another feature of Asian religions common to both Hindus and Buddhists, namely, reincarnation. The idea of reincarnation is simple: when one body dies, a person is placed into a new body with a new social situation determined by one's past life. In Seasons 2 and 3 of *The Good Place*, the Soul Squad is given hundreds of opportunities to make different choices, each reincarnation leading to growth, adaptation, and moral improvement.[8] And in Season 4, reincarnation becomes officially codified in the new system: life becomes not a *test* but rather a *classroom*, and the afterlife becomes not a place of reward and punishment but a *test* one can take over and over again. This "test" may look "just like your regular life," says Michael ("You've Changed, Man"), but the goal is moral improvement. Both Hindus and Buddhists believe in reincarnation as a metaphysical reality. In a Buddhist text, one character sees that "the decease and rebirth of beings depend on whether they have done superior and inferior deeds.... Over and over again they are born, they age, die, pass on to a new life, and are reborn."[9] Or, as expressed in the *Bhagavad Gita*, a Hindu text: "Worn-out garments are shed by the body: worn-out bodies are shed by the dweller."[10] The term for this seemingly endless cycle of birth, death, and rebirth is *samsara*.

Indian Philosophy, Hindu Religion, and *The Good Place*

Hindus and Buddhists both believe in reincarnation, but their understandings of it are *very* different. In fact, the matter over which they disagree is central to understanding which of the Asian religions *The Good Place* is most like. The key question is this: what exactly gets reborn? In answering this, we are inevitably drawn to the doctrine that separates Hindus from Buddhists, the concept of an immaterial essence, the *soul*.

Consider first the Buddhist idea of the "no-self" or "no-soul," what they refer to as *anatta*. According to this core Buddhist doctrine, the appearance of a person in her multiform complexity does not mean that there is some essential or unified "self" underneath. For the Buddhist, there is no "ghost in the machine," no immaterial "driver" controlling the vehicle of the body, no thinker of thoughts who is distinct from the thoughts it has. Using Buddhist imagery, just as one might observe bubbles floating down the Ganges River and realize there is nothing inside the bubbles, "the student of the Buddha beholds all corporeal phenomena, sensations, perceptions, moods, and thoughts.... He watches them, examines them carefully; and, after carefully examining them, they appear to him empty, void and without a self."[11] For Buddhists, there is "no self" in there. That's why some Japanese Zen paintings represent the self as a black circle with an empty middle: there's no one in there, just an ever-shifting, always-in-flux conglomeration of impressions.

Now, compare this Buddhist understanding with a Hindu one. Contrary to Buddhism, in Hinduism someone really is "in there." Hindus have two words that express different understandings of the soul: the first word, *jina*, refers to the part of the self that is contained in the body; and the second word, *atman*, refers to the part of the self that transcends corporeal boundaries. According to the *Katha Upanishad* and other sacred Hindu texts, one's inner *atman* is not an illusion, but rather a real and distinct thing.[12] In Hinduism, reincarnation continues until a person's *atman* is liberated from its corporeal existence, a process known as *moksha*.

In Buddhism there is no atman, no "self" or "soul" to be reborn from one body to the next. So how can reincarnation make sense in Buddhism? Here we will mention just one potential reply: there are ways to speak about the self or soul that don't require it to be one unified thing but *do* allow it to be reborn. If this is true, the self is like a pile of sand or a ball of yarn. The pile and ball are real, but upon closer inspection, they are made of other smaller parts that may present themselves to the world as one thing. Buddhists refer to the reincarnated "stuff" as *skandas*, a point the Buddha drove home to help his followers remove their desires and attachments, thereby contributing to enlightenment. Buddhists extend this notion of flux beyond the self to the entire universe. Thus, there is a kind of impermanent permanence in which the world is always in flux, consistently inconsistent.

According to this Buddhist doctrine (*anicca*), not only humans, but *everything*, lacks an essence. "Regard this phantom world as a star at dawn, a bubble in a stream," the Buddha taught, "a flash of lightning in a summer cloud. A flickering lamp—a phantom—and a dream."[13]

In light of the fact that the Soul Squad is having an actual afterlife experience, and in light of the fact that the four humans certainly seem to remain unified through time despite the resetting of their memories, we can conclude that *The Good Place* is closer to a Hindu version of reality than a Buddhist one. Some immaterial essence, a soul, really moves from one iteration of the self to the next. Whereas the Buddhist tradition advocates *anatta*, the Hindu tradition posits an inner *atman* to refer to the soul that is reborn.

The Good Place mirrors the Hindu tradition not only in reincarnation but also in the identification of the right "aims" or "goals" of life. Hinduism suggests that there are four aims in life, the first two of which fall on the Path of Desire. The first aim in life is pleasure: pure, unalloyed, sensory stimulation—food, drink, sex, and so on. This, of course, is the problem that confronts Jason, who struggles with impulse control, and Eleanor, who struggles with selfishness. Eleanor was preoccupied only with her own pleasure (for example, getting drunk before she could be the Designated Driver and "banging it out" with a hot bartender). In the Hindu tradition, pleasure is not inherently bad or evil. In fact, the religion offers suggestions on how to attain it (see the *Kama Sutra*) if, indeed, that is what one wants. However, the Hindu tradition also cautions that focusing one's life on pleasure will be ultimately unsatisfying because pleasure is fleeting and overly concerned with the self. A person's focus—herself and her own desires—is too small.

If one moves from pleasure to the next goal in the Hindu Path of Desire, success, one seeks wealth, power, and/or fame. These are not bad in themselves, argues Indian philosophy, but just as with pleasure, if one pursues them exclusively one will not be satisfied. On this much, Hindus are still in agreement with Buddhists. Part of the "core doctrine" given in the Buddha's first sermon involves seeing one's desires and then realizing that one must remove those desires.[14] Hinduism offers a different explanation for why our typical desires are unsatisfying, however. Desire itself is not the problem in Hinduism, but rather desiring the wrong things for an inappropriate duration. The image of a donkey moving forward because its driver mounted a carrot atop its harness originated in ancient Hindu texts.[15] Pursuing success exclusively has terrible consequences, Hindu philosophy tells us, because it focuses on an entity too small to give true fulfillment (the self). In *The Good Place*, Tahani's fundraisers and name-dropping were attempts to succeed, but she ended up in The Bad Place because her focus was always on what her success afforded her: acceptance in her parents' eyes and the eyes of those around her. Tahani conveys this to John in Season 4's "Chillaxing," when she says, "I was so obsessed with status" but "if all you care about in the world is the velvet robe, you will always be unhappy."

Only when one makes the journey from the Path of Desire to the Path of Renunciation does one begin to make real progress in Hinduism. The third aim of life on the Hindu journey is, therefore, much more satisfying to the person who has become disillusioned with selfishness. Instead of success, one pursues service to others. When pursuing this third aim of life, the self begins to expand, and not in ways that jeopardize the success of others. This is not compassion as Buddhists understand it; nor is it a "no greater love than laying one's life down for one's friends" sort of thing. This is duty, plain and simple. Clearly, *The Good Place* shows the value of this sort of moral progress. More than once, Eleanor sacrifices her own happiness and success for her friends, to the point of accepting her fate in The Bad Place, which finally increases her Point Count (her *karma*). What's more, after the Judge tests the four in "The Burrito," Eleanor is the only one who passes the test. But for the benefit of the other three, she turns down her opportunity to go to The Real Good Place. Only the Judge knows her selflessness in that moment. Eleanor acts in service to the other three.

Duty, though, is not the final goal of life on the Path of Renunciation in Hinduism. The whole point of the Hindu tradition is that the soul, the inner *atman*, seeks release from the strictures of the never-ending cycle. In short, the self seeks to be liberated and join the Infinite. Nothing short of this realization can really satisfy a person. Chidi, exemplar of others-centered, duty-driven behavior, represents the ultimate futility of duty to others. Nothing in this world, not even duty to others, not even the greatest Goodness, Truth, and Beauty, can ultimately satisfy a person. When one realizes that all earthly pursuits will inevitably result in this same unfulfilling cycle, Smith says, "This is the moment Hinduism has been waiting for."[16] In this moment, the self wants to join not only that which is larger, or even much larger, but infinitely larger. The final goal of life in Hinduism is *moksha*, release from the endless cycle of birth, life, death, decay, and rebirth.

This is the point at which the shackles of the world no longer hold a person, and the person approaches *infinite* being, *infinite* bliss, and *infinite* knowledge. The interesting point Hinduism makes is that this infinite is already inside a person. It is their inner *atman,* or "soul," connecting with the God of the Universe, or *Brahman.* In Hinduism, the self realizes it is one with the cosmic Self. In short, not even duty to others allows one to realize that one was a god all along. Chidi makes this clear using the Buddhist imagery of a wave retreating back into the ocean in the final episode ("Whenever You're Ready"), but this is a thoroughly Hindu concept as well.

In *The Good Place,* each character, in his or her own way, prepares for their release from the cycle of *samsara,* and each has come to accept reality as it is, accepting whatever their afterlives throw at them.[17] In Hinduism, recognizing the *oneness of all that is* enables a new kind of life here and now. It enables a person to see others as sources of divine light, to consider *who* they are, not what their current circumstances might look like. The Indian greeting *namaste* simply means, "The divinity within me salutes the divinity within you." And if the Soul Squad has shown viewers of *The Good Place* one thing, it's that relationships that are initially difficult can turn into something beautiful by the end, so much so that a person is willing to sacrifice everything to maintain them. Through all of the drama, "The soul's progress through these ascending strata of human wants does not take the form of a straight line with an acute upward angle," Huston Smith says, but rather "it fumbles and zigzags its way toward what it really needs."[18] And according to *The Good Place* and Hinduism, what a soul really needs is to be released and reunited with the infinite universe.

Meaning Making and Religious Pluralism

In the end, we may ask the same question Eleanor does at the start of the show: which of the world's religious stories will end up being right about the afterlife, if any of them? This question has given birth to three main perspectives: exclusivism, according to which only one religion is true and the rest false; inclusivism, according to which one religion is true but adherents of the others will partake in its benefits;[19] and finally pluralism, according to which there are either many paths up the same afterlife summit or multiple summits to which people go.

Neither *The Good Place* creators nor the best philosophers today can answer this question definitively for us before we experience the afterlife for ourselves. The religious journey is one that individuals and communities must take for themselves. But surely, we can appreciate the manifold ways in which great art invites us to ponder such questions. We would do well to remember that the search is worthwhile on its own, and perhaps *not* knowing also has its rewards, as Michael's journey illustrates in the finale, when he chooses to live as a human. In the words of Janet in "Pandemonium," "If there were an answer I could give you to how the universe works, it wouldn't be special. It would just be machinery, fulfilling its cosmic design.... But since nothing seems to make sense, when you find something or someone that does, it's euphoria.... Isn't that remarkable?" Eleanor, speaking for all of us trying to appreciate the journey, simply says, "I guess all I can do is embrace the pandemonium, find happiness in the unique insanity of being here. Now."

Notes

1   Todd May, *Death* (New York: Routledge, 2014), 19.
2   Christopher M. Moreman, *Beyond the Threshold: Afterlife Beliefs and Experiences in World Religions*, 2nd ed. (Lanham, MD: Rowman & Littlefield, 2018), chap. 2.
3   See, e.g., John 3:16, 5:24, 5:28–29, 11:25, 14:2–3; Rev. 1:18, 20:11–15.
4   Qur'an 17:100, 30:40.
5   Huston Smith, *The World's Religions* (New York: Harper One, 1991), 64.
6   Ibid., 68.
7   Ibid., 64–65.
8   This can be compared to Nietzsche's eternal recurrence, as discussed by James Lawler, "Beyond Good and Evil Places: Eternal Return of the Superhuman," Chapter 17, this volume.
9   Edward Conze, trans., "The Buddhacarita of Ashvaghosha," in *Buddhist Scriptures* (London: Penguin, 1959), 49–51.
10 *Bhagavad Gita*, II:22.
11 See, e.g., Sumyutta Nikāya 22.95 in Nyanatiloka Mahathera's edition and translation, *The Word of the Buddha* (Kandy, Sri Lanka: Buddhist Publication Society, 1981), 12.
12 See, e.g., Katha II, IV, and V in Juan Mascaro's edition and translation of *The Upanishads* (London: Penguin, 1965), 9–15, 19–20, 24, 59–60, and 63–64.

13 *Vairacchedika*, 32.

14 See, e.g., the Buddha's first sermon: Samyutta Nikāya 56.11 in Nanamoli Thera's translation of the *Dhammacakkappavattana Sutta* ("Setting Rolling the Wheel of Truth"), in *Three Cardinal Discourses of the Buddha* (Kandy, Sri Lanka: Buddhist Publication Society, 1972), 7–8.

15 Smith, 16.

16 Ibid., 20.

17 This is one of the other ways in which *The Good Place* represents the Hindu tradition: each character is on his/her own journey toward the Infinite, and it connects to the various "yogas" suggested in Indian philosophy: Eleanor repeatedly sacrifices her afterlife in The Real Good Place for the bad because of her friends, like India's "way of love"; Chidi embraces the "way of knowledge"; Tahani's is the way of work; and Jason, who is hardest to fit into one of the Hindu yogas, is perhaps closest to the "way of psychophysical exercise." After all, Jason is in a 60-person dance crew.

18 Smith, 66.

19 For example, twentieth-century Catholic thinker Karl Rahner argued that there are "anonymous Christians," people who do not profess Christianity but who, nonetheless, will be redeemed. For Rahner and other inclusivist Christians, God is in the business of salvation whether a person realizes it or not.

19
Who Are Chidi and Eleanor in a Past-(After)Life? The Buddhist Notion of No-Self

Dane Sawyer

> You should abandon desire for whatever is non-self.... You should abandon desire for whatever does not belong to self.
>
> —Buddha[1]

In "Janet(s)," an episode from Season 3, Eleanor tells Chidi that she has seen past reboots of their lives as "soulmates" when they were in The Good Place's neighborhood. Particularly surprising for Eleanor is the discovery that she and Chidi were in love in at least one of those reboots. Rather than welcome such news with excitement and enthusiasm (as Eleanor hopes), Chidi simply dismisses the importance of their past life together, claiming that while some person loved Eleanor, it is not the current Chidi, and thus cannot be the "real Chidi." In sum, Chidi claims that because he has no memory of that event, the Chidi who fell in love with Eleanor cannot be the "real Chidi."

As Chidi rightly suggests to Eleanor, this is a classic example of the philosophical issue of personal identity. In the show, Chidi appeals to philosophers John Locke (1632–1704) and Derek Parfit (1942–2017) to help clarify the philosophical conundrum for Eleanor, Jason, and Tahani. But it might be more helpful to consider early Buddhist thought.

Buddhism comes up several times in *The Good Place*. Jason Mendoza's early persona is Jianyu (a Buddhist monk who on Earth took a vow of silence). Eleanor writes a paper for Chidi on dharma, and the concept of karma is mentioned occasionally. Tahani becomes a Tibetan Buddhist monk and lives in a monastery for a time. David Hume (1711–1776) is mentioned as holding a similar view of the self as Buddhism. Perhaps most importantly, in the last episode of the series, Chidi directly uses the wave analogy from Buddhism to explain his decision to leave The Good Place.

According to Buddhism, what we think of as a "self" or "soul" is merely a convenient designator, a useful fiction, that doesn't correspond to any actual thing in the world. In fact, the Buddhist view might be right. Neuroscientists have poked around the brain in search of a self or soul, but they have never found a "self" running the show.[2] If Buddhism is right that there is no self, a number of interesting problems arise for Chidi and Eleanor as they attempt to figure out who the "real Chidi" is.

Would the "Real Chidi" Please Stand Up?

> Why do you assume 'a person'?
> ...[Y]ou have adopted a wrong speculative view.
> This is only a heap of processes
> There is no person to be found here.
> —Buddha[3]

When we wake up in the morning, we do not worry about whether we are the same person we were yesterday and will be tomorrow. I personally don't expect to go to bed one night and wake up the next day as a mirror centaur, a flying shrimp, or a Janet. Why? One obvious answer is that I have an essence, some part of me that continues to exist, day after day, and this is what the word "I" refers to. This essence could either be a particular part of me (such as my mind or soul), or it might refer to me as a whole person.

What it means to be a person is complicated. Consider this simple sentence: she is the same person but not the same. When we say she is the "same person," we mean she is a separate, individual person, with a particular body, that is numerically distinct from someone else. For example, Jason is one person, Tahani another. On the other hand, when we say a person is "not the same," we usually mean the person has undergone some qualitative difference, for instance, that her personality, characteristics, or preferences have changed. In other words, what makes someone qualitatively unique is what that person is like. On the show, Eleanor is trying to become qualitatively different by becoming a better person; she is trying to change so that she will no longer be the person she used to be. In short, she is the "same person" who wants to "not be the same."

This raises a philosophical problem: how much of one's essence would have to change before that person would no longer be the same person? Think about it: how much do you have in common with the toddler version of you, the 10-year-old you, the teenager you, and so forth? In some ways, you are obviously different, in others, similar, and maybe in some ways the same. Some people reflect back on earlier times and are ashamed of the person they used to be. This reaction only makes sense if there is some enduring, permanent part of them. So how can Buddhism respond?

The Buddhist Critiques of the Self: What the "Fork" Is a "Chidi"?

> When matter, feeling, perception, formations, [and] consciousness exist, it is through clinging to consciousness, through insisting upon (interpreting) consciousness, that such a view as this arises: "This is mine, this is I, this is my self."
>
> —Buddhaghosa[4]

Buddhism rejects what many Western and Eastern traditions call the self or soul. For Buddhists, instead, there are "five aggregates," or pieces, that make up what we commonly call our selves. When we bring these five aggregates together, we may experience the illusion or sense of self, but if we look closer we won't find a self at all. Rather, we will just find these five aggregates: form, feeling, perception, mental formations, and consciousness. Form (*rūpa*) is anything corporeal or physical, namely the body. Our bodies are one identifier that distinguishes who we are, a way of recognizing that we are talking to Jason or Tahani, and not Chidi or Eleanor.

Feeling (*vedanā*) is a little trickier to explain. In English, we often use the word "feeling" to refer to intuitions, emotions, and sensations, but when Buddhists use the term "feeling," they simply mean the sensations we experience, which are categorized as pleasant, unpleasant, or neutral. If a feeling is pleasant, we tend to grasp for it; if unpleasant, we usually feel aversion or want to push it away; if neutral, we tend to pass over or miss it in indifference or boredom. As an example, consider the frozen yogurt shops in the Good Place neighborhood. Michael claims that frozen yogurt is somewhat pleasurable to eat but tends toward bland neutrality, leaving the person eating not fully satisfied.

The third aggregate perception (*saññā*) explains our experience of recognizing a cup of coffee as a cup of coffee, and not as a smoothie. *The Good Place* cleverly plays on perception by deceiving the characters in the first season to believe they are in The Real Good Place, when they are actually in The Bad Place. In other words, perception often deceives us, and a large part of our suffering, according to Buddhists, results from the ways we mis-know reality.

The fourth aggregate is our mental formations or dispositions to act (*sankhāra*). This aggregate explains the primary mental activities that drive our daily lives. For instance, complex emotions are a part of the fourth aggregate, but so are thoughts, habits, inclinations, and decisions. Thus, for Buddhists, emotions embody a level of cognitive judgment. For instance, anger is not merely an irrational reaction but also embodies simple mental judgments, such as that one has been wronged and feels offended. Therefore, Buddhists defend the idea that emotions are a product of mental activity and are not "feelings," as they are often characterized in Western culture. Mental formations explain much of our craving behavior and habits. For instance, Jason doesn't just see or think of jalapeno poppers, he craves and wants them.

The final aggregate is consciousness (*viññāna*). Buddhists understand consciousness much differently than thinkers in the West. For the Buddhist, consciousness is merely the awareness of a physical or mental state. Thus, consciousness is awareness itself, and does not contain a "self" inside it. Consciousness is simply awareness of the other four aggregates, so that when one senses pain (the feeling aggregate), it is consciousness that is aware of that pain. In this sense, consciousness is similar to a flashlight in a dark room: it illuminates the room and is simply aware of whatever it is pointing at (but to make this analogy complete, we would have to get rid of the flashlight and only keep the beam, since the beam is all consciousness is—awareness of whatever is being shined at).

Every "Thing" Changes

One who sees consciousness as impermanent fully understands... [and] abandons the perversion of perceiving permanence in the impermanent. He crosses the flood of ignorance.

—Buddhaghosa[5]

So at this point one might be thinking, "Okay, big forking deal, we know that Eleanor is still Eleanor and not someone else; she has not become Jason or Janet." In other words, maybe Eleanor is who she is because of the unique makeup of her five aggregates, and, therefore, the self might indeed still be real. But according to Buddhism, the five aggregates are impermanent, and anything impermanent cannot legitimately be considered a self.

The body (form) is the easiest place for us to start. The body is constantly changing, such that approximately every seven years, our bodies have undergone an entire overhaul. In other words, the body cannot be considered the self, because it is impermanent and transitory. It is possible, of course, that one's body could change, but something else about the person remains that same. Is it true that one's personality stays the same over one's lifetime? No. Those who experience serious head trauma or brain injuries often display a change in their personality after the injury, and many people who suffer from dementia or Alzheimer's become, over time, quite different people, sometimes with radically contrasting personalities. More practically, people undergo major personality changes throughout life—a formerly happy person becomes clinically depressed, or a previously angry person learns how to be more compassionate.

In *The Good Place*, Eleanor's entire journey to becoming a better person is predicated on the belief that she can indeed change herself for the better. If change is possible, it is because that part of the self is capable of change. Perhaps consciousness is the self. Many people simply take it for granted that their selves are in some way either closely connected to or identical with their conscious experiences. Usually, people simply assume that their consciousness of experience is their "self" having that experience. However, for Buddhists, a careful look at consciousness will not show evidence of a self but rather the fleeting awareness of a rapid succession of sensations, thoughts, feelings, and perceptions. Buddhists argue that when one searches for the self in consciousness, all that one ever finds are individual experiences, not an unchanging or eternal self. It's the relationship between these conscious experiences that allow us to believe we have a self, when in fact all we have are individual mental events. Because these events proceed in a continuous process (possibly guided by time's nature as "Jeremy Bearimy"), we have a tendency to create the illusion of some permanent thing that is having all of these experiences, rather than merely seeing the succession of one event to the next.

The Self as a Useful Fiction

> Just as the word 'chariot'
> Refers to an assemblage of parts,
> So, 'person' is a convention
> Used when the aggregates are present.
> —Buddha[6]

So, if there is no self, does that mean there are no persons? It might sound as if the Buddhist answer would be yes, but Buddhism doesn't deny the existence of persons. Instead, Buddhism merely claims that there is no need to have a "self" acting behind all the aggregates in order to have a person. Rather, all that is needed is a conglomeration of aggregates that are constantly interacting and affecting each other. These interactions give rise to a sense of self, but one that is ultimately illusory, for there is nothing else besides the aggregates. A simple example will help clarify this point, and the example will also help us understand Chidi's argument with Eleanor about their relationship.

Let's consider a chariot. The word "chariot" clearly makes sense of a particular arrangement of objects and pieces. When all of these pieces are together in a specific way, we perceive a chariot. But if we were to scatter all of the parts on the ground, we would no longer have a chariot, just a mess. Words such as "chariot" and the "self" are convenient and pragmatic designations and concepts that help us navigate the world effectively but do not actually refer to something permanent and unchanging. In other words, conventionally there is a person, but ultimately there is none. Buddhists speak about two kinds of truth: conventional truth and ultimate truth. From an ultimate perspective, there are no chariots and no persons in the world, but from an everyday and practical perspective, there are chariots and persons. Chidi makes a similar point when he discusses the wave and ocean analogy in the final episode: I (a person) am like a wave that exists for a while before it crashes on the shore, and it is true to state that the wave is conventionally real, yet the wave is just one manifestation of water, and once the wave crashes ("I" die), the water remains (the universe and life itself). Conventionally, a wave is real; ultimately, it is not and is just water.

Back to Janet's void: Chidi claims that the Chidi who fell in love with Eleanor is numerically distinct from the Chidi that now stands before her. In one sense, Chidi is clearly correct—they are numerically distinct people, two different Chidis from two different timelines.

One could also argue that the Chidi who fell in love with Eleanor is qualitatively different—he is decisive in a way he isn't in other instances in the show (that is, he is acting out of character).

At the same time, however, Eleanor is right that Chidi is using philosophical arguments to avoid considering his feelings for her. As is common between couples, they are arguing about different issues: Eleanor is arguing about the conventional sense in which the person she fell in love with is obviously Chidi (she didn't fall in love with Jason), while Chidi is talking about the ultimate sense in which numerically the Chidi who fell in love with Eleanor is not the Chidi in Janet's void. The Buddhist would claim that both of these perspectives need to be maintained, the ultimate and the conventional, not one over or against the other.

Now let's consider Eleanor's "defragmenting of self" in Janet's void. As Chidi dismisses Eleanor's prodding to discuss their relationship, Eleanor's sense of self begins to "crumble," which, coincidentally, begins to take down Janet's void from the inside. Eleanor is having an "identity crisis." The show presents this crisis as a "world shattering event," and the characters all attempt to bring Eleanor back, trying to get her to do something "Eleanor-y" to regain a sense of her memory. This point in the show is dramatic.

From a Buddhist perspective, however, what Eleanor might be going through is not so much an identity crisis as a confrontation with the idea of no-self. Her disintegration and fragmentation could be understood as a step toward enlightenment and nirvana as opposed to a doomsday problem that needs immediate solving. According to Buddhists, clinging to our sense of self adds suffering to our lives. Eleanor's attachment to recapturing Chidi's love and the desire to have him say "I love you" causes much of Eleanor's suffering in this scene. Indeed, the desire to control or change what cannot be altered in life is a recipe for added suffering. By contrast, the Buddhist path encourages equanimity, as Tahani figures out in Season 3 while at the Tibetan Buddhist monastery.

Buddhist equanimity does not, however, involve ignoring the suffering of others. In fact, compassion is one of the chief virtues of Buddhism. Notably, the act that helps Eleanor recapture her sense of self is a kiss from Chidi, an act that helps Eleanor rediscover her self-narrative, her continued consciousness, as well as her memory. The Buddhist view is that once we adopt the position that there are no independent selves separate from all of reality, our natural stance toward all in the world should be compassion. Because we all suffer, harming others causes more suffering for others and ourselves. Over the course of *The Good*

Place, the characters transform from selfish and self-obsessed people who don't understand the amount of harm they are causing to themselves and others into people who have come to grips with the consequences of their past deeds (what Buddhists call karma). This, in turn, motivates them to alleviate the suffering of themselves and of others. In other words, they end up trying to follow the Buddhist path or at least something like it, as the last episode suggests by having the main characters decisively choose when they will no longer exist in The Good Place, a point of view that remarkably resembles final nirvana in Buddhism—the point at which a person is no longer reincarnated because he or she has ended the cycle of desire, attachment, and clinging.

Notes

1 *The Connected Discourses of the Buddha* (Samyutta Nikāya), trans. Bhikku Bodhi (Boston: Wisdom Publications, 200), III, 68–69, p. 909.

2 See Francisco J. Varela, Evan Thompson, and Eleanor Rosch, *Embodied Mind: Cognitive Science and Human Experience* (Cambridge, MA: MIT Press, 1991); and Robert Wright, *Why Buddhism Is True: The Science and Philosophy of Meditation and Enlightenment* (New York: Simon & Schuster, 2017).

3 John J. Holder, ed., *Early Buddhist Discourses*, trans. John J. Holder (Indianapolis, IN: Hackett Publishing, 2006), 87.

4 Bhadantācariya Buddhaghosa, *The Path of Purification* (Visuddhimagga), trans. Bhikkhu Ñānamoli (Onalaska, WA: BPS, Pariyatti Editions, 1991), XIV, 218, p. 484.

5 Buddhaghosa, XIV, 229, p. 486

6 Holder, *Early Buddhist Discourses*, 87.

Part VIII

"SOMETIMES A FLAW CAN MAKE SOMETHING EVEN MORE BEAUTIFUL"

Hell Is Other People's Tastes

Darren Hudson Hick and Sarah E. Worth

> Time is up. In preparation for your trip to The Bad Place, please put on these fedoras.
>
> —Shawn ("Mindy St. Claire's")

Much ink has been spilled in philosophy over the question of whether morality is an objective or subjective matter: whether there is some fact about the rightness or wrongness—praiseworthiness or blameworthiness—of an action or a person. There is a similar, parallel debate in *aesthetics*, the philosophical study of beauty and art, about whether beauty and its opposite are objectively or subjectively determined. In the world of *The Good Place*, the answer to the moral question seems fairly firmly determined: right and wrong are objective matters, and there is a fact about whether your actions (and, by extension, you) are good or bad. Exactly what determines the rightness or wrongness of an action in *The Good Place* is a more complicated question, and is the subject of other chapters in this book. Here, however, we are interested in what *The Good Place* has to tell us about aesthetics, and in particular about the idea of taste. Aesthetics has to do with beauty and perception—and not necessarily with "shoulds" and "oughts"—but aesthetics and ethics are tied together in some interesting ways in *The Good Place*.

On its face, *The Good Place* is about ethics: about what it means to be good, and what it means to be in The Good Place. But (spoiler alert), it turns out that Eleanor, Chidi, Jason, and Tahani aren't in The Good Place; they're in The Bad Place. And although ethics explains what landed them there, what makes The Bad Place bad turns out to be significantly aesthetic in nature. And the torture that our characters undergo in The Bad Place tells us a lot about aesthetics.

The Good Place and Philosophy, First Edition. Edited by Kimberly S. Engels.
© 2021 John Wiley & Sons, Inc. Published 2021 by John Wiley & Sons, Inc.

Eleanor's Clown Nook

Eleanor's hell-home, a primary-colored neomodern bungalow with a clown nook, appears to be the epitome of an objectively ugly thing. But we are told in the first episode that it has been designed to precisely suit the tastes of Eleanor Shellstrop. And it turns out that our Eleanor Shellstrop isn't that Eleanor Shellstrop. That Eleanor Shellstrop—the "Real Eleanor"—shows up seven episodes later in "Most Improved Player." "Real Eleanor" intuitively knows how to activate the staircase leading to the bedroom, while our Eleanor has been living with the constant irritation of having to haul herself up. Our Eleanor does not belong in The Good Place; she is in the wrong place. Eleanor discovers that she is literally taking someone else's place, and that Eleanor's place is a triumph of tackiness. Our Eleanor's tastes are pretty ... basic, leaning toward hotel lobby art, horizontal stripes, and hot mailmen. Average. And the average person will find the clown nook abhorrent.

But "Real" Eleanor Shellstrop turns out to be a fiction as well. There is no "Real" Eleanor. And this makes some sense. After all, what possible person would want to live in Eleanor's kitsch-cottage? Well ... somebody would. Somebody is willingly buying the crap that they're selling on the Home Shopping Network, after all. Somebody buys black-light posters and velvet Elvis paintings. And (speaking of Elvis) have you been to Graceland?

From the outside, Elvis Presley's Colonial Revival mansion appears surprisingly modest and tasteful. It would not look out of place on the main street of Colonial Williamsburg. The inside is a different story, once described as "the Taj Mahal of aesthetic misjudgment."[1] The pinnacle of the Graceland aesthetic is the Jungle Room, described by *Rolling Stone* as a "breathtakingly garish tiki-tinged lair."[2] The Jungle Room is festooned with enormous hand-carved furniture, some pieces featuring armrests carved like dragons. The floor is covered with thick, green shag carpeting, and one wall features a trickling waterfall covered in plastic vines. And, indeed, a Polynesian-styled tiki bar sits at one end of the wood-paneled man-cave. Elvis had the means to decorate his home any way he chose, and he chose—at great expense—the Jungle Room. Eleanor's home might appear to the average viewer as somehow objectively tacky, the sort of kitchiness that couldn't possibly appeal to anyone's taste. But people are funny. Eleanor's clown nook has nothing on the Jungle Room.

Tahani's Mansion and Jason's Bud-Hole

Tahani Al-Jamil is a woman of refined tastes, liking only what is best and rejecting all else. Her home in the afterlife is a colossal mansion that somehow retains a classic elegance. Everything is marble, gold, and crystal, but without looking like the inside of Trump Tower. It's classier. Modernist still-life paintings adorn the walls. And Tahani is very concerned with her style. Naturally, then, she is paired in The Bad Place with Jianyu, a silent Buddhist monk apparently entirely disinterested in grandeur, fashion, Impressionist painting, or even conversation.

The Buddha, Gautama, started on his path of enlightenment when he rejected the luxury of his princely upbringing, choosing the simple robes of a holy man and eschewing worldly goods. Buddhist monks follow the Buddha's example. Tahani's lifestyle and opulent mansion literally represent everything that the Buddha rejected. Aesthetically speaking, then, Tahani and Jianyu are polar opposites. But it turns out that Tahani can actually have two opposites—both the same person—because Jianyu is actually Jason Mendoza, an amateur Floridian DJ and drug dealer. Jianyu was non-aesthetic, but Jason's tastes—to Tahani, at least—would be anti-aesthetic.

While publicly pretending to be Jianyu, Jason hides in his "bud-hole" inside Tahani's mansion, which is exactly what you would expect an amateur DJ and drug dealer's living room to look like if he lived in his mom's basement. Mismatched, overstuffed furniture faces the flat-screen TV and overflowing media shelf. Posters of bikini-clad models and sports cars dot the walls. As Eleanor describes it: "It's like, '12-year-old boy' meets '13-year-old boy'" ("Tahani Al-Jamil"). The bud-hole is like an undeveloped frat-boy version of Elvis's Jungle Room. And, like Elvis, Jason could have literally anything he wanted, and this is what he wanted. Since Jason has to live publicly as Jianyu, his aesthetic bud-hole is the hole-away-from-home where he hides his own tastes. Jason's torture—both on Earth and in The Bad Place—is pretending to be someone else, pretending that he doesn't have the tastes he does.

Of course, when Tahani discovers the bud-hole, that Jianyu is actually Jason, and that he can talk, things are no better for her. Tahani's torture is people who don't appreciate her refined tastes. Jianyu won't, and Jason can't.

No Good Place for Chidi

Part of Chidi's torture is that he isn't allowed to appreciate The Good Place (he isn't in The Good Place, but he doesn't know that). Instead, Chidi has to spend his afterlife teaching undergraduate philosophy— a familiar hell for some of us. What Chidi wants to do in paradise, he says, is "paradise things, like rowing out on a lake, with a good bottle of wine, reading French poetry" ("Category 55 Emergency Doomsday Crisis"). We never see the inside of Chidi's home, but we get a glimpse of it from the outside: it's an apartment overlooking what can only be described as a Parisian alleyway—quiet, colorful, and speckled with blooming flowers and café bistro tables. But Chidi moves out of his apartment on his third day in paradise so that he can live in Eleanor's guest room and teach ethics full-time. Chidi has a particular image in mind of what paradise should be like, but he doesn't get to enjoy it.

"Oh Cool, More Philosophy—That Will Help Us!"

Whether there is some fact about whether a thing is beautiful is a debate as old as Western philosophy. The ancient Greek philosopher Pythagoras—he of hypotenuse fame—believed that beauty was a quantifiable principle of nature, and that we could find the source of beauty in the harmony, order, and regularity of beautiful things. On this view, there is some fact of the matter about whether a sunset or a song is beautiful, and we know we have encountered something beautiful because it pleases the soul. The only task that remains is to determine the precise mathematical arrangement of parts that made the thing—and would make another thing—beautiful. Pythagoras took the first step in this direction when he discovered the precise mathematical relationships behind harmonic musical sounds, setting off a hunt for further formulae of beauty that would engage philosophers and artists for centuries.[3]

Pythagoras and his followers had detractors, though. Another group of ancient Greek philosophers, the Sophists, believed that beauty was strictly in the eye of the beholder. On this view, there is no mathematical formula of beauty to be found because beauty is always relative to the perceiver. And this, the Sophists believed, is because all truth is relative, aesthetic and ethical included. As the Sophist Protagoras famously declared, *man is the measure of all things*.[4] If you find a sunset or a song beautiful, then it is beautiful to you, and if you do not, then it isn't. There's no further work to be done, and no debate to be had. Impressionist paintings of ballerinas please Tahani's soul, and playing *Madden 18* pleases Jason's soul, and there is nothing more to be said about it.

But, of course (philosophy being philosophy), there is more to be said about it. By the time Western philosophy reached the Enlightenment in the seventeenth and eighteenth centuries, a paradox of sorts had risen to the surface. On the one hand, it seems true that there is no disputing about taste: *de gustibus non est disputandum*. The familiar Latin proverb had, by the Enlightenment, become an accepted truism: people like what they like and dislike what they dislike, and there's no point in debating it, and no accounting for it. On the other hand, it seems equally true that the work of musician Sebastian Bach (of '80s hair-metal band Skid Row) is generally inferior to the work of Johann Sebastian Bach (of the Baroque period). This is how philosopher David Hume (1711–1776) sets up the Problem of Taste: how can we reconcile the idea that taste is entirely subjective with the notion that Bach's *Tocatta and Fugue in D Minor* is unproblematically superior to Skid Row's "Makin' a Mess"?

Hume's proposed solution rests in the distinction between *sentiment* and *judgment*. Sentiment, Hume argues, is your liking or disliking of a thing—simply how you feel about that thing. Eleanor likes "full cellphone battery" frozen yogurt and when she says so, she's making a claim about her feelings, her preferences. Gunner likes "folded laundry" frozen yogurt, and when he says so, he's making a claim about his mind, his tastes. Eleanor's sentiment and Gunner's sentiment are not at odds with each other; they're not disagreeing about anything. The issue isn't which is better; it's which each likes more. According to Hume, however, judgment is an assessment of something outside of oneself, and not merely a matter of preference, and so you could be wrong in your judgments. To declare one artwork (or yogurt flavor) superior to another is to make a judgment about those works and their relative quality. Hume suggests that one person may be a better judge of such matters than another person. So, Hume asks, what makes one judge superior to another?[5]

To begin, one's sense organs may be in a sound or defective state. Exposure to loud noise, inner ear infections, and buildup of earwax can all cause temporary hearing loss. Someone with defective hearing is unlikely to be picked as a judge on *American Idol*. Likewise, color-blindness is going to be a hindrance for a critic of modern art. At the very least, an ideal judge should have properly working sense organs.

But, more than this, Hume suggests, the ideal judge must develop a certain *delicacy* of taste—a capacity for fine discrimination and a disposition to be calmly affected by beauty. One isn't born with such a capacity, but must work to develop it and refine it. The more refined one's taste, the more one is able to observe and discriminate fine details, and so better appreciate subtle features one otherwise would have missed. Better judges have trained themselves to make better assessments than those who haven't, or who are less practiced. One's taste is improved—made more delicate—through practice, by exposure to and contemplation of more and more works.[6] Tahani appears to reflect the aesthetic ideal that Hume imagined, if anyone does. Her life on Earth gave her access to the world's great art and the luxury of the freedom to contemplate it.

Judgment is a matter of understanding, and we tend to be victims of our own sentimentality, preferring the things that we are used to (hence Jason's bud-hole). The ideal judge must free himself from all prejudices—that is, work to put aside his personal preferences and circumstances, and become as much as possible a "man in general." The closer one approaches this ideal, Hume suggests, the better a judge of artistic beauty one will become.

The Metaphysics of Taste in The Good Place

Presumably, The Good Place—if there is such a place—should be a paradise, containing the very best of everything. The first hint that we're not in The Good Place, then, comes during Eleanor's initial tour of the neighborhood. As she points out, there are a lot of frozen yogurt shops. Michael responds: "People love frozen yogurt. I don't know what to tell you" ("Everything Is Fine"). On Earth, we have to make trade-offs. We love frozen yogurt because it's close to ice cream, but without all the fat and calories. As Michael says to Eleanor, "There's something so human about taking something great and ruining it a little so you can have more of it" ("Jason Mendoza"). In paradise, we can presume, ice cream wouldn't come with the bad stuff, just the good taste.

In the world of *The Good Place*, torture is what you deserve for doing bad things. And aesthetically bad things are a kind of torture. When the neighborhood of Michael's design descends into chaos, he meets with Tahani and Jason for frozen yogurt. Tahani orders "everything" yogurt: "I can't believe they managed to mix one million flavors together, and yet, somehow, I can taste each individual one. It's remarkable!" ("Flying"). Michael licks at his "no-flavor. It's all I deserve, really." Just desserts.

Aesthetically bad things are what you deserve for doing bad things. What it means to do bad things in the world of *The Good Place* is an objective matter.[7] What it means to be aesthetically bad, however, is a subjective one. Jason's bud-hole might be torture for Tahani, but it's paradise for Jason. Michael isn't lying on Day 1 when he tells Eleanor that "every detail" of the neighborhood "has been precisely designed and calibrated for its residents" ("Everything Is Fine"). It's just that the details are calibrated for torture, not pleasure: for aesthetic discomfort.

Even The Medium Place is wildly subjective. Mindy St. Claire is the sole resident of The Medium Place, where the afterlife is an aesthetic compromise. Mindy's music selection consists entirely of Eagles live tracks and William Shatner spoken-word poetry. She has an endless supply of room-temperature beer. Her video library consists entirely of VHS copies of *Cannonball Run II* and *The Making of Cannonball Run II*. Eternal mediocrity. But what's medium for one person isn't medium for another. When the Judge considers sending the characters to their own Medium Places, she says, the characters would have to be split up: "That's the thing about Medium Places. It has to be tailored to what's medium for the individual, so if you're all together, it ain't medium" ("The Burrito").

Hell Is Other People's Tastes

In some ways, *The Good Place* appears to treat aesthetic goodness and badness as if they were objective matters. In Version #11 of The Good Place, Eleanor is paired with Sebastian, who writes her a "three-hour spoken-word jazz opera." This is when—for the eleventh time—Eleanor determines she's in The Bad Place: "No version of heaven for anyone would ever include three hours of this" ("Everything Is Great, Part 2"). When Shawn is getting ready to send Tahani and Chidi to The Bad Place, he tells them they will need to wear fedoras—no further explanation is needed. But torture isn't being forced to endure objectively bad things: some people like bad things. Given her tastes, Tahani should hate to wear a patterned fedora, but Chidi's plaid fedora fits his style just fine. It may be that nobody would like a three-hour spoken-word jazz opera, but that doesn't mean it's thus objectively bad. Things that are objectively bad are bad regardless of what people think of them.

Let's assume for the sake of argument that some things really are, objectively, more beautiful than others, and that some artworks are just better than other works. If that's the case, does it mean that paradise should resemble the Louvre, filled with only the very best art, the most beautiful things? Tahani might like an eternity in the Louvre, but Eleanor would be bored by it. Jason would be confused. And Chidi would imagine he would like this, but he would be in no way prepared to appreciate its beauty. Chidi imagines a paradise of drinking fine wine and reading French poetry in a rowboat, but he knows nothing about wine or poetry, and has never stepped foot in a rowboat. When Eleanor actually puts him in a rowboat with a bottle of wine, a loaf of bread, and some French poetry, he is literally and figuratively adrift. He hollers from the middle of the lake: "I've never actually done this before! This is a theoretical fantasy! How do you row a boat?!" ("Tahani Al-Jamil"). Chidi doesn't appear to know what his tastes are, which seems appropriate. After all, Chidi's defining characteristic is his uncertainty. He seems to believe that there is some objectively valuable thing, just as he seems to believe that there is some fact about what is right and wrong. Chidi imagines liking the greatest things—because we should like great things—but he has no experience liking such things.

Chidi seems to assume that once he's put in that rowboat with some wine and poetry, things will take care of themselves. But, Hume might suggest, Chidi needs a guide (as Chidi guides Eleanor in ethics) to appreciating what's beautiful about beautiful things. Judgment requires understanding, and understanding requires knowledge. Truly, fully appreciating good art (or wine, or rowing) requires knowledge about the thing being appreciated and a sustained immersion in it. So, we might imagine, an eternity in the Louvre with the right guide should be paradise for Chidi. But taste isn't that easy.

Contemporary philosopher Theodore Gracyk notes:

> [J]udgment requires background knowledge about the object, but knowledge does not itself create our preferences. Someone may 'get' twelve-tone music, knowing quite a bit about the history of music and understanding what has been accomplished. It does not follow that the person ever wants to hear it.[8]

Proper judgment may require knowledge, but knowledge does not guarantee appreciation. We appreciate different things, and the subjectivity of preferences might simply be unavoidable. Hume requires the ideal judge to be a "man in general," but surely any fully developed person will have a unique set of preferences. Our tastes are personal; they are what make us *us*. There is no reason to suppose that an eternity of wine and French poetry would actually be paradise for Chidi.

In "Chidi's Choice," we walk in on a conversation between Jason and Tahani:

JASON: Number five is number one. Number seven is number two. Number three and number four are tied for number three.

TAHANI: What are you talking about?

JASON: I'm ranking my favorite *Fast and the Furious* movies. You said you wanted to know who I am, and this *is* the best way to get to know me. ("Chidi's Choice")

The *Fast and the Furious* franchise has grossed in excess of $5 billion in ticket sales. You may think the movies are detestable, but a lot of people like them. These fans of *The Fast and the Furious* are in what Ted Cohen (1939–2014) calls an "affective community"—a group connected to each other by their group preference.[9] You might feel a bond with the select group of people who, like you, carry a great appreciation for twelve-tone music, or Mongolian throat-singing, or terrifying clown paintings. And you might also feel a bond with the enormous community of *Fast and Furious* or *Harry Potter* fans. Being connected to a narrow group of appreciators, Cohen notes, doesn't seem inherently better than being connected to a wide group of fans. Your tastes are your tastes, and they overlap in complex ways with the tastes of others, but it seems unfounded to say that you should like "better" art.

Just as Eleanor, Jason, Tahani, and Chidi carry their personalities and memories into the afterlife, so too do they retain their preferences. Our tortures, like our tastes, will be personal. The Bad Place is about torturing its residents, and it does this by making them uncomfortable.

The Good Place is a sort of extended version of Jean-Paul Sartre's (1905–1980) existentialist play *No Exit*, where three characters find themselves in the afterlife, a single room that they're locked in together. It becomes apparent that Joseph, Inès, and Estelle are three people wholly unsuited to live with each other—like a nightmare sitcom—and they will spend eternity in that room together. Hell, they discover, is not an afterlife of physical torture. No, as Sartre says, hell is other people. The first thing that Joseph, Inès, and Estelle notice is that their room contains three sofas. Estelle bursts into laughter.

JOSEPH [*ANGRILY*]:	There's nothing to laugh about.
ESTELLE [*STILL LAUGHING*]:	It's those sofas. They're so hideous. And just look how they've been arranged. It makes me think of New Year's Day—when I used to visit that boring old aunt of mine, Aunt Mary. Her house is full of horrors like that.... I suppose each of us has a sofa of his own?[10]

Hell is someone else's sofa. In *The Good Place*, hell is other people's tastes. The aesthetic punishments that Eleanor, Chidi, Tahani, and Jason are forced to endure have nothing to do with what's actually good or bad, but with what hurts. *The Good Place*'s creator, Michael Schur, notes:

Eleanor's house is utopia for someone, but that someone is not Kristen Bell's character.... All of the furniture is very aesthetically pretty but it looks really uncomfortable to sit on. It's like when you go to someone's house who has the exact opposite vibe as you, and you're like, "God, if I had to live here I would kill myself." [11]

But, of course, Eleanor can't kill herself. She's already dead.

Notes

1   Karal Ann Marling, *Graceland: Going Home with Elvis* (Cambridge, MA: Harvard University Press, 1996), 223.
2   Jordan Runtagh, "Inside Elvis Presley's Legendary Man-Cave Studio," *Rolling Stone*, August 8, 2016, https://www.rollingstone.com/music/music-features/inside-elvis-presleys-legendary-man-cave-studio-248975/.
3   See D. H. Hick, *Introducing Aesthetics and the Philosophy of Art* (London: Bloomsbury, 2017), 2–3.
4   Wladyslaw Tatarkiewicz, *History of Aesthetics*, vol. 1 (London: Continuum, 2005), 97.
5   David Hume, "Of the Standard of Taste," in *Essays, Moral, Political, and Literary*, ed. Eugene F. Miller (Indianapolis, IN: Liberty FundBooks, 1987), 226–249.
6   Ibid.

7 The point system seems a particularly good indicator of this.

8 Theodore A. Gracyk, "Having Bad Taste," *British Journal of Aesthetics* 30 (1990), 120.

9 Ted Cohen, "High and Low Thinking about High and Low Art," *Journal of Aesthetics and Art Criticism* 51 (1993), 155. See also Ted Cohen, "High and Low Art and High and Low Audiences," *Journal of Aesthetics and Art Criticism* 57 (1999), 137–143.

10 Jean-Paul Sartre, *No Exit, and Three Other Plays* (New York: Vintage Books, 1955), 10.

11 Lara Zarum, "How 'Superstore' and 'The Good Place' Use Production Design to Elevate the Ordinary," *Flavorwire*, January 11, 2017, http://flavorwire. com/597170/how-superstore-and-the-good-place-use-production-design-to-elevate-the-ordinary.

Why Everyone Hates Moral Philosophy Professors: The Aesthetics of Shallowness

T Storm Heter

In his introductory comments to a panel discussion on NBC's *The Good Place* at the North American Sartre Society annual meeting in 2018, Todd May suggested that the show be understood as a form of postmodern art that bridges high and low culture.[1] *The Good Place* features a comical satire of moral philosophy, exemplified most prominently in the figure of Chidi Anagonye, whose spectacularly bad decision-making abilities reveal what we could call a postmodern aesthetic strategy of favoring surfaces over depth. Chidi's faults as a moral philosopher are exaggerated, to the point of slapstick, as a way to focus the viewer's visual gaze on surfaces, rather than the traditional appeal to intellectual and artistic depth. Chidi is a spectacularly "flat" character in the sense that his choices (or rather his nonchoices) are predictable and cringe-worthy. As we'll see, this flatness is an intentional aesthetic maneuver, akin to the way visual artists like Andy Warhol abandoned perspective in their art and turned to one-dimensional illustrations that forced viewers to focus on surfaces.

Hell Is Ordinary People

In the first episode, Chidi Anagonye introduces himself to his supposed soulmate Eleanor with a grandiose description of his job as a philosophy professor: "I've spent my entire life in pursuit of fundamental truths about the universe" ("Everything Is Fine"). Chidi does not yet

The Good Place and Philosophy, First Edition. Edited by Kimberly S. Engels.
© 2021 John Wiley & Sons, Inc. Published 2021 by John Wiley & Sons, Inc.

know that, like Garcin in Jean-Paul Sartre's *No Exit*,[2] this supposed soulmate is actually his torturer. "Hell is other people" encapsulates the plot twist of *No Exit*. The characters expect hell to be a torture chamber with racks and red-hot pincers, but it turns out that the worst kind of torture for human beings is not physical, but mental. And this torture is mundane—not the stuff of Guantanamo Bay, but the stuff of *Friends*—being stuck in a room (an apartment, business suite, or regional branch office) with ordinary people and their ordinary bullshit.

The demon Michael plays a role parallel to the valet in *No Exit*. In Sartre's play, the characters already know they are in hell, but in Michael Schur's sitcom the characters think they are in The Good Place until a major plot twist at the end of Season 1 reveals that they are in The Bad Place ("Michael's Gambit"). In *No Exit*, the characters are surprised with the visual appearance of hell: a banal drawing room with second empire furniture. The victims are trapped in a claustrophobic space, with only a few objects around them. Most of all, there are no shiny or sharp surfaces. The absence of mirrors is a literary device representing the struggle for recognition or being seen, both literally and figuratively. Humans are dependent creatures who are set up psychologically to need other people. This makes us easy victims.

The characters in *No Exit* are obsessed with why they are in hell. They pretend, in bad faith (a Sartrean concept describing how we hide the truth from ourselves), that they don't know why they are damned. The audience, however, can see that each character has a single tragic flaw. Garcin is cowardly; Inès is cruel; and Estelle is vain. Sartre's artistic use of the tragic flaw alludes to the Greek sense of the tragic in which a protagonist's complex desires and drives are reduced to a single character trait that ultimately causes her or his downfall.

Michael Schur has a talent for writing situation comedies that are about being trapped in a room with a bunch of quirky people. *The Office* and *Parks and Recreation* are about the drama of being stuck, if not in hell, then in the modern equivalent of hell: a boring workplace. Writing this type of comedy requires being good at phenomenology. Schur (and his team of writers) are skilled at depicting the lived experience of *being with*. Phenomenology, a philosophical movement that takes the firsthand, conscious experience of individuals as its focal point, is a philosophy of the mundane: it reveals ordinary, everyday experience. What makes *The Good Place* phenomenological is its attention to the banality of space. Frozen yogurt shops adorn every corner, in a rough equivalent to the Parisian second empire furniture in *No Exit*. When Eleanor gets a tour of her new house, we learn that in The Good Place, everybody's house matches their personal style. One can imagine "Hell is the suburbs" scrawled on the whiteboard in *The Good Place* writers' room.

As a non–*Homo sapiens*, Michael makes for a humorous phenomenologist of the human mind (and body). In the episode "Existential Crisis," a grumpy Michael mocks our parochial species: "Let me just get into the mindset of a human. 'Oh, I'm a human and my breathing tube is next to my eating tube. Oh and my arms end in stupid little sticks.'" To really learn to be human, Chidi thinks Michael needs to grasp finitude. Chidi explains that Michael is going through an existential crisis, a "sort of anguish people go through when they contemplate the silent indifference of our empty universe." By the end of Season 4, the human characters glimpse the zombie-like existence of The Real Good Place and they face their own existential crises: once one has done everything on one's bucket list, is (the after)life worth living?

The Good Place is a phenomenologically rich commentary on the ordinary. However, to grasp this richness, the viewer must come to terms with the over-the-top flatness of each character. By a "flat" character I mean one who does not show growth over time. We expect characters to learn from their mistakes and become more emotionally complex, but in *The Good Place*'s first three seasons, this often does not happen.

Why Does Everyone Hate Moral Philosophers?

Eleanor's voice is a primary vehicle through which *The Good Place* critiques philosophy. She is court jester—both fool and sage. A terrible human whose selfishness is on full blast, she is right about one thing: Chidi doesn't know how to live. The more books he reads, the more hopeless he is at living the good life.

Chidi's character flaw is indecisiveness. As a self-described "professor of ethics and moral philosophy," he takes every opportunity to lecture about the history of philosophy. Yet his obsessive need to talk about philosophy leaves him impotent to act. He is a perpetual deer in the headlights, frozen by options. At the beginning of the show we cringe while hoping Chidi will decide. We expect him to grow and to find some further complications deep within his psyche that will make indecisiveness less a necessity of moving the plot along and getting laughs, and more a necessity of the progress of his soul. But for the first three seasons, this does not happen. No human would be this stubborn, dumb, or repetitive. He is outrageously flat—he does not become more sophisticated or grow from his mistakes. We are denied when we hope for some extra depth to Chidi's indecisiveness in the next episode. Chidi is Chidi; he'll never learn. In Season 4, "The Answer," Chidi gets back a note that he had given Janet before his reset. It reads, "There is no answer. But Eleanor is the answer." The logically contradictory note is enough to prime Chidi's flesh-like memories of loving Eleanor. His (after)lifelong indecisiveness is abruptly gone.

Chidi's indecisiveness predates his becoming a professor. Through flashbacks to his youth in "Chidi's Choice," we learn he was a hated boy on the playground. His closest friend on earth, Uzo, knows him so well that he plans a fake wedding to test Chidi. Can he plan a bachelor party? No, he can't—too many options for dates and venues. Can he deliver a speech as best man? No, because then he'd have to select among the 11 versions he drafted. Chidi is so spectacularly bad at making decisions that he causes his own death. His best friend forgives him for messing up the wedding, and he offers to buy him a beer. Disastrously, Chidi must pick the bar. He stands frozen on the sidewalk, unable to pick the bar, and gets smashed by an air conditioner. Uzo, Chidi's oldest friend, both "hates" Chidi and also still wants to be his friend.

It is Eleanor who *really* hates Chidi, though. In the pilot she proclaims, "That's why everyone hates moral philosophy professors." Chidi won't lie to protect Eleanor after she tells him that she doesn't belong in The Good Place. When Janet is murdered, Chidi again refuses to lie. The pattern repeats: Chidi gets a stomachache and Eleanor gets pissed.

Right off the bat, Eleanor searches for why Chidi is so insistent about not lying. "I'm just asking you to fudge a little bit. You must have told a few white lies in your life. I mean, what was your job?" When Chidi tells her his profession, Eleanor's response is a simple, sanitized "Motherforker" ("Everything Is Fine"). The dramatic tension that binds Eleanor to Chidi is now in place. The student-teacher relationship is psychological torture. The lover-loved relationship, the awkward roommate relationship, the odd-couple relationship—all these, too, are concrete relations with others in the existentialist sense. Chidi is stuck with Eleanor, whom he can never satisfy. Eleanor is stuck with Chidi, whom she can never satisfy. By the end of the show, Eleanor has become capable of reading a dense philosophy book and even understanding its main point. She gives Chidi her blessing to both love her, and also to leave her by walking through the door.

Eleanor hates Chidi, but she also, of course, *loves* him. Sartre suggested that love and hate were pretty much the same. No fan of emotions, Sartre compared them to a person attempting magic. In *The Emotions: Outline of a Theory* he claimed that emotions are choices. Passion is not something that wells up from inside and overpowers reason.[3] Passion is a mode of consciousness, akin to visual perception. We choose whom we love and how we love, whom we hate and how we hate. Clearly, Michael Schur and the writers' team have chewed upon and swallowed a bit of existentialist thinking: Chidi and Eleanor are condemned to be free, and condemned to be in bad faith or self-deception about their freedom.

Philosophy and Depth

The appeal to depth is a mainstay of philosophical thinking. Shallowness has been understood as a fault, failure, and deficiency in aesthetics, epistemology, and ethics. Calling someone shallow is an insult to their intelligence, emotional maturity, and artistic sensibility. The appeal to depth is also a mainstay of aesthetic criticism and was especially prevalent in nineteenth-century Europe in the Romantic period, when authenticity was understood as letting out something from deep inside a person.

Depth metaphors were a central feature of the emerging notions of autonomy, individuality, and freedom in European modernity. A range of cultural fields (literature, painting, music, high theory) articulated new notions of the self, of the will, and of the human. A figure thus emerged: the man (or woman) who is measured by his intellectual and emotional depth. This sense of self was connected to notions of moral responsibility, criminal liability, authorship, and copyright rules. While European moral philosophers mostly thought emotions clouded ethical decisions, poets and artists saw emotions as something inside that needs to get out. An underlying assumption of this view is that each person has a privileged access to their own emotions. Thus it is important for the artist to dig deep and release what is theirs alone to give to the world—the private contents of their own mind, which are supposedly deep inside.

The appeal to depth remains a mainstay of philosophical thinking. In contemporary epistemology the appeal to depth is revealed in the definition of knowledge as "justified, true belief." The question of how to justify a belief is the question of how we can have reasons that "back up" assertions. "Gettier problems" (named for Edmund Gettier) are generated when we form true beliefs, but fail to have the right reasons for those true beliefs.[4] Let's say we're staring at a field and we see sheep.[5] We form the belief "There are sheep in the field." Little do we know that the sheep we are gazing at are not sheep, but clever dogs dressed in elaborate sheep costumes! The rub consists in the fact that our belief is "true" (factually accurate) because, unbeknownst to us, there are real sheep in the field somewhere, although we can't see them. The problem of depth is twofold: first, our own mind lacks the depth it needs for knowledge—we've formed a belief for the wrong reasons. We do not have the right justification backing up our reasons. Second, our lack of mental depth mirrors the lack of depth in the fake sheep. The sheepiness of the sheep is all outside, a trick of appearance, a cover for what's below.

Michael's experiment—creating a fake heaven—is consistent with the long-standing philosophical device of providing "thought experiments" like Gettier's that generate skepticism about experience. In *Discourse on Method*, Descartes (1596–1650) presents another classic thought experiment—one that would not be out of place in the writers' room of *The Good Place*.[6] He imagines a hoax where a carpenter creates a mechanical "monkey or any other rational animal." Such machines would have "the organs and outward shape of a monkey." That is, on the *surface*, the machines would be indistinguishable from genuine simians. "We would have no means of knowing that they were not of exactly the same nature as these animals."[7] The proposed standard for having a mind is the ability to use language. In other words, Descartes is arguing that human nature is depth, and nonhuman animal nature is shallowness. Humans have experiences inside that they can communicate by "letting it out."

Michael's version of the mechanical monkey test would probably be more galling: something like secretly replacing the family dog with a robot and seeing if anyone notices. Michael does, after all, kick Teacup the dog into the sun, remarking, "Everyone, it is a mere construct of a dog, it feels no pain or joy or love." Teacup's owner is left almost speechless: "Teacup doesn't love me?" If Teacup is a "mere construct of a dog"—that is, the mere surface appearance of a dog—then no, Teacup does not have emotional depth and is incapable of love.

From fake sheep and fake barns to the idea that life is a dream, philosophers have been fascinated with the possibility that surfaces mask reality. Philosophers have thought of themselves as "deep thinkers" who probe beneath the obvious, providing "reasons," "justifications," and "motives" for their actions and beliefs.

Depth and Existentialism

In 1936 Sartre published *The Transcendence of the Ego*, a critique of Edmund Husserl's phenomenological method.[8] With an artist's flair he offered a single devastating argument: the self is not "inside" consciousness, but is "outside." In other words, *existence precedes essence*. While Sartre is remembered for his formulation of existentialism, it is now widely accepted that existentialism was developed by a network of intellectuals, among them Simone de Beauvoir and Frantz Fanon. But what exactly does "existence precedes essence" mean? It means that the nineteenth-century, Romantic model of a "self" residing "inside" a person's consciousness is faulty.[9]

Sartre argues that Husserl is half right: we need to use phenomenology (analysis of first person experience) to capture experience. But Husserl was overly fond of introspection, whereas existential phenomenologists favor analyzing actions as they unfold in time. Introspection distorts the experience of choosing by freezing it in the past. The stakes of this debate are high. The Husserlian/Romantic model of selfhood amounts to bad faith. We do not discover our motives, reasons, and emotions inside of us; rather, we create those motives, reasons, and emotions via our engagement with the world. Existentialism points to an ethics of self-creation, not self-discovery. On the existential view of consciousness, *I am my outside*. The radical implication is that our commonsense way of speaking about what is "inside/outside" of the self is mistaken. Our self is entirely outside and constructed in our interaction with the world, not hidden within us waiting to be revealed.

Chidi's Tragic Flaw

Through the first three seasons, Chidi's inability to commit makes him a flat character: he doesn't pass through stages of moral development. What makes Chidi's flatness funny is how it is exaggerated, like a giant fake nose. We can't stop staring at the train wreck—or rather trolley wreck—that is Chidi trying to decide something. The American group Devo sings, "In ancient Rome there was a poem / About a dog who found two bones / He picked at one, he licked the other / He went in circles, he dropped dead." Sounds like Chidi, right? The song alludes to the story of Buridan's Ass, a parable in which a hungry donkey has two stacks of hay. Both are equally good tasting. The donkey starves because he is unable to pick one to eat. The story comically illustrates a couple of assumptions. The first is that not-choosing is a choice. Second, the story illustrates the stupidity of being paralyzed by a choice between two outcomes that are equal. Humans have the capacity to ask themselves: what is at stake in this choice? Is this choice significant or insignificant?

For Chidi, overthinking things leads to paralysis, just as it does for Buridan's donkey. The donkey dies because it has opposite and equal desires that cancel out, hence it cannot act. Chidi, on the other hand, doesn't appear to have any desires at all. He's all brain. His problem is that of (what Sartre called) moral "sincerity"—he is so sincerely concerned with moral imperatives that all decisions appear to him equally good (or bad). Once Chidi does become capable of decisions and love, it is through what Sartre would call a radical "conversion." Sartre asserted that all humans have a "basic project" that frames desires, choices, and character. The move from one basic project to a different one has no rational justification. Chidi makes just such a leap when he accepts the belief "There is no answer, but Eleanor is the answer."

Chidi's indecisiveness can be contrasted with Jason's dumbness, Eleanor's selfishness, and Tahani's love of fame. Jason is so dumb (so flat) that he does not exercise real freedom of choice. He moves through life with the simple desires of a teenage boy. Shallowness of two other sorts are revealed by Eleanor's selfishness and meanness, and Tahani's obsession with social status. Unlike Jason, Eleanor and Tahani are smart enough to have willful choices; but they fail to make the right choices. Janet, by contrast, develops the ability to choose and hence is one of the least flat characters: she learns to lie, falls in love, and even creates a rebound boyfriend. The lesson of how a Janet can become a person echoes the master-slave section of *The Phenomenology of Spirit*, where Hegel argues that through the struggle for freedom and recognition the slave achieves more self-consciousness than the master.

The portrayal of Chidi as the philosopher who is unable to commit is the driving comedic force in *The Good Place*. But as Michael Schur has made clear on numerous occasions, *The Good Place* makes fun of philosophy because *there is something philosophical about making fun of philosophy*. *The Good Place* is an Andy Warhol moment in modern television: Warhol flattened the surfaces of his work and made fun of Pollock, Kline, and de Kooning (all very morally serious artists who spent many nights being drunk Chidis arguing over aesthetics in the Cedar Street Tavern). Warhol's pop aesthetics, featuring Coca-Cola bottles, Campbell's soup cans, and Brillo boxes, is about gazing at shiny surfaces and allowing ourselves some ironic detachment.

My Love-Hate Relationship with Professors of Ethics and Moral Philosophy

In "The Trolley Problem" we watch the existential dynamic of love-hate, teacher-student unfold as Michael commits himself to understanding human psychology. Michael, the rude student who is doubtlessly "just playing devil's advocate," interrupts Chidi's classroom lesson by snapping his fingers. Instead of talking about trolleys, Chidi is now driving one. What better way to call out the "armchair philosopher" and "Monday morning quarterback" than make him throw the ball and brace for the blitz? After traumatizing Chidi, Michael apologizes: "You specifically asked me if there was a way I could connect with the material more. I'm trying, you guys." Mental note to all us professors: never close your eyes while teaching ethics.

The trolley problem episode works as comedy on two levels. For the lay audience, the premise of the trolley problem is the joke. Moral philosophers set up their teachings around elaborate hypotheticals that bear little resemblance to reality. For philosophers and students in ethics classes, the joke has to do with the switch from analysis-paralysis to driving-deciding. We philosophers get a glimpse of ourselves in the mirror; what a distance we've drawn between theory and reality. Watching Chidi drive the trolley and get his hands dirty showcases the impotence of philosophy—all talk, no action. That's why everyone hates us.

But before we throw all ethics under the trolley, let's pause to acknowledge that the trolley problem arises within a specific tradition of ethics. Existential thinkers—like Sartre, de Beauvoir, Fanon, and others—developed searing critiques of mainstream ethics.

Asking "What would you do in this situation?" the trolley problem is an "ethical dilemma." Because it is dramatic and the choices are inescapable, this type of problem is very useful in the classroom. Other examples include the "ticking bomb" scenario, where we must decide whether to torture one to save a hundred; the "sinking boat" experiment, where our lifeboat is too small and someone must go overboard; and the "transplant" case, where a surgeon can save many lives by letting one patient die and harvesting her organs. Perhaps the most cringe-worthy of these ethical dilemmas is that of "Jim and the Indians" from Smart and Williams's *Utilitarianism: For and Against*.[10] Look up that last one for yourself (or don't).

While *The Good Place* does a brilliant job of making fun of moral dilemmas, philosophers outside of the mainstream ethical traditions have been making similar critiques for years. For example, Hugo Adam Bedau's *Making Mortal Choices: Three Exercises in Moral Casuistry* expresses a pragmatist critique of traditional ethics.[11] The pragmatist critique can also be found throughout the work of James D. Wallace, especially *Ethical Norms and Particular Cases*.[12] I consider my writings about existential ethics to be consistent with Bedau's and Wallace's pragmatic critique. My book *Sartre's Ethics of Engagement: Authenticity and Civic Virtue* argues that existential ethics is nothing like Kantian or utilitarian thought.[13] As the title of my book suggests, existentialism is a philosophy of *engagement*.[14] Ethics turns out to be about the messy details of life more than about the universal truths of humankind. Schur's comedy shares this spirit: messiness and humanity go hand in hand.

Conclusion: The Aesthetics of Shallowness

In drawing this chapter to a close, let's return to the theme of shallowness. *The Good Place* uses the postmodern strategy of gazing at surfaces to articulate a critique of philosophy. Pre-conversion Chidi is flat, not deep: he lacks change, he is repetitive, he prevaricates. Chidi is flat, not deep, in a second sense. He tries too hard to provide reasons, justifications, and intellectual backing for his actions, but this attempt at intellectual depth is a complete failure. Intellectual depth is a ruse. As Warhol would put it—everyone has their brand. Some people's brand is to pretend to hate and reject branding—but that's just one more brand. *The Good Place* is effective as a piece of "serious" art precisely because it offers an effective critique of moral seriousness. This ironic strategy of forcing us to look at shallow, shiny surfaces is what keeps viewers coming back.

Notes

1   May commented in his introduction, "It's because it occupies an extremely unique place in modern culture. We're living in a period in which … the line between what's traditionally called high culture and what's traditionally called popular culture has become effaced.… All over there are people who are taking what used to be a high culture, in the context of some form of entertainment and then melding them together. What to me makes *The Good Place* so unique is that it's not doing that. It's doing something else. It's operating at the level of popular culture and popular entertainment. It's not melding the two. It's operating in that, but bringing in themes associated with high culture. And because it's doing that it really gets a wide audience. And that audience is getting involved in philosophy in ways … allowing them to at once be entertained and yet have things to think about afterwards. And I don't know any other television show or any other work at this point that is doing that idea of going into that part of the culture and introducing these themes."

2   Jean-Paul Sartre, *No Exit and Three Other Plays* (New York: Vintage, 1989).

3   Jean-Paul Sartre, *The Emotions: Outline of a Theory*, trans. Bernard Frechtman (Citadel Press, 2000).

4   Edmund Gettier, "Is Justified True Belief Knowledge?" *Analysis* 23 (1963), 121–123.

5   Roderick Chisholm, "Knowledge and Belief: 'De dicto' and 'de re'," *Philosophical Studies* 29 (1976), 1 –20.

6   René Descartes, *Discourse on Method*, trans. Ian Maclean (Oxford: Oxford University Press, 2006).

7   Ibid., 46.

8   Jean-Paul Sartre, *The Transcendence of the Ego: A Sketch for a Phenomenological Description*, trans. Sarah Richmond (London: Routledge, 2004).

9   Ibid., 9–12.

10 J.J.C. Smart and Bernard Williams, *Utilitarianism: For and Against* (Cambridge: Cambridge University Press, 1973).

11 Hugo Adam Bedau, *Making Mortal Choices: Three Exercises in Moral Casuistry* (Oxford: Oxford University Press, 1997).

12 James D. Wallace, *Ethical Norms and Particular Cases* (Ithaca, NY: Cornell University Press, 1996).

13   T Storm Heter, *Sartre's Ethics of Engagement: Authenticity and Civic Virtue* (London: Continuum-Bloomsbury, 2006).

14   I will also note that James D. Wallace—my graduate mentor while I studied for my PhD at Illinois from 1995 to 2003, and father of novelist David Foster Wallace—was the only member of the faculty who treated me with unconditional decency. Wallace is a "mensch," as we say in Yiddish. Wallace taught me that ethics is indeed *engagement*—he taught me how to engage students as humans first and foremost; he taught me how to carry my humanity with me into the workplace.

Part IX

"OH COOL, MORE PHILOSOPHY! THAT WILL HELP US."

Part IX

OH COOL, MORE
PHILOSOPHY THAT
WILL HELP US

An Epistemological Nightmare? Ways of Knowing in *The Good Place*

Dean A. Kowalski

"Oh cool! More philosophy! That'll help." More Shellstrop sarcasm. But by now, and as Eleanor did (mostly), you've come to realize that learning about philosophy is not all bad. It can be helpful. One of the more vivid examples of this pertains to knowledge. Are there different ways or types of knowing? What does it mean to know anything in the first place? What can we say about how we come to know anything?

These are questions of epistemology—the study of knowledge, which is one of the major branches or sub-areas of philosophy. Recall Chidi's reply to Eleanor's sarcastic quip: "Don't you see the problem? We can't learn from our mistakes because our memories keep getting erased. It's an epistemological nightmare!" Chidi thinks he is helping Eleanor better understand their constant reboot predicament. Unconvinced and exasperated, she retorts, "Ugh. Even your nightmares are boring!" By the end of this chapter, you'll have learned some epistemology by revisiting some of your favorite *The Good Place* moments. As a result, we may be in a better position to understand Janet's character, especially in terms of her allegedly knowing everything, and how this might have real-world applications. I'll do my best to make it neither a nightmare nor boring, and certainly not a boring nightmare. Everything will be fine!

Three Types of Knowledge

Philosophers distinguish between three types of knowledge, corresponding (roughly) to three different ways of knowing. The first type, "competence knowledge," is knowing how to perform some task successfully.

The Good Place and Philosophy, First Edition. Edited by Kimberly S. Engels.
© 2021 John Wiley & Sons, Inc. Published 2021 by John Wiley & Sons, Inc.

Before you learned how to ride a bike, you didn't know how. Chidi knows how to write a 3600-page manuscript, but he does not know how to print a newspaper or map a neighborhood. He has competence knowledge regarding being an author, but he lacks competence knowledge with respect to being a newspaper editor or a cartographer (especially as the former requires meeting deadlines and the latter rouses his diagnosed directional insanity).

The second type, "acquaintance knowledge," is knowing someone or something in a personally familiar or intimate way.[1] Now that Tahani has met and interacted with Jason Mendoza—in all sorts of ways—she knows him in ways that she didn't prior to her arrival in The Good Place. For that matter, she knows him in ways that Eleanor does not. This insight reminds us that one can also become familiar with certain sorts of qualitative experiences only by having them. If you've never had a headache, you cannot know what it's like to suffer one. Michael, as a superior being, never had a headache—until he read Chidi's burdensome tome. He laments, "I mean that thing is unreadable. I literally learned what headaches were because that thing gave me a headache."

There are two intriguing examples of acquaintance knowledge in *The Good Place*. The first involves Michael encountering his humanity, including (upon Chidi's prodding) coming to grips with his mortality. There are two parts to Michael's coming to know about humanity. First, in "Team Cockroach," Michael divulges that human form is not his natural state. He explains, "Everyone in the Bad Place Bureau of Human Affairs gets randomly assigned a human body so we can get the feel of how best to torture you. I gotta say, it took me a long time to get used to the hanging bits." Michael and his co-workers can read about torturing humans and perhaps they might consult Janet for additional information, but they cannot know what it is truly like for a human to be tortured unless they assume human form (and perhaps suffer it for themselves).

The second part involves Chidi's ploy to exploit Michael's human form so that he better understands the point of studying ethics. In "Existential Crisis," Chidi explains, "Before I can teach Michael to be good, I have to force him to think about what we used to think about. That life has an end and, therefore, our actions have meaning." Of course, Chidi is successful, which spins Michael into an existential crisis (hence the episode title). The angst that afflicts Michael is another unsettling experience (like a headache) that he now knows about only because he has suffered it. Furthermore, Michael unsuccessfully attempts to cope with his new knowledge in very human ways (at least those stereotypical for middle-aged men). But by his own admission, all Michael ever really wanted was to know what it was like to be human. It seems impossible for him to accomplish that goal without taking human form.

The second intriguing example involves Janet's glitching episodes. When Jason and Tahani begin to experience growing pains in their budding relationship, they turn to Janet for counseling in "The Trolley Problem." After Janet (instantaneously) reads every book ever written on psychotherapy, she does her best to help. During their sessions, Janet's thumb surprisingly separates from her body and floats away, and she unexpectedly croaks like a frog. When Tahani and Jason later thank Janet for her part in making their relationship stronger, she replies, "Congratulations. I am very happy for the both of you." Immediately, the entire neighborhood experiences earthquake-like tremors. Janet subsequently appears to Michael. He asks, "What's the matter? What is wrong?" To which she answers, "I am wrong. I can't stop glitching."

Janet was programmed to make humans happy; in fact, she is evidently made happy when she helps them. Interestingly, after 802 reboots, she somehow gained the ability to lie. She lies to Tahani and Jason about how it makes her happy when she makes them happy by improving their relationship. In truth, she is not made happy by this because she, on some level, still loves Jason. Thus, perhaps Janet is glitching because she is attempting to cope with human emotions that she is ill-equipped to experience. She is gaining acquaintance knowledge of love, envy, sadness, and deceit (including self-deception perhaps). However, Janet has no effective way to process this knowledge because she is not a (human) girl.

Janet's problem conveys the philosophical insight that one's acquaintance knowledge is limited by facts about the person in question. A blind person will never know exactly what it is like to see the color red. Janet's predicament is akin to a person who is born blind but regains her vision and cannot immediately process what she sees. Of course, after some effort and practice, the newly sighted person will more effectively process what she sees, and there is some reason to think that Janet will keep evolving in analogous ways. However, strictly speaking, Janet's original programming does not allow for her to experience emotions as humans do. Hence the glitches.

Despite such interesting insights, the third kind of knowledge, called "propositional knowledge," gets the most philosophical attention.

It involves grasping what the facts are or being aware that such and such is the case. Imagine someone who claims, "I know that Jacksonville, Florida, is the home of the Jaguars," or someone else who asserts, "I know that *The Good Place* aired for four seasons." Such claims to knowledge refer to statements that express descriptions of how things (actually) are. The first pertains to a fact about Jason's favorite NFL football team and the second pertains to a hilarious NBC television show. Thus, they are examples of "propositional knowledge."

The Requirements of Propositional Knowledge

There are three generally accepted conditions that must be met for someone to have propositional knowledge: belief, truth, and justification. Propositional knowledge begins with a belief. A belief is the mental acceptance of some statement about how things supposedly are. After all, if you have no awareness of some state of affairs, it certainly seems odd to claim that you know about it. If you (unlike Jason Mendoza) have never even heard of Blake Bortles, then you cannot know that he is an NFL quarterback. You are (non-culpably) ignorant of facts about this person because you are completely unfamiliar with him. But it seems intuitive that ignorance is opposed to knowledge. Thus, one cannot know a statement unless one first believes it.

Yet belief alone is not sufficient for knowledge. Recall the early episodes when Michael asserts to each of the four main characters that he or she has died and is now in The Good Place. Tahani especially readily believes him. However, it seems odd to claim that Tahani can know that she is in The Good Place when actually she is not. This is similar to someone claiming to know that Kristen Bell is taller than Jameela Jamil. A natural reaction to someone claiming to know this is that he or she is mistaken. Jamil is much taller than Bell. This is another instance of someone being ignorant of the facts, but, again, ignorance is opposed to knowledge. Therefore, it seems that propositional knowledge requires *true* belief.

True belief, though, is not enough for propositional knowledge. In one way, this should be obvious, because it might be a lucky guess that something you believe turns out to be true. Just as knowledge cannot consist of ignorance, *guessing* about a topic is opposed to *knowing* it. However, there are also more interesting examples leading to the position that true belief is insufficient for knowledge. Recall neuroscientist Simone Garnett's Season 4 belief that she is not in The Good Place. Her belief is true, but not for the reasons she offers. She surmises that she must be hallucinating, because there is no such thing as an afterlife. Rather, she is in the experimental Medium Place. Because the experiential Medium Place neighborhood is not The Good Place, her belief is technically true, but it seems doubtful that she knows she is not in The Good Place, despite her claim to the contrary. Her belief lacks proper connection to the facts.

Simone's example leads us to the position that a true belief must be accompanied by some sort of grounds or evidence that properly establishes its connection to the truth, which (optimally) in some way accounts for its being believed in the first place. Philosophers have long held this sort of view. Consider Plato's (428–348 BCE) classic statement:

> True opinions ... are a fine thing ..., but they are not willing to remain long, and they escape from a man's mind ... until one ties them down by [giving] an account of the reason why. After they are tied down ... they become knowledge, and then they remain in place.... Knowledge differs from opinion in being tied down.[2]

If one can provide an account of, or reason why, one's belief is true, we are much more apt to hold that one's knowledge claim is genuine. Thus, in Simone's case, she doesn't actually know she is not in The Good Place because her belief lacks adequate justification; she doesn't believe for the right reasons. Without proper grounds or evidence for her belief, it is too much like a lucky guess and, thus, not knowledge.

Justification, Sources of Knowledge, and Chidi's Nightmare

Propositional knowledge requires justified, true belief,[3] but philosophers never stop asking questions: How much justification must one have in order to know? Does one need so much that it is impossible to be mistaken about what one believes? Does knowing some truth mean knowing it for certain? After all, if someone claims to know something, but then readily admits that she could be mistaken, it seems natural to conclude that person does not *know* it.

René Descartes (1596–1650) held something like this view. His mission was to doubt everything he once believed until he discovered a belief that he could not be mistaken about. Descartes went so far as to hypothesize the existence of a malicious being possessing vast power who constantly deceives him. He writes:

> I will suppose ... that there is an evil demon, supremely powerful and cunning, who works as hard as he can to deceive me. I will say that sky, air, earth, color, shape, sound, and other external things are just dreamed illusions that the demon uses to ensnare my judgment.... If I do not really have the ability to know the truth, I will at least with-hold assent from what is false and from what a deceiver may try to put over on me.[4]

The possible existence of such a being was enough for Descartes to not believe anything as true until he could be absolutely certain that he wasn't being fooled into believing some falsehood.

Michael represents much of Descartes's hypothetical demon. He works as hard as he can to deceive Eleanor, Chidi, Tahani, and Jason about their surroundings. Furthermore, as made clear at the end of "Best Self," the neighborhood Michael designed—the sky, air, earth, and its colors—is little more than a virtual reality shared-dream illusion in which Michael attempted to have the four humans unwittingly torture each other for a thousand years (which makes you wonder about Jason's gastric difficulties with "fro-yo"). However, most of us would have difficulty fully accepting Descartes's very cautious and conservative approach to acquiring knowledge. How could you come to learn anything new? Indeed, most of us are prone to the sort of approach Eleanor represents at the end of Season 1. Despite Michael's best efforts, and even though Eleanor might be mistaken, she surmised that she and her three friends were actually in The Bad Place. Holy motherforking shirtballs! But she wasn't merely guessing they were in The Bad Place either. She had good reasons to believe it, and those reasons led her to a true belief. So, most contemporary philosophers agree that propositional knowledge requires less than complete justification. You don't need to know that you know—you just need to know. Having good reasons for your beliefs being true seems sufficient for knowledge.

Philosophers tend to discuss two basic sources of knowledge: the proper use of one's senses (perception) and the proper use of one's reason. Each has its place in knowledge acquisition. We learn about our surroundings by encountering them. This invariably occurs via the five senses. It's difficult to understand how anyone could know how impeccably smooth Tahani's skin is unless you touch it (or try to apply facial cream to it). It's likewise difficult, perhaps more so, to know how the frozen yogurt flavor "New Cellphone Battery" tastes unless you sample it. In fact, this involves two senses because it apparently tastes the way a new fully charged cellphone battery makes you feel. Thus, it's clear that perception, although occasionally faulty, is a viable source of knowledge.

Yet sometimes one gains knowledge of some fact through the careful use of one's reason without any direct perceptual experience. The classic examples involve abstract objects or ideas. Everyone knows what (exact) circles are, what it means for two things to be perfectly equal, or that the number 7 is prime, but we have never perceptually experienced any of these in the way Eleanor knows how clam chowder tastes at Little Bit Chowder Now.

Chidi's approach to ethics also serves as a plausible source of knowledge. Recall Eleanor's worry in "Derek" that it was wrong to not tell Chidi about their romantic relationship in a previous version of the neighborhood. Should she tell him because keeping secrets is just like lying? Is keeping a secret from someone you care about especially morally objectionable? According to Chidi, "It's okay to keep a secret as long as that secret isn't harming anyone, and telling them that secret might cause harm." Because Chidi's response covers all cases of keeping a secret, it seems that the implicit argument, if successful, brings Eleanor knowledge without any direct perceptual input from the five senses. Moreover, if you believe, as Chidi does, that there are moral principles that cover all cases, then they are known apart from experience.

We often blend the two epistemological sources. Recall in "Janet and Michael" how Michael and Janet attempted to determine what was causing her glitches. Initially, Michael was convinced that he was the problem. He lied to Janet the first moment they met and he has been telling bigger lies ever since to hide that first one. But Janet interjects that if it were true that Michael's initial lie was the source of the problem, then she would have been glitching all along. Since this wasn't the case, they discovered that there must be a different source. Their discovery results from experience and a deductive inference.[5]

Philosophers often discuss two additional sources of knowledge. These sources pertain more to self-knowledge. The first is introspection. This occurs when you turn your "mind's eye" inward to discern internal facts about yourself, for example, how sad you feel because Tahani doesn't grab your butt in public. The second is memory. Unlike the first three sources, memory preserves rather than procures knowledge. You can remember what you experienced or reasoned about in the past. In either case, you can recall what you've previously come to know.

Memory is very important to one's sense of self. By remembering how you wronged your friend yesterday, you can properly make amends today without further damaging your relationship. Imagine if you couldn't remember your past. How could you make any long-range plans? If your past experiences have changed you in distinctive ways, but you don't recall the specifics of the relevant circumstances, how could you truly know who you are now or who you are becoming? In light of all this, we can see why Chidi claims that he and his three friends are living an "epistemological nightmare." They have changed as a result of being together, but because Michael constantly reboots them, each is barred from knowing who he or she is, and who each has become as a result of their interactions. It's indeed a frightening way to live.

A Debate about Justification (and Janet)

Some contemporary philosophers attempt to specify what kind (and not merely how much) justification is required for knowledge. This contemporary debate arises as a result of conflicting interpretations of Plato's classic statement about how one's beliefs must be "tied down" to the truth "by giving an account."[6]

The older of the two views is called internalism. Internalists, as the name suggests, stress the importance of a person providing an account of the reasons or evidence he or she has for believing that a statement is true. Moreover, internalists require that a person has done her due diligence in investigating the matter to discern the difference between proper and faulty evidence. Thus, for internalists, justification primarily depends on what is happening "inside" a person. Given her cognitive perspective and the reasons she has, is the belief reasonably held? If so, then she is sufficiently justified in holding it.

The newer of the two views, not surprisingly, is called externalism. Externalists focus on how a belief arises in the relevant circumstances, and they downplay the importance of one's internal cognitive perspective. That is, externalists stress how a belief is "tied to the truth" and reinterpret the requirement of "providing an account" to mean something like how, in an impartial sense, one's belief is appropriately generated in response to one's environment.

Thus circumstances external to the person are just as important as what is going on "inside" the person.

Perceptual knowledge is invariably interpreted via externalism. One need not be able to explain exactly how vision works and how it consequently plays a role in forming perceptual beliefs. Rather, it is sufficient that vision, assuming that it is not defective in some way, reliably produces perceptual beliefs that are likely to be true, which certainly seems to be the case.

Although this debate about justification may seem, well, academic, it has an intriguing application to how we might interpret Janet's character. Sometimes, as in the Season 1 episode "The Eternal Shriek," Janet describes herself by saying, "I am simply an anthropomorphized vessel of knowledge built to make your life easier," or "I am an informational delivery system," as she does in "Someone Like Me as a Member" from the same season. But other times, as she does in the Season 3 episode "Snowplow," she claims to know (literally) everything and agrees with Michael that she is a genius. In the Season 3 episode "The Ballad of Donkey Doug," when attempting to help Chidi break up with Simone, Janet tells him, "I do know everything about you and Simone and computer programming and virtual reality and artificial intelligence and the human brain and everything else." In fact, in the Season 2 episode "Derek," she even goes so far as to claim, "The whole point of me is that I know everything!" So, does Janet know everything? Does she know anything?

If you're inclined to believe that Janet does not *really* know anything, but rather acts more like a search engine, then you probably agree more with the internalists. Janet is merely a tool, and tools don't know anything because they cannot offer good reasons for how they behave. The externalist might respond that Janet is no mere piece of software. She regularly and reliably marshals and conveys true beliefs. Moreover, when Michael uses the random object generator program in "Janet and Michael" when attempting to determine why Janet is glitching, she immediately and successfully returns with a 14-ounce ostrich steak impaled on a novelty pencil that reads, "Lordy, Lordy, look who's 40." Perhaps the internalist would object that Janet is no different than the mysterious red-green cube that Michael uses to determine whether one of the humans is telling the truth. Just as the cube is merely relaying truth, but doesn't know anything, neither does Janet. In turn, the externalist might argue that Janet, unlike the cube, acts as if she has beliefs, and can marshal and convey the sorts of beliefs that we would expect of someone who possesses various different instances of knowledge about the world, including oddities involving ostrich steaks and novelty pencils (unlike the cube). Thus, at the very least, the internalist/externalist debate can explain why the show seems to waver on how Janet's character is portrayed.

"Here Comes the Egghead ..."

It's true that philosophical debates can be difficult to resolve completely, and Chidi takes a lot of flak for this fact. But it's clear that the internalist/externalist debate has some intriguing implications, especially in our current age of sophisticated artificial intelligence. Could IBM's Watson succeed at *Jeopardy* without in some sense *knowing* the answers to the questions?[7] As artificial intelligence continues to progress, it may seem only natural, at least eventually, to admit that such beings possess knowledge. Studying epistemology, and internalist and externalist accounts of justification especially, can explain why.

Notes

1 For more on acquaintance knowledge, see Louis Pojman, *What Can We Know?* (Belmont, CA: Wadsworth, 2001), 2. Some philosophers refer to it as "objectual knowledge." See Robert Audi, *Epistemology* (New York: Routledge, 1998), 16–17.

2 Plato, *Five Dialogues: Euthyphro, Apology, Crito, Meno, and Phaedo*, trans. G.M.A. Grube (Indianapolis, IN: Hackett, 2002), 97e–98a.

3 To be fair, Edmund Gettier's brief but influential 1963 article, "Is Justified True Belief Knowledge?" has raised some doubt about the adequacy of the justified true belief account.

4 René Descartes, *Meditations on First Philosophy* (1641), trans. Ronald Rubin (Claremont, CA: Arete Press, 1986), 5.

5 In deductive logic, the premises of an argument, if true, guarantee the truth of the conclusion. You can thus extend your knowledge by crafting logically proper deductive arguments.

6 For a thorough but accessible introduction to the debate between these two camps (internalism and externalism), see Jack S. Crumley, *An Introduction to Epistemology* (Mountain View, CA: Mayfield, 1999), 157–187.

7 See the PBS *Nova* episode "The Smartest Machine on Earth" (2011).

What's the Use of Free Will?

Joshua Tepley

The issue of free will is always lurking in the background of *The Good Place*, a show deeply concerned with making choices, doing the right thing, and moral responsibility. The episode that puts this issue front and center is "The Worst Possible Use of Free Will," the key parts of which take place in a public library and at a local diner (both of which, coincidentally, are used after hours to shoot pornos). In this episode, Eleanor becomes convinced that she doesn't have free will, and Michael tries to convince her that she does. This chapter offers a careful analysis of the arguments exchanged between these two characters. What are their arguments? Are these arguments any good? Is Eleanor's rejection of free will justified? Or does Michael's defense of free will get the upper hand?

Free Will

In ordinary language, "free will" means something like "done without coercion or compulsion." If I give my wallet to an armed robber, I can justifiably tell people afterward that I didn't do so "of my own free will." I was coerced. Actions done under hypnosis, under the influence of drugs or alcohol, or while sleepwalking aren't done freely in this sense, either.

It's tempting to say that this is all there is to free will: acting on one's own desires, without being coerced or compelled to do so. But it's not. There's another, deeper sense of "free will" that interests philosophers: the ability to do otherwise.

The Good Place and Philosophy, First Edition. Edited by Kimberly S. Engels.
© 2021 John Wiley & Sons, Inc. Published 2021 by John Wiley & Sons, Inc.

To see what this means, and how it differs from the ordinary-language sense of "free will," imagine being in a situation in which you can choose between two flavors of frozen yogurt—chocolate and vanilla—and, in fact, you choose chocolate. Suppose further that nobody had a gun to your head, you weren't under hypnosis, and the vanilla frozen yogurt didn't look poisoned or gross. In the everyday sense of "free will," you clearly did this "of your own free will." But there's another sense of "free will" we might wonder about. Could you have done otherwise? Could you *really* have chosen vanilla? Knowing you were uncoerced, not under hypnosis, and acting on your own desires doesn't tell us one way or the other.

This sense of "free will"—the ability to do otherwise—is what philosophers have in mind when they ask whether or not we have free will. It's also the sense that Eleanor and Michael are debating in this episode.

The Case against Free Will

The following dialogue contains the core of Eleanor's case against the existence of free will (the ability to do otherwise):

ELEANOR: I didn't choose to fall in love with Chidi, because some all-knowing demon, *you*, brought us together and scripted our lives.
MICHAEL: That's ridiculous. I didn't make you kiss Chidi by that lake.
ELEANOR: You kind of did. You orchestrated the whole "pet day" thing, manipulated us into choosing specific animals, made my lizard run away, which led to Chidi coming to help me find it, which led to us kissing, which led to us falling in love. None of that was my choice. Everything in my life has been determined by my upbringing, my genetics, or my environment. And everything in my afterlife was determined by *you*. There is no such thing as free will.

There's a lot going on here. Let's start with Eleanor's claim that everything she does is determined by her upbringing, her genetics, or her environment. What Eleanor means by "determined" is *caused*, where "caused" means *made to happen, given the laws of nature*. If a spark "causes" an explosion, this means that the spark, together with a number of other factors (such as the presence of fuel and oxygen) and the laws of nature, makes the explosion happen. In other words, given the spark, these other factors, and the laws of nature, the explosion had to happen. So, according to Eleanor, given her genetics, her upbringing, her environment, and the laws of nature, she must do everything she does.

Does it follow that Eleanor doesn't have free will—the ability to do otherwise? Not quite. One further assumption must be made, namely, that she had no control over these factors: her genetics, her upbringing, her environment, and the laws of nature. If any of these were under her control, then their jointly causing her behavior wouldn't take away her free will. In order for this argument to work, we must assume not only that all of Eleanor's actions have causes, but also that she had no control over those causes.

It's safe to say that Eleanor never had any control over her genetics, her upbringing, or the laws of nature. But what about her "environment"? What does that even mean? Presumably, the situation in which she finds herself—including where she lives, what job she has, and who her friends are. But why think she never had any control over these things? She might have had no control over them as a child, but why not as an adult? Why couldn't she freely change her friends, quit her job, or find a new place to live? Eleanor can't say that she had no control over these things because she had no free will, for that would simply beg the question—that is, presuppose the truth of what she's trying to prove.

At any rate, this argument faces another problem: why think that these three factors, combined with the laws of nature, completely specify everything Eleanor does? Perhaps some things Eleanor does are unavoidable, given her genetics, the way she was raised, and her current life situation. But everything? Is what she eats for lunch fixed by these factors? Or what time she goes to bed? Or which route she takes to work? This is extremely doubtful.

Determinism

Perhaps I've been interpreting Eleanor's argument too narrowly. Maybe her genetics, her upbringing, and her environment are meant to be examples of things that determine her behavior. In the very next scene, when a waitress asks her if she wants a drink, Eleanor responds: "Maybe I do, maybe I don't. But whatever I choose will be the result of millions of biological, genetic, and societal factors that are entirely outside my control." This list is different from the one she gave earlier, which suggests that what really matters for her argument isn't the specific factors she mentions but rather the existence of causes in general. Perhaps Eleanor's point is that each of her actions has some group of factors, possibly including but not necessarily limited to the ones she mentions, that caused her to do it.

The idea that everything, including human behavior, has a cause of some sort is called "determinism." More precisely, determinism is the view that *everything that happens is caused by other things that happen.*

Suppose determinism is true. Does it follow that there's no such thing as free will? Perhaps, but to prove that free will doesn't exist, it isn't enough to show that all of our actions have causes. It must also be shown that we had no control over those causes. And why think that? Everyone agrees that we never had any control over our genetics or our upbringings, but why think that we never had any control over any of the causes of our actions, whatever they happen to be?

Here's why. According to determinism, everything has a cause. Since causes precede their effects in time, it follows that the causes of our actions occurred before those actions happened. Regardless of what those causes were, they themselves must have had causes, too— if determinism is true. And so did those causes, and the causes of those causes, and the causes of those causes, and so on, back in time, until we reach a massive group of causes that occurred before we were born. We definitely didn't have control over anything that happened before we were born, so we definitely didn't have any control over the causes of our actions, either. And this means that determinism rules out free will.[1]

Compatibilism

There are different ways of responding to the "argument from determinism." Some people bite the bullet and admit that we don't have free will. People who say this are called "hard determinists." They think that determinism is true and that determinism rules out free will, so we don't have free will. Others simply deny determinism. People who accept the incompatibility of free will and determinism but insist that we have free will anyway, and so deny determinism, are called "libertarians" (not to be confused with political libertarians).[2] Libertarians about free will don't say that nothing is caused; they simply say that some things—namely, free human actions—are either uncaused or have special causes not governed by the laws of nature.

Despite their differences, libertarians and hard determinists both think that determinism rules out free will, a view known as "incompatibilism." A third way of responding to the argument from determinism is to deny incompatibilism. This view, not surprisingly, is called "compatibilism." According to compatibilists, determinism does not rule out free will.

But we just saw how determinism apparently does rule out free will. So, how can anybody be a compatibilist?[3]

Compatibilists use a number of strategies to reconcile free will and determinism, but the simplest, and most common, is to insist that free will isn't the ability to do otherwise. Remember I said earlier that, in ordinary language, acting "of one's own free will" means, more or less, acting on one's own desires without being coerced or compelled? According to the compatibilists I have in mind, that's the only kind of free will there is—or, at any rate, the only kind that matters. And if that's all free will is, then it's perfectly compatible with determinism, for nothing in this definition of "free will" requires that our free actions were uncaused or that we ever had any control over their causes.

However, this compatibilist strategy faces two major problems. First, in order for this definition of "free will" to be compatible with determinism, the word "compelled" has to mean something that includes abnormal states like hypnosis, drunkenness, and sleepwalking but excludes causal determinism. Why is a person who does something in her sleep "compelled" to do so, but not a person who does something as a result of causes that occurred before she was born? This is far from clear.

Second, compatibilism saves free will from determinism by changing the topic. The problem of free will starts as the problem of whether we can ever do something different from what we actually do, and compatibilists change it into the question of whether we can ever act on our own desires without being coerced or compelled to do so. That's a simple bait and switch.

So, it seems to me, compatibilism isn't the way to go. Free will—in the sense we should be talking about—is the ability to do otherwise, and this sort of free will really does seem to be incompatible with determinism. Is that the end of free will? Not necessarily. Remember, the argument from determinism depends upon the truth of determinism. While there are reasons to think that determinism is true, they are far from conclusive. Adherents of free will can simply reject determinism. And this is exactly what Michael should have said in response to this argument from Eleanor: determinism isn't true—at least in the case of free human (and demonic!) actions.

Michael's 15-Million-Point Plan

Our discussion so far has focused on just one of Eleanor's arguments against free will—the argument from determinism. But there's another argument contained in the little dialogue quoted in the "The Case against Free Will" section: Michael's manipulation of her in the afterlife based on his 15-million-point plan. Eleanor likens him to a puppeteer who pulled a bunch of strings, making her—a puppet—do what he wanted. Setting determinism aside, did Michael's elaborate plan take away Eleanor's free will?

It's easy to tell what a compatibilist would say: free will requires acting on one's own desires without being coerced. Michael's plan involved a great deal of coercion, so it must have taken away some of Eleanor's free will—in particular, when she acted according to his plan. But it's doubtful that it took away all of it. First, despite having 15 million points, Michael's plan wasn't detailed enough to determine everything Eleanor did. His plan included specific ways in which Eleanor and Chidi would torture each other, but did it also include which flavor of frozen yogurt she ate? Or how many shrimps she engorged at the neighborhood welcome party? Or what outfit she put on each morning? No way. Second, Michael admits that Eleanor did a number of things that surprised him, such as announcing to the neighborhood that she was the source of their problems. Since these things were unexpected to Michael, they couldn't have been parts of his plan. So, in these cases too, Eleanor acted freely—according to the compatibilist's definition of "free."

That's what a compatibilist would say. But I argued earlier that compatibilism isn't a winning strategy. It avoids the problem of determinism by changing the topic, which doesn't really solve the problem. So, what about incompatibilism—more specifically, libertarianism? What would libertarians say about Michael's plan in the afterlife? Did it take away Eleanor's free will?

Let's consider an extreme case of coercion: a robber puts a gun to your head and demands a dollar. You have one in your pocket, so you give it to him. Assuming you sometimes have the ability to do otherwise, did you have it in this particular case? Could you have refused to give the robber the dollar and taken a bullet instead?

I don't think so. Why not? Because you have a very good reason to give the robber a dollar (to save your life) and a comparatively bad reason not to do so (to save a dollar). In situations like this, when you have what appears to be an all-things-considered good reason to do something, you can't do otherwise. But if that's right, then do we ever have free will? Most of the time we have what appear (to us, at least) to be all-things-considered good reasons for doing what we do. If this is always the case, then we never have free will.

When Is the Will Free?

Thinking along these lines, the libertarian philosopher Peter van Inwagen argues that there are just a few situations in which people actually have the ability to do otherwise.[4] Here are three.

First, there are situations in which the alternatives are so equal in a person's mind that it's not obvious which of them to pick. Choosing between chocolate and vanilla frozen yogurt is a good example—assuming you want frozen yogurt in the first place, and your desires for chocolate and vanilla are more or less equal.

Second, there are situations in which one's immediate desires conflict with what's in one's own long-term self-interest. Should I eat this piece of cake? Have another drink? Smoke a cigarette? I want to do these things right now, but doing them—at least repeatedly—will harm me in the long run.

And third, there are situations in which what you perceive to be your moral duty conflicts with what's in your own self-interest. An example is being asked to tell the truth when doing so will get you into trouble but lying won't.

There may be other situations in which a person has the ability to do otherwise, but these three will suffice for our purposes. The only way that Michael's plan can take away Eleanor's free will assuming she has any free will to begin with—is by preventing her from being in these three situations. Does it?

Not at all. Eleanor finds herself in these situations all the time. Not only is she frequently able to make trivial choices about what to eat, what to drink, and what to wear, but she has to decide day by day, and sometimes minute by minute, whether or not to keep studying ethics with Chidi—something she has no immediate desire to do but will, she thinks, improve her long-term chances of being allowed to stay in The Good Place. And in the finale of the first season, Eleanor has to decide whether or not to tell the truth about being the source of the neighborhood's problems, even though she knows that doing so might earn her a one-way ticket to The Bad Place. So, while Michael's 15-million-point plan probably took away some of Eleanor's free will—by forcing her into situations in which there was just one obvious thing for her to do, given her desires, preferences, and values—it clearly didn't take away all of it.

In Defense of Free Will

Let's take stock. I've examined two arguments from Eleanor against the existence of free will. The argument based on Michael's 15-million-point plan fails to show that Eleanor had no free will in the afterlife. Michael's plan took away some of her free will, assuming she had any to begin with, but neither compatibilists nor libertarians should think that it took away all of it. The other argument, based on determinism, is much stronger, but it can be avoided by denying determinism—the view that everything has a cause. This is a heavy price to pay, but so is giving up on free will (more on which later in this chapter).

Of course, showing that Eleanor's arguments against free will aren't convincing doesn't prove that we have free will. Is there any good reason to think that? In his conversation with Eleanor, Michael says (or does) a number of things—four, by my count—that can be construed as arguments for the existence of free will.

First, Michael explains that, his 15-million-point plan notwithstanding, Eleanor did many things he never anticipated—such as falling in love with Chidi and announcing to the neighborhood that she was causing their problems. In his words: "I tried to script your whole afterlife, and I devised a 15-million-point plan to torture you. You made choices I never saw coming. I call that free will." Undoubtedly, Michael is being truthful: Eleanor really did do things he never planned or anticipated. But does it follow that she did such things freely? Of course not. Human beings are extremely complex. The fact that Michael couldn't predict some of Eleanor's actions doesn't prove that those actions couldn't have been predicted in principle. It only proves that human beings are complicated and that Michael isn't omniscient (all-knowing).

Second, Michael attempts to demonstrate that he has free will by doing something spontaneous: dumping iced tea on Eleanor's head. "Why did you do that?" asks Eleanor. "Because I have free will,"

Michael replies. The underlying idea seems to be this: free actions are uncaused, and this action—which was done for no reason—had no cause. Therefore, it was a free action. Is this a good argument? Not at all. Why think that Michael's dumping iced tea on Eleanor's head was done for no reason? In fact, we know what his reasons were: to snap Eleanor out of her funk, to punish her for being so annoying, and to demonstrate that he has free will. And even if these weren't his reasons, it wouldn't follow that his action had no cause. Failure to find a cause—for example, through introspection—doesn't prove that there's no cause to be found. Causes, like good friends, are sometimes hard to find.

Third, Michael claims that Eleanor's denial of free will is just a defense mechanism, an attempt to avoid feeling vulnerable after being reminded of her relationship with Chidi. And at the end of the episode, Eleanor admits to Michael as much: "I'm sorry. You were right. I was scared about what it all meant, and I went back to one of my favorite moves: turn on the ol' Blame Hose." But even so, this doesn't prove anything about free will. The cause of Eleanor's rejection of free will might have been an unconscious desire to avoid feeling vulnerable, but this wouldn't undermine the reasons she gave for this rejection. In fact, this type of objection, which attacks a belief or an argument on the basis of its origins, or genesis, is so clearly fallacious that philosophers have given it a name: the genetic fallacy.

The Use of Free Will

Michael's fourth and final argument on behalf of free will comes in the following dialogue, which occurs after Eleanor fails to be convinced by his other three arguments:

ELEANOR: Whatever. Who even cares?
MICHAEL: I do. Because if everything is determined, and we have no free will, then all the stuff we're doing to put more good into the world is pointless. And I want to believe that it matters.

Michael's not arguing that free will exists. He's explaining why he's going to believe in it anyway. Why? Because if there's no free will, then everything he does is pointless. He doesn't want to believe that everything he does is pointless, so he's going to believe in free will. Presumably, Michael thinks that the same line of reasoning will appeal to Eleanor—and to everyone else, for that matter. If we don't have free will, then everything we do is pointless. So, if we don't want to believe that everything we do is pointless, then we ought to believe in free will.

How good is this argument? Well, for one thing, it presupposes that believing what makes you happy is more important than believing what you think is true. I find this both dubious and despicable. But let's set this problem aside in order to focus on the other premise of Michael's argument, namely, that everything we do is pointless without free will. Is that true?

Suppose, for a moment, that we don't have free will—the ability to do otherwise. Everything we do, we must do given the past and the laws of nature. If this were true, then what would follow? Could we still make plans? Experience pleasure? Help other people? Achieve our goals? I see no reason why not. None of these things require the ability to do otherwise. So, what would be missing from our lives if we didn't have free will?

Moral Responsibility

The only thing I can think of is moral responsibility. It makes no sense to praise or blame people for what they do if they can't do otherwise. After all, why don't we blame people for having certain parents? Or for getting sick? Or for sneezing? Because they can't help these things. These things aren't under their control. And if all of our actions are like these, then it makes no sense to blame (or praise) us for any of them, either.

The thesis that people are morally responsible for their actions only if they could have done otherwise is called the "principle of alternative possibilities."[5] If this principle is true, then moral responsibility doesn't exist without the ability to do otherwise, or what I've been calling "free will." But surely we are, sometimes, morally responsible for our actions. And in that case, we have a good reason to believe in free will—and this reason doesn't rely on the dubious (and despicable) assumption that being happy is more important than finding truth. It's not exactly Michael's reason, I admit, but we can give Michael some credit for getting us to think about what we'd be lacking if we didn't have free will.

Determinism versus Moral Responsibility

Where does this leave us? Eleanor offers an argument against free will that can be avoided only by denying determinism. An argument inspired by one of Michael's arguments implies that free will can be denied only by giving up moral responsibility. So, we must reject one of these two: determinism or moral responsibility. But which one? Should we be libertarians? Or hard determinists? I'll let you decide— if you can.

Notes

1 For a much more rigorous presentation and defense of this argument, see chapter 3 of Peter van Inwagen, *An Essay on Free Will* (Oxford: Oxford University Press, 1983). The rest of this book is also highly recommended.
2 According to political libertarians, the role of the state ought to be minimized in order to promote individual liberty. For a classic articulation and defense of this position, see Robert Nozick, *Anarchy, State, and Utopia* (New York: Basic Books, 1974).
3 For an accessible, book-length defense of compatibilism, see Daniel C. Dennett, *Elbow Room: The Varieties of Free Will Worth Wanting* (Cambridge, MA: MIT Press, 1984).
4 See Peter van Inwagen, "When Is the Will Free?" *Philosophical Perspectives* 3 (1989), 399–422.
5 Not all philosophers accept the principle of alternative possibilities. For a classic paper arguing against this principle, see Harry G. Frankfurt, "Alternate Possibilities and Moral Responsibility," *The Journal of Philosophy* 66 (1969), 829–839.

From Clickwheel through Busty Alexa: The Embodied Case for Janet as Artificial Intelligence

Robin L. Zebrowski

As we watch Michael, Janet, and the Soul Squad navigate four seasons of transformative adventures, it becomes clear that no one (including Janet) really understands what Janet is. In Season 1, she claims to be "simply an anthropomorphized vessel of knowledge built to make your life easier" ("The Eternal Shriek"). Throughout the series, though, she undergoes a change at least as radical as the one the humans undergo, which at first glance appears to be of a very different nature. Janet's transformation seems as mysterious as that of the humans, too, and at least part of it can be attributed to the same cause: other people.

Philosophers have long been exploring the possibility of artificial consciousness. Currently there are at least two independent strands of thought concerning the underlying metaphysics of AI. On the one hand, we can ask if computers can ever possibly be the kinds of things that have minds. Of course, this involves a lot of tough philosophical questions about what minds are and how they work. On the other hand, we might be agnostic about what minds are and how they work, and yet still ask worthwhile questions about artificial minds in our quest to make more sense of minds in general.

By considering Janet, we can discover a bit about the nature of minds (at least as they're conceived in the universe of *The Good Place*). Additionally, we can learn why Janet is becoming the kind of person she is as the series progresses. She's not a robot and not a girl, but as she grows and develops the ability to have experiences, she's clearly a person. Here, it helps to realize that a person does not necessarily need to be human. Rather what we mean by a person is a being with certain kinds of rights, privileges, and responsibilities. So, we can watch as Janet develops from an automated being, like today's algorithms, to a person with thoughts and experiences rather than just statements, semantics rather than pure syntax. As we'll see, Janet supplies a blueprint for how we ought to think about artificial intelligence in the twenty-first century: embodied, social, and surprising.

Embodiment Matters

Our human forms of embodiment, the many various ways real bodies appear in the real world, structure our experiences, memories, thoughts, and language in ways both subtle and important. On *The Good Place*, we have bodies in the afterlife, and they must be real enough that they can be filled with pins and butthole spiders. The brain matters for thinking, sure, but so do our bodies and our environments. In fact, our minds couldn't exist as they do without the kinds of bodies we have in the kinds of social and physical environments we inhabit.

We tend to think of our minds as things locked away inside our heads. The usual reasoning goes: sure, your mind needs input, which it gets from your senses, and it provides output, in the form of your body moving or speaking or thinking. We mostly think of the mind as a little computerized soul-thing, chugging away in the head. We might even think our mind would be fundamentally the same if we put it in a different body. This is how we get all those highly questionable body-swap movies, and how we can make sense of the episode "Janet(s)." That's the one where all of the characters look like Janet in her void, but we can recognize their mannerisms and language quirks well enough to distinguish them. In reality, though, minds are not ethereal, disembodied computers.

Consider language. There is robust evidence that our bodies help structure not just the words we use, but also how we actually conceptualize many different ideas. Concepts are the building blocks of thought, and our languages reveal how we formulate and grasp these concepts. (See what I did there? I used both "reveal" and "grasp" metaphorically, because my mind doesn't grasp, my hands do, but "understanding an idea" is so abstract that one of the ways we make sense of it is to use the language of our bodies to help us actually conceptualize it.

Many abstract ideas work this way.[1]) When Janet reports that she might be the most advanced Janet in the universe because of her more than 800 reboots, her first demonstration is embodied: patting herself on the head and rubbing her stomach, not solving mathematical equations (because any simple calculator can do that). In a book about the importance of bodies for cognition, Andy Clark says that our brains are "bad at logic and good at Frisbee."[2] This means behavior is never just a matter of code running on an abstract system, but of the interface where body and mind meet environment.

Scholars have studied how embodied ways of conceptualizing the world differ across cultures.[3] But how do you make sense of a void? Janet's void is both a place and not a place. She goes there, she sends Derek to "a corner" of it, but a void can't be a place to go. So my body's experiences in a world like ours really can't help me conceptualize the void. To make this a bit clearer: imagine you are a spherical being floating in space without gravity or other objects and perceiving in all directions at once. The very concepts of up, down, in front of, behind, to the side of, and so on would not make sense to you.[4] And you use those concepts to understand many more things! As Lakoff and Johnson remind us, "the cat is behind the tree or in front of the car only relative to our capacity to project fronts and backs onto cars and trees and to impose relations onto visual scenes relative to such projections."[5] The future is in front of you and vision is used to make sense of understanding, if you see what I mean. Bodies matter for the complex kind of reasoning our minds do, and the spaces those bodies occupy matter, too (even when they're a void).

Researchers in robotics recognized the importance of having a body in the real world as a method of building AI way before the mainstream AI community did.[6] When Rodney Brooks, a roboticist, wrote a now-legendary paper explaining why embodiment matters in AI, it was rejected from every journal for years until it was eventually published in the most prestigious AI journal.[7] People argued that he misunderstood the work of AI because bodies couldn't matter, only thinking mattered, and yet Brooks was busy designing robotic creatures that could solve problems no other AI systems could touch (literally!). The Mars Rovers owe a debt of gratitude to his early work that demonstrated ways to deal with unpredictable environments without heavy computation: you let the body do the work and leave the brain out of it. If you have a robot with four wheels and two motors, and you program it to perform some action, what happens if you switch the locations of the motors, or turn two of the wheels into articulated legs, but don't change the code? Wildly different behaviors! Why? Because embodiment matters to how we experience the world and how intelligent behavior emerges.

Wisdom and Social Abilities

Janet loves to remind us she's not a robot and not a girl. And while her embodiment establishes that she might be a candidate for the kind of thing that has a mind (and therefore is a person), we still don't really know what she is. Janet does admit that with every reboot, she gains "wisdom and social abilities," and we might think the social aspect is a bit of a weird inclusion. Wisdom, sure, but social abilities? It turns out that social abilities, and the fact that Janet is a social being, play a huge role in her development as the kind of creature we'd consider a person, and having the kind of experiences we'd consider characteristic of a mind.

The idea of people being who they are and having a sense of selfhood has a rich and complicated philosophical history. But one common idea is that your sense of who you are as well as the actual metaphysical truth about what you are heavily depend upon your social world. Throughout the first three seasons, Janet herself recognizes the ways she is changing. The change is subtle early on, so it's easy to continue to see her as the Busty Alexa that Eleanor sees at first. But even by the end of Season 1, in "What's My Motivation," Janet is aware of her development. She tells Jason that she now has the capacity to love and hate, and as Eleanor decides to summon a train, Janet says, "Now that I can think and feel, I don't belong here either." But much of Janet's most interesting development comes when she recognizes herself as a being in relation to her friends. Her relationship with Jason prompts Janet to stop being an anthropomorphized vessel in a void and start being something we'd rightly call conscious, and even a person. She's able to pack away Derek and get over her heartbreak "now that I know I can talk to my friends about it" ("Janet and Michael"), and in the Season 3 finale ("Pandemonium"), when Jason says that for a robot, Janet makes a really good girlfriend, she corrects him with "I'm one out of three of those things." It is the relationships that change Janet, and the social aspects of those relationships are doing a lot of philosophical work for her.

Since we don't get to see any other Good Place Janets, it's hard to know how different our Janet's experience is from other Janets'.

But we do know that Eleanor and Jason's experiences in the fake Good Place are unlike the experiences of regular real Good Place residents. When they treat Janet as a confidante and include her in their schemes, they enable Janet to participate in a neighborhood in a (presumably) different way than most Janets. This, along with her 800-something reboots, positions her as a unique system in the universe.

Janet's participation in the life of the neighborhood is meaningful in many ways, and it is difficult to untangle from the other interesting pieces of her identity. But that participation is likely tied up with her growth from not-a-robot into a full, experiencing person, and we can make some sense of this idea through a concept called "participatory sense-making."[8] Much philosophical and scientific research on social cognition focuses on individuals, and how they exist and grow as the people they are when in social interactions. But participatory sense-making turns this upside-down, offering us a way to understand how we make meaning in the world when we start from social coordination as the unit of study, rather than individuals engaged in such coordination. The kinds of meaning we can make, and the ways we understand ourselves and our world, change in a fundamental way when we're involved in socially interactive situations. If we think about Janet learning that she has feelings for Jason and how those feelings are interacting with her role in the community, we'll remember that she only came to this understanding through an emotion-laden conversation. Participatory sense-making is "the coordination of intentional activity in interaction, whereby individual sense-making processes are affected and new domains of social sense-making can be generated that were not available to each individual on her own."[9] Thus, "it constitutes a level of analysis not reducible, in general, to individual behaviors,"[10] which is why when the residents of Neighborhood 12358W interact with Janet and treat her as a person, it offers opportunities for Janet to actually *become* a person. She quite literally could not have done this alone.

Many philosophers have understood the formation of the self to be in various relations to the social world, in contrast to the more traditional idea of the self as some core, stable, unchanging kernel somehow attached to a life. Frantz Fanon (1925–1961), for example, argued that self-identity is a process of mutual recognition in a social world, a world where relations of social power like race can enable or limit one's ability to be the person they want to be. Another version of this comes to us from traditional Ubuntu philosophy, where we are taught things like "I am because we are, and since we are, therefore I am."[11] When considered in this context, Janet's transformation begins to make perfect sense (as do the transformations of the rest of our protagonists). Most of us hold an unexamined concept of selfhood that likely comes to us from René Descartes (1596–1650). He likened the mind to the self, and famously said, "I think, therefore I am." (If we loosen our definition of "thinking," we might see this a bit like Eleanor's life on Earth: she was all that existed or mattered, the center of her own universe, owing nothing to anyone.)

Though the fake Good Place is remarkably free from prejudice of the kinds we're very used to in our own world, Janet's unique status oddly, but not maliciously, gets called out many times. No one seems to hold that status against her, but the fact of it being called out is still noteworthy. Janet can very likely never escape from being at least partly constituted by the labels she is given by the humans, even if they don't accurately capture her existence. She is called a girl and a robot repeatedly, while remaining steadfast in denying that's what she really is. Fanon, a black man living under colonial rule, wants to be "a man among other men,"[12] as Janet presumably wants to be recognized for what she truly is. But, Janet carries the history of everything resembling her that came before: robot and girl alike. Perhaps the most useful way to make sense of Janet's transformation is that it's really a transformation for us, the viewers. We transform from understanding ourselves (and Janet) as Cartesian subjects, centers of our universes and possessing selfhood by some magical metaphysical nature of humanity, to making sense of Janet (and ourselves) as people in relation to other people. But this notion of a self created only through other selves, "A person is a person through other persons,"[13] is a revelation that pushes us closer to the main point of the show: that we owe things to one another by virtue of being people in social relationships. And we become people through *having* those social relationships.

A Moral Neighborhood

Janet's position in the social order sets up more than just her capacity to develop the kind of mind she does, and to become the person she does. It also enables her participation in the kind of moral social order that the entire show is about. Chidi loves to present abstract ethical theories and then watch everyone squirm as they realize the impossibility of living up to those various standards (as he would be the first to demonstrate). But plenty of philosophers have focused on the role of the social community with regard to building and sustaining an ethical world.

One of the most visible philosophical works in the show is T.M. Scanlon's *What We Owe to Each Other*, which first appears early in Season 1 when Chidi tries to explain contractualism to Eleanor.[14] He asks her to imagine a group of reasonable people trying to decide the rules for a new society. Eleanor quips, "Like if your Uber driver talks to you, the ride should be free?" Scanlon's argument is that morality, at its core, is a contract among reasonable social beings. Indeed, Chidi sums it up perfectly in his three-hour video lecture on YouTube that Eleanor watches in "Somewhere Else." Building off Scanlon's work, he says, "I argue that we choose to be good because of our bonds with other people and our innate desire to treat them with dignity." And as we now know, it is Scanlon's book that Eleanor returns to in the series finale—the work is never done. If Janet has, as I argue, really developed into a conscious, experiencing person, with a mind and feelings, then she, too, counts in this moral calculation that Chidi and Scanlon argue for. She has those bonds with the group, and she factors into the social contract as someone to treat with dignity (even Michael is horrified when he believes she's been marbleized). The language of people owing something to each other recurs throughout the series (or not owing, as when young Eleanor requests emancipation from her parents), and it's a reminder that relevant moral questions always involve other people.

Possibly the most famous experiment in building a neighborhood, aside from *The Good Place*'s Neighborhood 12358W, is Hull House in Chicago. Jane Addams (1860–1935), along with co-founder Ellen Gates Starr, built the neighborhood as a social experiment. Importantly, Addams thought that "knowing one another better reinforces the common connection of people such that the potential for caring and empathetic moral actions increases."[15] In other words, she built a neighborhood with the goal of having people live together, since this would necessarily increase their knowledge of one another and therefore also result in a caring, moral community. Education was a core value, and Addams didn't believe that the success of one member or a small number of members in the group counted as progress. The only way for improvement to matter is if it is improvement of the group. She writes:

> What he does attain, however, is not the result of his individual striving, as a solitary mountain climber beyond the sight of the valley multitude, but it is underpinned and upheld by the sentiments and aspirations of many others. Progress has been slower perpendicularly, but incomparably greater because lateral.... He has not taught his contemporaries to climb mountains, but he has persuaded the villagers to move up a few feet higher.[16]

The humans of *The Good Place* have learned this lesson, refusing the Judge's offer of letting individual tests determine whether they move on or not. In "The Burrito," the Judge clarifies, "So, if you all pass, you're in. And if even one of you fails, you're all effed, right? Terrible idea." But if morality is fundamentally tied to the social world, as Addams argued, then the humans are living (despite being dead!) this philosophy in the same way Addams did, always ensuring the theory is put into practice.

So where does Janet fit in? Well, by the time the group has come together to make this decision, I would argue that Janet is fully a person. She says, in "Somewhere Else," "I'm not a girl. I'm also not just a Janet anymore. I don't know what I am." And wondering what you are is about the most human, conscious act a person can undertake.

Not Just a Janet Anymore

The history of AI theory is a history of asking what kinds of processes underlie the human capacity for the kinds of thoughts and felt experiences we have. Theorists have spent a lot of time and ink debating whether thought is computation, how much the squishy meat stuff that makes up our brains matters, and whether nonhumans could possibly have minds. But for the last couple of decades, theorists have also started taking embodiment claims seriously. Questions about the felt quality of experiences, along with the particular details of how varied sorts of human bodies work in physical, social, and cultural environments, have finally started to impact the ways we think about AI. Between philosophy and science fiction, we've explored a huge number of ways AI might emerge. But the intersection of social morality and embodiment, the intersection where Janet comfortably rests, has been underexplored.

Janet is a refreshing way to think about AI going forward. Indeed, she is a model for how AI researchers and philosophers ought to think about the emergence of a mind, of thoughts and feelings that a system previously lacked. The most important lesson about AI that we learn from Janet is that it isn't just a question of getting the weightings right in the neural network or creating the optimal symbol system. Rather, it's heartbreak, friendship, and participation in a social world that matter. Ultimately, that's what makes Janet's emergence as a person possible.

Notes

1 George Lakoff and Mark Johnson, *Philosophy in the Flesh: The Embodied Mind and Its Challenge to Western Thought* (New York: Basic Books, 1999); and idem, *Metaphors We Live By* (Chicago: University of Chicago Press, 1980).

2 Andy Clark, *Natural Born Cyborgs: Minds, Technologies, and the Future of Human Intelligence* (New York: Oxford University Press, 2003).

3 Lera Boroditsky and Paul Thibodeau, "Metaphors We Think With: The Role of Metaphor in Reasoning," *PLoS ONE* 6 (2011): e16782; and Lera Boroditsky and Alice Gaby, "Remembrances of Times East: Absolute Spatial Representations of Time in an Australian Aboriginal Community," *Psychological Science* 21 (2010), 1635–1639. (See, in general, Lera Boroditsky's entire body of experimental work.)

4 Lakoff and Johnson, *Philosophy in the Flesh*, 34.

5 Ibid., 35.

6 For a discussion, see Josh Bongard and Rolf Pfeifer, *How the Body Shapes the Way We Think: A New View of Intelligence* (Cambridge, MA: MIT Press, 2007).

7 Rodney Brooks, *Cambrian Intelligence: The Early History of the New AI* (Cambridge, MA: MIT Press, 1999).

8 Hanna De Jaegher and Ezequiel Di Paolo, "Participatory Sense-Making: An Enactive Approach to Social Cognition," *Phenomenology and the Cognitive Sciences* 6 (2007), 485–507.

9 Ibid., 497.

10 Ibid., 492.

11 John Mbiti, *African Religions and Philosophy* (Johannesburg: Heinemann, 1969).

12 Frantz Fanon, *Peau noire, masques blanc* (Black skin, white masks) (Paris: Editions de Seuil, 1952), 112.

13 This analysis of the Ubuntu philosophy in contrast with a Cartesian view of selfhood is courtesy of Abeba Birhane, "Descartes Was Wrong: 'A Person

Is a Person through Other People'," *Aeon*, April 7, 2017, https://aeon.co/ideas/descartes-was-wrong-a-person-is-a-person-through-other-persons.

14   T.M. Scanlon, *What We Owe to Each Other* (Cambridge, MA: Harvard University Press, 1998).

15   Maurice Hamington, "Jane Addams," *The Stanford Encyclopedia of Philosophy*, Summer 2019 ed., ed. Edward N. Zalta, https://plato.stanford.edu/archives/sum2019/entries/addams-jane/.

16   Jane Addams, "A Modern Lear," in *Jane Addams and the Dream of American Democracy*, ed. Jean Bethke Elshtain (New York: Basic Books, 2002).

Why It Wouldn't Be Rational to Believe You're in The Good Place (and Why You Wouldn't Want to Be There Anyway)

David Kyle Johnson

I'm a neuroscientist, so I get what's going on here.
—Simone ("A Girl from Arizona, Part 1")

The Good Place is, obviously, about moral philosophy. But one reason everyone hates moral philosophers (especially other philosophers) is that they think everything is about ethics. It's not. And the same is true for *The Good Place*. Indeed, it raises two very interesting non-moral questions: (1) could you ever actually know you were in The Good Place? And (2) would you even want to be? As I shall now show, the answers to these questions are "no" and "hell no," respectively.

Cartesian Skepticism about The Good Place

When I pose questions about whether you could ever know you were in The Good Place, you probably think back to Season 1 and its big reveal: everyone thought Eleanor, Chidi, Tahani, and Jason were in The Good Place, but they were actually in The Bad Place. In an effort to torture them, the demon Michael had deceived them. So, one might wonder, even if The Good Place and The Bad Place were real, how could one ever know that they were actually in The Good Place (instead of the victim of some elaborate hoax)?

Interestingly, this harkens to the concerns of a philosopher named René Descartes (1596–1650). In his famous *Meditations on First*

The Good Place and Philosophy, First Edition. Edited by Kimberly S. Engels.
© 2021 John Wiley & Sons, Inc. Published 2021 by John Wiley & Sons, Inc.

Philosophy, Descartes looked for an unshakable undoubtable belief upon which to ground his endeavor for scientific knowledge. An early candidate he considered was his belief that the physical world existed. But he then soon realized that belief was not indubitable. After all, he'd had dreams where he was completely convinced that what he was experiencing was the physical world. How could he know for sure that he wasn't dreaming?

Now, contrary to common opinion, that didn't make Descartes doubt the existence of the physical world. After all, the ideas in his dreams came from his waking experience of the physical world—and if so, the physical world exists. But then Descartes considered another possibility. What if "some malicious, powerful, cunning demon has done all he can to deceive me [and] the sky, the air, the earth, colors, shapes, sounds, and all external things are merely dreams that the demon has contrived as traps for my judgment"?[1]

In other words, what if a demon (perhaps named Michael) had tricked Descartes into thinking that a physical world exists when it doesn't? Descartes didn't actually think he was being tricked, mind you. But he concluded that the fact that he couldn't prove that he wasn't being tricked entailed that he couldn't *know* that a physical world existed (even if it did). And so, in the same way, one might wonder: "Even if I did arrive in The Good Place, how could I ever know that a demon (named Michael) wasn't fooling me into thinking I was, when I wasn't?"

Now, the answer to that question might be similar to the solution that I think works for Descartes's problem. How can I know the world is real when I can't prove that it is? Because knowledge doesn't require proof. It doesn't require certainty. Since Plato, knowledge has been defined as "True belief with an account"—or, as philosophers put it today, "justified true belief." But a belief can be justified, even if it is not certain. To quote my favorite contemporary philosopher, Ted Schick:

> [K]nowledge doesn't require certainty, [it] doesn't require enough [justification] to put the claim beyond any possibility of doubt, but rather enough to put it beyond any reasonable doubt. [And a] proposition is beyond a reasonable doubt when it provides the best explanation of something.[2]

Although it's possible that a demon is deceiving me into thinking that a physical world exists when it doesn't, that is not the best explanation for my experience. That a physical world exists is a much better explanation.

And thus I can know that the physical world exists. In the same way, although I could never know for certain that Michael wasn't fooling me into thinking that I was in The Good Place when I wasn't, that I was in The Good Place could be the best explanation for what I was experiencing. For example, if, unlike Eleanor, I had no reason to think I didn't deserve to be there, and there weren't things that bothered me—in other words, if the place I was in really was good—then "I am in The Good Place" would be the better explanation for the wonderful experiences I was having.

The Good Place as a Good Explanation

But now you are probably asking yourself:

> But wait a minute. What makes one explanation better than another? Why is (for example) "A physical world exists" a better explanation for my experiences than "I am being fooled by a demon"? Or why would "I am in The Good Place" be a better explanation than "I am in The Bad Place"?

This is a great question. Clearly you're paying attention.

For the answer, we can once again turn to Ted Schick. In the sixth chapter of his book, *How to Think about Weird Things*, he lays out what explanations must be to, by definition, be good explanations. They must be:

TESTABLE:	make novel observable predictions
FRUITFUL:	get the predictions they make right
WIDE SCOPING:	explain a vast number of phenomena, and not raise unanswerable questions
SIMPLE:	not unnecessarily invoke new entities or forces
CONSERVATIVE:	cohere with what we already have good reason to believe[3]

These are called the "criteria of adequacy." A good explanation need not always meet all these criteria, but all things being equal, the explanation that is more adequate—that adheres to the most (when compared to other explanations)—is the one we should prefer.

When it comes to Descartes's concerns, we can see why "A physical world exists" is a better explanation than "A demon has created a dream world to fool me." First, unlike a physical world, the hypothesis that the demon exists is not testable (and thus also can't be fruitful). He's not observable, and he'd sabotage any test you performed to see if he existed. It's not wide scoping because it raises unanswerable questions (like "How does the demon create this dream world?" and "Why is he intent on fooling you?").[4] And since the demon hypothesis also requires the existence of the demon, his dream world, and an elaborate deception, it's not as simple as the physical world hypothesis.[5]

When it comes to the Good Place versus Bad Place hypothesis, the big giveaway is simplicity. The Good Place hypothesis doesn't require a grand deception and all the planning that would be necessary to keep it afloat. The Bad Place hypothesis does. In this respect, it's essentially a conspiracy theory; and one of the (many) reasons conspiracy theories are irrational is because of the grand assumptions one must make to believe that such grand deceptions exist.[6] And while both hypotheses raise unanswerable questions—we are dealing with an ethereal afterlife here, after all—the Bad Place hypothesis seems to raise more. Why would a demon create a place that truly seems good to torture me? How is that torture? Since the Good Place hypothesis is simpler and wider scoping than the Bad Place hypothesis, it would be the preferable explanation.

But this raises a different question. If you found yourself in a situation like the one Eleanor and Chidi found themselves, would "I am in The Good Place" and "I am in The Bad Place but being fooled" be the only two possible explanations? It seems not. Recall that, at the beginning of Season 4, Simone suspects that The Good Place is just a product of her imagination.

> You know, clearly, I was in some kind of horrible accident. I'm on my deathbed, and this entire thing is just a hallucination constructed by my damaged brain as it slowly shuts down. It's not real, so I'm just gonna wander around until I wake up or die. See you later, figments of my imagination! ("A Girl from Arizona")

Since she's a neuroscientist, she's aware that this could be an explanation for what she is experiencing. But is it really the better explanation for what she is experiencing? This is the question I have in mind when I wonder whether one could ever know that they were in The Good Place.

Scientific Skepticism about The Good Place

Sadly, it seems "I am hallucinating" would in fact be the better explanation for what one was experiencing if they found themselves in The Good Place. Why?

Elsewhere, I have explained why justified belief in things like demons and miracles is impossible.[7] In order for such beliefs to be justified, "A demon did it" or "A miracle occurred" would have to be the best explanation for some event or experience. But such explanations are, by their very nature, not wide scoping, simple, or conservative. They raise unanswerable questions, invoke extra entities, and violate physical laws. And on the rare occasions they are testable, they have always failed the test. Natural explanations will always be better, so thinking that there is one will always be more rational—even if you can't figure out what it is. Of course, it's logically possible that supernatural forces have violated physical laws. But it's also possible that you simply are not smart or observant enough to figure out what really happened. And that will always be the better explanation because it is simpler, wider scoping, and more conservative. The supernatural explanation invokes supernatural entities, raises unanswerable questions about how supernatural entities interact with the natural world, and conflicts with well-established causal closure principles. The natural "I missed it" explanation does none of these things, and aligns quite nicely with what we know about the powers and limits of human perception, memory, and intellect.[8] Indeed, although you may think what occurred defied the laws of physics, it's more likely that you are simply wrong about what the laws of physics allow.

And this line of reasoning is not a stubborn, pigheaded, irrational refusal to believe in the supernatural. Indeed, it employs exactly the same logic that one employs at magic shows—a logic that avoids what I have elsewhere labeled the "mystery therefore magic" fallacy.[9] When I see the magicians Penn & Teller do something I can't explain, I don't conclude that they have magic powers. I conclude that there's a natural explanation I'm not smart enough to detect. And this would be true, even if I were an expert at detecting such natural explanations. After all, Penn & Teller themselves have a show (*Fool Us*) where they are fooled by other magicians at least once an episode. But never, upon being fooled, have Penn & Teller said, "Well then, I guess you have magic powers." The fact that magic, miraculous, or demonic explanations are never justified is just a consequence of the fact that they are, by definition, inadequate explanations. And this would be true even if magic, miracles, and demons were real.

And so, even if The Good Place was real and we were in it, we could never be justified in believing that we were. That we were experiencing a hallucination caused by our brain as it slowly shuts down would be the better—simpler, wider-scoping, and conservative—explanation. The Good Place is an extra entity that raises unanswerable questions, and our being in The Good Place conflicts with facts that we have good reason to believe.

What kind of facts, you ask?

Well, for example, discoveries in neuroscience have shown that the functioning of my brain is necessary for the existence of my mentality. When certain parts of a person's brain cease to function, specific parts of their mentality disappear, and once their brain shuts down, that person no longer experiences anything. In other words, our mentality is not housed in a separable entity, called a soul, that can float away from our body when we die.[10] So the idea that our soul can float away to some afterlife, like The Good Place, conflicts with well-established science.

Of course one might argue that since, in The Good Place, one seems to have a body and brain, one could still have experiences. But consider the fact that if someone went looking for Eleanor's body on Earth, they would presumably find it lying in her coffin. At best, what's in The Good Place is a copy of Eleanor's earthly body. But if what's in The Good Place is a copy of your earthly body, then it's not really you; it's just someone who looks and acts like you. Indeed, contemporary philosopher Peter Unger has argued that in order for our personal identity—the fact that we are one and the same person—to be preserved, it must be the case that the physical continuity of our body (or, more specifically, our brain) is preserved over time.[11] Since, when you die, your brain ceases to function, your personal identity ends there.

Now, this particular difficulty can be overcome. To preserve your personal identity into the afterlife, Michael could just swoop in and steal and heal your body before you die (and replace it with an inanimate replica). Interestingly, this is what Christian philosopher Peter van Inwagen suggests that God *must* do if he is to fulfill his promise to propel faithful Christians into the afterlife: God must be a body snatcher.[12] But even if Michael did this to Simone (or Eleanor, or you) for all the reasons I laid out here, she would still be more justified in believing that she was the victim of a hallucination.

Sadly, not even all brain experts realize this. In his book, *Proof of Heaven*, neurosurgeon Eben Alexander claims he had an experience while in a coma induced by an *Escherichia coli* infection that could only be explained by his soul floating away to heaven. But not only did later reports reveal that the coma was actually induced and maintained *medically* (not by his *E. coli* infection), his argument that his experiences couldn't have been the result of a hallucination is fallacious. He assumes his experiences happened when he was in the coma, but they would have actually occurred while he was being weaned off his anesthetics and in a "conscious but delirious" state.[13] Indeed, near-death experiences cannot ever provide evidence of an afterlife for much the same reason that "It's magic" could never be the best explanation for anything. For the reasons we have discussed, there will always be a better natural explanation. And for the same reason, "I'm hallucinating" would always be the better explanation for whatever you experienced in The Good Place.

Now, Simone did eventually come to believe that she was in The Good Place. One presumes that, since the experience lasted a long time, Simone eventually concluded that it couldn't be a hallucination. In reality, however, this line of reasoning is unsound. As anyone who has watched *Inception* knows, time passes in dreams (and hallucinations) differently. What's more, one might hallucinate the memories of a year's worth of experiences, or the feeling that years had passed when they hadn't. So, again, you really could never know that you were in The Good Place ... even if you did spend millions of bearimies there.

But the prospect of spending millions of bearimies in The Good Place raises the prospect of spending an eternity there ... and this raises the second question I want to address: would you actually want to end up in The Good Place?

Cosmic Coachella

The prospect of spending an eternity in The Good Place might seem—well, *good*. But as Eleanor and company discovered when they went there, it probably wouldn't be. To begin to understand why, it's important to realize that merely existing is not an intrinsic good—a good in and of itself. It's only instrumentally good as a means of attaining pleasurable experiences or what philosophers call eudemonia: a kind of life worth living. This fact is often cited in debates about euthanasia; if one is facing only a future of illness and pain, it makes sense to want to end one's life early.[14] But to establish that mere existence is not something to preserve for its own sake, one need look no further than The Bad Place. Everyone would prefer non-existence to having their penis flattened forever.

But the biggest worry about an eternal life in something like The Good Place was made famous by the philosopher Bernard Williams: boredom.[15] If you really lived forever, no matter how great you had it, you would eventually become bored. You'd do everything you've ever wanted to do— visit Greece and Paris, taste what fully understanding the meaning of *Twin Peaks* feels like, sniff the bedpan that Stone Cold used to beat up Vince McMahon ... and then you do it again, and again ... and again. Eventually, you will have done it all, so many times, that you are sick of it—all of it. And then there you will be, with all of eternity to do ... what? All the things you are now sick of doing? Drink milkshakes? Ask Janet for random objects? Nothing at all? As Patty (Hypatia of Alexandria) put it (in the show):

> On paper, this is paradise. All your desires and needs are met. But it's infinite ... [y]ou get here and you realize that anything's possible, and you do everything, and then you're done. But you still have infinity left. This place kills fun, and passion, and excitement, and love, till all you have left are milkshakes. ("Patty")

Although it might take a while, The Good Place would eventually, and inevitably, turn into The Bad Place. Immortality would become torture.

As a way out of this problem, Williams considers the possibility of making boredom "unthinkable" by magically stripping you of the psychological ability of being bored. Or perhaps infinity just turns you into what Eleanor calls "a happiness zombie" that is just "too far gone to care" about the boredom. "[W]hen perfection goes on forever, you become this glassy-eyed mush person." Williams argues that this wouldn't solve the problem, however, because such an existence isn't really desirable. From an objective standpoint, no one would want to be this dumbed down. As, again, Patty put it:

> I used to be cool, man. I studied so much things. Art and music and the, um, the one with the number piles? Where I'd be like, "Two!" and you'd be like, "Six!" [Math?] Yes! And then I came here where time stretched out forever, and every second of my existence was amazing, but my brain became this big dumb blob.

Even Jason is too complex of a person to not look past the problem. "Go-karting with monkeys got boring really fast." And no one wants to be exponentially dumber than Jason for eternity.

Alternately, maybe one could become so involved in some pursuit that one becomes oblivious to the boredom. Williams imagines a philosopher—much like Chidi—so bogged down in an eternal pursuit of knowledge that he never notices how bored he is. But again, Williams argues, this solution doesn't work. While knowledge is intrinsically valuable, intellectual pursuits seem to only fit into a life of variety in which they can be applied. No one would really want to live like that.

A second problem with both these suggestions is that it's not clear that a person so dumbed down, or so lost in their work, would still be the same person. According to Williams, in order for some depiction of the afterlife to be desirable to me, two conditions must be met. (1) The life actually has to be attractive—the kind of life I would want to live. And (2), the person living the life actually has to be me. And if you eternally strip me of the ability to be bored, either by dumbing me down or eternally distracting me, it's not clear that it really is me.

In an attempt to meet these conditions, Williams also imagines someone who lives a series of consecutive lives, one after the other, where there is no memory overlap. This is exactly like Michael's suggestion to fix The Good Place: "What if we do what I did to you in the original Neighborhood? Erase their memory every once in a while? That way, paradise would seem fresh and new" ("Patty"). But this wouldn't work either. First, as Chidi is quick to point out, "You were doing that to torture us. Actual paradise can't use the same playbook as hell." And second, as Williams points out, such a solution would violate the second condition. Even if each of these consecutive persons has the same body, they wouldn't all be the same person. The psychological break caused by the memory wipe would seem to create a new person. Notice that, if I told the first person that the fifth one was going to be tortured in a hundred years, the first person would feel no sense of dread. They wouldn't think that they were going to feel the torture.

All in all, given an eternal existence, it doesn't seem that you can meet both conditions at once. To make an eternal life desirable, you'd have to break the identity condition; but preserving the identity condition would make the life undesirable. And so it doesn't seem that you should want to be in The Good Place at all. Eternal life, even in some place as good as The Good Place, would eventually become torture.

Conclusion: The Meaning of Life

Now, of course, everything I laid out in the last section is what motivates the crew to "fix" The Good Place by letting its inhabitants choose to leave.

> We're gonna set up a new kind of door ... when you feel happy and satisfied and complete, and you want to leave the Good Place for good, you can just walk through it, and your time in the universe will end. ("Patty")

But would setting up (what we might call) an "oblivion door" really work? Would that make (what we might call) Michael's "Better Place" be a place you'd really want to end up after you die?

I think so. As Williams points out, even though (1) given what we've discussed, a desire for immorality is irrational, and (2) as Epicurus pointed out, the state of being dead is itself nothing to dread—it's still perfectly rational to want to live a longer life rather than a shorter life. And this is what a Better Place would allow you to do.

One thing to still worry about might be that you would never be presented with challenges; Janet could just do everything for you. And that could very easily strip existence of meaning. But it doesn't seem that this problem would be unavoidable. Consider Michael, who is trying to learn to play guitar in the last episode. Janet offers him "a magic guitar that plays all the notes for you. It's the number one request among men over 50 who have gotten in here." But he quickly replies, "the whole point is to learn how to do stuff without using afterlife magic." Notice that Tahani *learns how* to do woodworking (from Nick Offerman); she doesn't just ask Janet for the perfect chair. Worst-case scenario: people would just learn the hard way that they need to do things for themselves ("Whenever You're Ready").

Another problem might be that no one would ever actually walk through the oblivion door; they would always be too afraid of non-existence. But I don't think this would really be a problem. First, for the reasons stated in this chapter, boredom really could get that bad. Non-existence would eventually be preferable. Second, everyone could easily come to embrace the Epicurean truth that non-existence really is nothing to fear because there is nothing *it is like* to not exist. As he put it in his Letter to Menoeceus,

Death is nothing to us, for good and evil imply awareness, and death is the privation of all awareness; therefore a right understanding that death is nothing to us makes the mortality of life enjoyable, not by adding to life an unlimited time, but by taking away the yearning after immortality.[16]

And third, I think it makes sense that, given long enough, everyone would reach a sense of peace, just as they do in the show, where they are ready for it to end. And if they don't, they can just use Chidi's final speech to get them there.

Picture a wave in the ocean ... you can see it, you know what it is.... And then it crashes on the shore, and it's gone. But the water is still there. The wave was just a different way for the water to be for a little while. That's one conception of death for a Buddhist. The wave returns to the ocean, where it came from, and where it's supposed to be. ("Whenever You're Ready")

The only real danger, it seems to me, lies not in a Better Place—but in the hope that one exists. Don't get me wrong; it'd be nice if one existed. But if you *truly believed* that this life will be followed with a paradise that lasts as long as you want, your life will have no urgency. Why bother doing anything now, why make the most of the time you have, if you think you'll have as long as you want in paradise to do it later? In a sense, really believing that a Better Place exists could turn people into the same kind of "glassy-eyed mush person" that being in The Good Place did. It could make you waste the one and only life that you likely have.

Yes, the concept of death might be scary. As Eleanor told Michael, "every human is a little bit sad all the time, because you know you're gonna die" ("Existential Crisis"). But it's that knowledge that "gives life meaning." That's why adding the oblivion door "restore[d] meaning to the people in the Good Place." Contemporary philosopher Julian Baggini would likely agree. As he points out in his book *What's It All About? Philosophy and the Meaning of Life*, a never-ending basketball game, or a truly never-ending movie, would be pointless. The conclusion of such things gives them meaning.[17] In the same way, our lives have meaning only if they have a conclusion.

And so it is also, with books about *The Good Place*.

Notes

1   René Descartes, *Meditations on First Philosophy*, ed. John Cottingham (New York: Cambridge University Press, 2013), 19.
2   Theodore Schick and Lewis Vaughn, *How to Think about Weird Things*, 8th ed. (New York: McGraw-Hill, 2019), 76–77.
3   Ibid., 180–190.
4   The existence of the physical world is at least in principle explainable, and indeed has been largely explained by science. For more on this, see my article "Does God Exist?" forthcoming in the journal *Think*.
5   One might also think that the demon hypothesis doesn't cohere with the common belief that the physical world exists, making it seem conservative. But to invoke that when comparing it to an "A physical world exists" explanation begs the question—it assumes the truth of what you are trying to prove. For more on this kind of refutation of Cartesian Skepticism, see Jonathan Vogel's article "Cartesian Skepticism and Inference to the Best Explanation," *Journal of Philosophy* 87, no. 11 (1990), 658–666.
6   For more on why conspiracy theories are irrational, see my chapter "How Fallacies Fuel Conspiracies," in *Conspiracy Theories: Philosophers Connect the Dots*, ed. Richard Greene and Rachel Robinson-Greene (Chicago: Open Court, 2020).
7   See David Kyle Johnson, "Justified Belief in Demons Is Impossible," in *Philosophical Approaches to Demonology*, ed. Robert Arp and Benjamin W. McCraw (New York: Routledge, 2017), 175–191; and David Kyle Johnson, "Justified Belief in Miracles Is Impossible," *Science, Religion and Culture* 2, no. 2 (2015), 61–74.
8   For more on such limits and powers, see chap. 5 of Schick and Vaughn's previously mentioned book, *How to Think about Weird Things*.
9   David Kyle Johnson, "Mystery Therefore Magic," in *Bad Arguments: 100 of the Most Important Fallacies in Western Philosophy*, ed. Robert Arp, Bruce Robert, and Steve Barbone (Hoboken, NJ: Wiley-Blackwell, 2018), 189–192.
10 For more on this, see my article "Do Souls Exist?" *Think* 12, no. 35 (2013), 61–75.
11 Peter Unger, "The Physical View," from *Identity, Consciousness and Value* (New York: Oxford University Press, 1990), 192–211.
12 Peter van Inwagen, "The Possibility of Resurrection," *International Journal for Philosophy of Religion* 9, no. 2 (1978), 114–121.
13 Esther Zuckerman, "The 'Proof of Heaven' Author Has Now Been Thoroughly Debunked by Science," *The Atlantic*, July 2, 2013, https://www.theatlantic.com/entertainment/archive/2013/07/proof-heaven-author-debunked/313681/.

14   For more on this, see my paper "More on the Relevance of Personhood and Mindedness: Euthanasia, Salvation, and the Possibility of an Afterlife," forthcoming in the journal *SHERM*.

15   See Bernard Williams, "The Makropulos Case: Reflections on the Tedium of Immortality," in *Problems of the Self: Philosophical Papers 1956–1972* (Cambridge: Cambridge University Press, 1973), 82–100.

16   Epicurus, *Letter to Menoeceus*, trans. Robert Drew Hicks, http://classics.mit.edu/Epicurus/menoec.html.

17   Julian Baggini, *What's It All About? Philosophy and the Meaning of Life* (Oxford: Oxford University Press, 2004).

Index

f = the subject appears in a footnote

The Good Place and Philosophy, First Edition. Edited by Kimberly S. Engels.
© 2021 John Wiley & Sons, Inc. Published 2021 by John Wiley & Sons, Inc.

I love
chemisery

Levi McCormack

CPSIA information can be obtained
at www.ICGtesting.com
Printed in the USA
BVHW040607190121
598094BV00018B/279